A+

for Students: Essentials

www.aplusforstudents.co.uk

The logo of the CompTIA Authorized Quality Curriculum (CAQC) program and the status of this or other training material as "Authorized" under the CompTIA Authorized Quality Curriculum program signifies that, in CompTIA's opinion, such training material covers the content of the CompTIA's related certification exam. CompTIA has not reviewed or approved the accuracy of the contents of this training material and specifically disclaims ant warranties of merchantability o fitness for a particular purpose. CompTIA makes no guarantee concerning the success of persons using any such "Authorized" or other training material in order to prepare for any CompTIA certification exam.

The contents of this training material were created for the CompTIA A+ Essentials (220-601) exam covering CompTIA certification objectives that were current as of 2006.

How to become CompTIA certified:

This training material can help you prepare for and pass a related CompTIA certification exam or exams. In order to achieve CompTIA certification, you must register for and pass a CompTIA certification exam or exams.

In order to become CompTIA certified, you must:

Select a certification exam provider. For more information please visit http://www.comptia.org/certification/general_information/exam_locations.aspx

Register for and schedule a time to take the CompTIA certification exam(s) at a convenient location.

Read and sign the Candidate Agreement, which will be presented as the time of the exam(s). The text of the Candidate Agreement can be found at http://www.comptia.org/certification/general_information/candidate_agreement.aspx

Take and pass the CompTIA certification exam(s).

For more information about CompTIA's certifications, such as its industry acceptance, benefits or program news, please visit www.comptia.org/certification

CompTIA is a not-for-profit trade information technology (IT) trade association. CompTIA's certifications are designed by subject matter experts from across the IT industry. Each CompTIA certification is vendor-neutral, covers multiple technologies and requires demonstration of skills and knowledge widely sought after by the IT industry.

To contact CompTIA with any questions or comments, please:

Call (1) (630) 678 8300 or email questions@comptia.org

A+

for Students: Essentials

Anthony Price

Hodder Arnold

A MEMBER OF THE HODDER HEADLINE GROUP

Orders: please contact Bookpoint Ltd, 130 Milton Park, Abingdon, Oxon
OX14 4SB. Telephone: (44) 01235 827720. Fax: (44) 01235 400454. Lines
are open from 9.00–5.00, Monday to Saturday, with a 24 hour message
answering service. You can also order through our website
www.hoddereducation.co.uk

If you have any comments to make about this, or any of our other titles,
please send them to educationenquiries@hodder.co.uk

British Library Cataloguing in Publication Data
A catalogue record for this title is available from the British Library

ISBN: 978 0 340 91580 6

This Edition Published 2007
Impression number   10 9 8 7 6 5 4 3 2 1
Year   2011 2010 2009 2008 2007

Cover photo Getty Images/Digital Vision/Magictorch
Typeset by Pantek Arts Ltd, Maidstone, Kent.
Printed in Malta for Hodder Arnold, an imprint of Hodder Education and,
a member of the Hodder Headline Group, an Hachette Livre UK Company
338 Euston Road, London NW1 3BH.

TABLE OF CONTENTS

Chapter 11 Laptops and portable systems   180

INTRODUCTION

The A+ qualification

The A+ certificate is *the* internationally recognised entry-level qualification for PC support technicians from the Computing Technology Industry Association (CompTIA). Candidates are required to pass two online exams in order to demonstrate that they have the skills and knowledge of a PC support technician with 'at least 500 hours of hands-on experience in lab or field'.

Prior to the 2006 exam specification, there were two compulsory exams, one on hardware and the other one on operating systems. However, with the increasing complexity of the modern PC technician's role in the workplace, the new exam specification allows for a degree of specialisation in the make-up of the qualification. To gain the qualification, all candidates must pass the *Essentials* exam – which covers both hardware and operating-system topics – and a second exam, chosen from one of three options:

- Field Service Technician (A+ 220–602)

- Remote Support / Help Desk Technician (A+ 220–603)

- Hardware / Bench Technician (A+ 220–604)

This book covers the requirements of the A+ Essentials exam.

About the Essentials exam

A+ Essentials is a 90-minute online exam which you will pass (or fail) there and then, on the day. It can be taken at any recognised test centre, and you will require two forms of identification – one of which needs to include your photograph, such as a passport or full driving licence. You should check current requirements with the centre when you book your exam.

The exam consists of 80 multiple choice / multiple response questions to be answered in 90 minutes. Each question presents you with a problem – sometimes accompanied by an illustration – and you are presented with four possible answers. You are required to indicate one or more correct answers from those listed. You need to read and think quickly in this type of test, but still be alert for the odd 'trick question'. Doing practice exams (more later) can help.

The pass mark is in the region of 60 per cent, though CompTIA reserves the right to alter this – or, indeed any other aspect of the qualification – at its discretion. To keep up to date with what's happening in the world of A+ certification, visit:

http://certification.comptia.org/

which lists all the CompTIA certifications, including A+. By following links from the CompTIA site, you can download detailed exam specifications and a handful of sample exam questions. Further practice questions, based on the content of this book, are available from:

www.aplusforstudents.co.uk

About you

You are intending to achieve the A+ certificate in order to work in a PC technical support role. You may be looking for an entry-level qualification in order to strengthen your CV, or you may be a working technician who needs to validate practical experience and workplace skills through A+ certification. You are probably following a college, or other instructor-led training course, though you may, of course, be working alone. You are aware of the value of practical hands-on experience, but you are also prepared to learn the necessary facts and figures to pass a theory exam. Above all, you are prepared to work to achieve your ambitions. No book, no training course, no video, is a substitute for your own efforts, but if you want to do it – to achieve A+ certification – this book can help.

About the book

A+ for Students: Essentials covers *all* of the objectives of the CompTIA Essentials exam. Each chapter begins with a summary of the objectives covered and works though them in a systematic way. There are suggestions for practical activities from time to time and each chapter ends with a brief summary and questions to help you test how much of the chapter has 'stuck'. There are also suggestions for further practical exercises in Appendix I.

About the author

Anthony Price is a former working PC technician who writes on the technical aspects of computing. He has written two self-instruction books *Teach Yourself Home PC Maintenance and Networking*, and *Teach Yourself PC Networking for Your Small Business*. He has a Master of Science degree in Information Technology and is also a qualified and experienced adult-education lecturer.

Practical exercises

It is possible, in principle at least, to pass the A+ certification exams without doing any practical work on a PC. There are, indeed, 'boot camp'-style intensive courses which take this approach. However, there are good reasons for doing some practical work:

1   If you don't yet have any work experience as a PC technician, A+ certification on its own is less likely to impress a potential employer than certification *and* hands-on experience.

2   Learning by doing is more effective than learning by rote. Changing a hard drive and breaking your finger nails while setting the jumpers is, somehow, a more effective

learning strategy than just reading about it or attending a theory class that never gets down to business on the tools of the trade.

3. Practical activity is more fun. If you don't enjoy messing with PCs, then why do you want to be a tech in the first place?

Working safely

Whether you are going to experiment at home, or in a classroom or lab, there are a few essential guidelines for working safely with PCs:

- *Always* power down and disconnect from the mains power source before you remove any covers or lids. PCs run on AC mains power – they are no more (or less) dangerous than any other household gadget that uses mains power.

- Once the machine is disconnected from the power, you need to remove the lid, cover, or side panel in order to access the inside of the machine. Covers and panels are usually secured by two or three screws with 'star'-style heads on them. Put these screws somewhere safe – a loose screw left inside a case can cause an electrical short, which will damage the hardware.

- Before you touch *any* of the internal components, you should touch a bare metal section of the chassis of the machine. This safely discharges any static in your body – or at least equalises it with any in the machine – so that there is no difference of potential between you and the machine. Having discharged any static in this way, you should always touch bare metal before touching any component. Remember, even though you can't see static, it can damage your system.

- Wearing a wrist strap that you attach to the chassis of the PC means that you are permanently 'touching' bare metal. If you want a wrist strap, you can buy one cheaply enough from your local PC shop. Just remember NOT to wear it if you are in contact with high-voltage equipment like a laser printer, where it could conduct a high voltage *to* you rather than static *away* from you.

- Be sure that you are aware of any local rules, laws, or Health and Safety requirements. You are responsible for your own safety as well as that of those around you.

- When dealing with any form of specialist equipment – like a laser printer or an uninterruptible power supply – read the product manuals and documentation before you start.

These, of course, are general guidelines to help you to stay out of trouble; not a comprehensive guide to every possible situation or a summary of the law as it may apply to you in your college, place of work or home.

Setting up a lab

If you are attending a college course as a student, you should have access to suitable hardware and software packages to carry out some practical exercises. If you are a member of college staff responsible for the kit, you should plan to have one PC that is capable of running Microsoft Windows® 2000 Professional and / or Microsoft Windows® XP for each student.

A PIII with 128 MB of RAM and a hard disk of (say) 10 GB will be sufficient for any practical activity suggested in this book. For the go-it-alone student, this 'play' machine should be in addition to their main (or family) PC. This type of machine can be bought second-hand for next to nothing. In a college, you can probably equip a lab entirely from PCs of that specification or better, when working PCs are being withdrawn from mainstream use.

Your work area should be well lit and there should be space to lay out components. You should also have suitable containers for screws, jumpers and 'bits'.

There are suggestions for practical work in the text, and Appendix I gives suggestions for further practical work that you can adapt according to your needs and available equipment.

Tools

- A Phillips #2 screwdriver is essential.

- Other screwdrivers – Torxx, stub handles, etc. will be needed occasionally.

- Pliers – useful with damaged screws, Molex connectors that are stuck, etc.

- A multimeter – mainly used for testing Power Supply Units (PSUs).

- A torch and a magnifying glass – PCs are dark inside and the writing on components is small.

- A wrist strap – these are mandatory in many workplaces when working on the inside of a PC.

- Internet access – whether you need to download software device drivers, update or patch an operating system, or look up a fact, the Internet is one of the working technician's major resources.

Practice exams, mock tests, etc.

There are many practice exams and mock tests available, some of them claiming to be a simulation of the CompTIA exams. Usually, if you read the small print, you will find a disclaimer stating that, for example, it may not be 100 per cent representative of the real exams. With this in mind, use every opportunity you can to answer test questions. They can be a good way of focusing your attention on the exam objectives and reinforcing your knowledge of the subject material. Each chapter of the book ends with some practice questions and there are also some pen-and-paper mock tests on the website at www.aplusforstudents.co.uk.

These are available for online use or you can download hard-copy versions in pdf format.

Any mock test that you do can be useful in building confidence and practising exam technique. However, no mock exam or practice test, including the ones presented in this book or on the website, are the real thing. The only test that *really* matters is the one you take on the day. Good luck.

Acknowledgements

Thanks are due to Tracey Williams for reading the original typescript with the eye of an A+ and Network+ qualified working PC technician; for checking the examples, and for correcting a number of errors. Thanks also to Kim Vernon for copy editing, to Pat Winfield (Bookworm Editorial Services) for proof reading, and to Roger Angove for some perceptive comments on networking. All of them have contributed to the accuracy and readability of the text. Any errors which remain are, of course, my responsibility.

Anthony Price, Truro, Cornwall, UK
anthonyp@elenmar.com
(May 2007)

CHAPTER 1
Motherboards and Power Supply Units

The motherboard – also known as the system board or main board – is the component that, literally, holds the other components together. Everything in the PC is attached one way or another to the motherboard and every piece of data and every control signal passes over its buses. It also delivers power to attached components. Because of its central role in both the physical construction of the PC and its operations and its relationship to all other components, it is true to say that if you 'know your way around' a motherboard you are well on your way to understanding the hardware side of the PC.

The Power Supply Unit (PSU) supplies power to one or more connectors on the motherboard and has to have a compatible 'form factor'.

Exam objective 1.1 (part)
Identify the names, purposes and characteristics of motherboards

    Form factor (e.g. ATX / BTX, Micro-ATX / NLX)
    Components
    Integrated I/O (e.g. sound, video, USB, serial, IEEE 1394 / FireWire, parallel, NIC, modem)
    Memory slots (e.g. RIMM, DIMM)
    Processor sockets
    External cache memory
    Bus architecture
    Bus slots (e.g. PCI, AGP, PCIE, AMR, CNR)
    EIDE / PATA
    SATA
    SCSI Technology
    Chipsets
    BIOS / CMOS / Firmware
    Riser card / daughterboard

Identify the names, purposes and characteristics of power supplies

    AC adapter
    ATX
    Proprietary
    Voltage

Motherboards

Form factors

The physical characteristics of motherboards – size, fixing points, general layout of components, and so on – are defined by their form factor. Early PCs were known as 'Advanced Technology' and many components associated with that era designated as AT by association. For this reason, the early motherboards were referred to as AT form factor motherboards. They are no longer used for building PCs, but their successors are. The important motherboard form factors for the A+ exams are: ATX, BTX, Micro-ATX and NLX.

The ATX form factor

This is the motherboard type that you will encounter most frequently when working in the field. The maximum size for an ATX board is specified as 12.0 in × 9.6 in (305 mm × 244 mm). This is similar to the size of the earlier AT specification but most of its other characteristics are different. The orientation of the board is rotated by 90 degrees – it fits across the width of a desktop case – and the mounting locations and power connections are different.

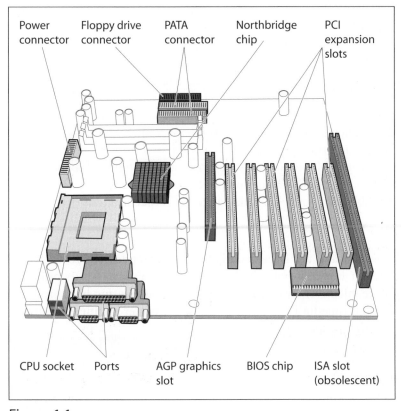

Figure 1.1

I/O ports on an ATX motherboard are in two rows at the back of the machine and feature PS/2 connectors for both mouse and keyboard and two nine-pin serial ports and a parallel (printer) port. There are probably, but not necessarily, other ports for USB, sound, LAN connection, etc.

The ATX mounts RAM and CPU away from the expansion slots and closer to the power supply fan. On earlier motherboards, the power supply fan pulled air into the case over the CPU and memory to improve cooling of these components, but this arrangement has been superseded. In order to reduce dust and dirt from the atmosphere entering the case, the ATX form factor uses a fan that pulls air across the components and expels it through the case vents. There is also provision for an additional fan on most ATX motherboards. Use of such a fan is recommended where there are many hot-running components such as multiple hard drives, etc.

ATX motherboards were the first to introduce support for soft switching options for the power supply, that is power can be turned off though software. ATX boards also provide a range of voltages: 12v, 5v and 3.3v through the one-piece 20-pin power supply connector.

All motherboard form factors are associated with the case type and the power supply unit. When buying or upgrading, all three elements must match.

The Micro-ATX form factor

This is a development (or variant) on the standard ATX specification. It is smaller – the maximum size being 9.6 in × 9.6 in (244 mm × 244 mm). The size reduction is achieved by reducing the number of expansion slots. A full-size ATX, for example, usually has five PCI slots, whereas a Micro-ATX will typically have three. Micro-ATX boards often have a lot of I/O ports built into the board – an on-board graphics chip, for example – and for this reason the Micro-ATX is popular with system builders when producing budget systems. With a few small modifications, it is possible to mount a Micro-ATX motherboard in a full-size ATX case, though the opposite is not possible – a full-size ATX board is physically too big to mount in a Micro-ATX case, even though in terms of fixing points, etc., it would otherwise be compatible. Other components, such as expansion cards and power supplies are compatible with both ATX and Micro-ATX specifications.

The BTX form factor

Like the earlier ATX specification, the Balanced Technology Extended (BTX) specification was devised by Intel. It was first published early in 2005 and one of its principal concerns was to deal more effectively with the seemingly ever-increasing heat problems associated with modern multimedia PCs, mainly through a better engineered airflow though the case and over the components.

The BTX specification also supports newer technologies such as PCI Express, Serial ATA and USB 2 as part of its original design rather than as additional features grafted on to the earlier specifications.

In terms of size, there are a number of options. The depth of the board is always 266.7 mm, but there are four widths described in the specification depending on the number of expansion slots supported.

The larger boards, unsurprisingly, have more fixing points in order to mount them securely in the case. Full-sized BTX boards will work with ATX power supplies because the power connector is the same and the direction of the airflow from the cooling fan in the PSU is unchanged. BTX motherboards have not (yet) been widely adopted by system builders.

The NLX form factor

There has always been a market for PCs described as 'slimline' or 'small footprint' and these rely on specially designed motherboards. Early PCs of this type were based on a now defunct specification called LPX. The key characteristic of these boards is that rather than fitting expansion cards into slots on the motherboard, the system bus is on a riser card that plugs into the motherboard. Expansion cards are then fitted into the riser card – or daughterboard – parallel to the place of the motherboard.

Just as the original AT motherboard became outmoded and was replaced by the ATX specification, the LPX was replaced by a new specification (from Intel) called New Low Profile Extended (NLX).

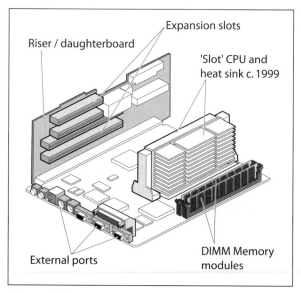

Figure 1.2

These motherboards were popular with system builders in the late 1990s – the era of slot processors – but have largely been superseded by newer specifications such as Micro-ATX (see page 9).

Two new motherboard types (not in the A+ spec)

There are two new motherboard types which may supplant the Micro-ATX in the future. These are Flex-ATX, which Intel describes as an 'Addendum' to the Micro-ATX specification, and Mini-ITX from VIA Technologies. Flex-ATX boards have a maximum size of 9.0 in × 7.5 in(229 mm × 191 mm) and have fixing holes and external ports that make them compatible with ATX and Micro-ATX cases. Mini-ITX are 6.7 in × 6.7 in (170 mm × 170 mm) and are intended to deliver low power consumption and quieter performance, particularly for the 'home theatre' market.

Components

Integrated input / output (I/O) ports

There has been a trend through time towards building I/O ports onto the motherboard instead of fitting them on expansion cards. The costs of budget systems, where high performance is not needed, can be reduced by using a motherboard that has built-in I/O. A workhorse PC that is used for word processing, email and web access can, for example, operate satisfactorily with an on-board graphics chip rather than the sort of top-of-the-range graphics cards needed for gaming or three-dimensional design work. The most common integrated I/O ports are: sound, video, USB, serial, IEEE 1394 / FireWire, parallel, Network Interface Card (NIC) and modem.

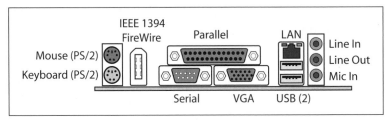

Figure 1.3

Sound

Like most on-board I/O ports, the sound ports tend to be adequate rather than outstanding in performance. When a higher quality of sound is required, it is possible to install a sound card in one of the expansion slots on the motherboard to replace it. When this is done, it is good practice to disable the on-board ports in the system BIOS set-up in order to save resources. In some instances, this may be essential for the new sound card to work properly.

Video

On-board video is popular in budget systems and is adequate for relatively undemanding applications. As with sound ports, it is possible to upgrade to a dedicated graphics card to obtain better performance. Disabling the on-board port in the BIOS set-up is generally recommended. Most on-board graphics use the Accelerated Graphics Port (AGP) chip and connect to the monitor through the standard VGA port. This is a female connector with 15 lines. The VGA connector and its alternatives such as DVI are considered in Chapters 4 and 5.

Universal Serial Bus (USB)

The Universal Serial Bus (USB) was developed to provide a simple, fast, general purpose interface between the PC and attached USB devices. Its key characteristic from the user's point of view is that it is 'hot swappable', that is it is possible to connect and disconnect installed devices without rebooting the PC. The connector at the PC end of the connection is known as a type 'A' connector. It is flat and rectangular in section. The attached devices use a type 'B' connector, which is smaller and almost square in section. USB supports data transmission rates of:

- 12 Mbps for 'fast' devices (this is the original USB 1 specification)

- 1.5 Mbps though a sub-channel for 'slow' devices, such as keyboards and mice

- 480 Mbps – introduced with USB 2.0.

USB allows for connection of up to 127 devices through USB hubs and there is even a USB 'bridge' that can be used to connect two PCs back-to-back 'laplink' style for data transfers. USB can provide power to low-power devices such as keyboards and mice: power-hungry devices such as printers need their own independent power supply.
USB is considered further in Chapter 5. There is also a website (www.usb.org) which is the home of the trade association.

IEEE 1394 / FireWire

IEEE 1394 is the standard defined by the Institute of Electrical and Electronic Engineers – a US-based standards organisation – as a rival technology to USB. FireWire is probably the best-known implementation of the IEEE 1394 standard and the name is the property of Apple Computer Inc. Other implementations of the standard are: iLink (Sony) and Lynx (Texas Instruments).

The 1394 connector is larger than the one used by USB and it is nearly square in section. The standard cable has six lines and – like USB – can be used to provide power to low-power devices. IEEE 1394 can support up to 63 attached devices. It is sometimes referred to as 'Serial SCSI'. IEEE 1394 is considered further in Chapter 5. There is a web site (www.1394ta.org – the 'ta' stands for trade association) where you can find news of the latest developments in this technology.

Parallel port

The parallel port has been part of every PC since the days of the original 8086 / 8088 systems built by IBM in 1981. Like most sub-systems of the PC, it has developed through time, but its appearance – a D-shaped female connector with 25 lines – is largely unchanged. Historically, its main use has been for printing, so it is frequently referred to as a 'printer port' or 'LPT1'. Modern parallel ports are almost invariably on-board and usually support bi-directional data transfers, though this may require you to change settings in the BIOS set-up utility. Parallel ports are considered further in Chapter 5.

Network port

Until relatively recently, network connectivity was usually through a port that was added as an expansion card in one of the motherboard slots, and this is still frequently the case. However, the growth in the popularity of networking in recent years and the almost universal adoption of Ethernet networking technology has resulted in Ethernet ports being built into the motherboard. In laptop / portable systems, the RJ45 port for Ethernet networking is almost a universal feature. Most ports support 10/100 Mbps transmission speeds and 1000 Mbps – Gigabit Ethernet – is becoming increasingly common.

Modem

The modem port is similar in appearance to the RJ45 network port, but it is smaller. It is known as an RJ11 (the 'RJ', stands for 'Registered Jack', by the way), which is widely used in the US telephone system. Internal on-board modems are slower in operation and may not be supported by all operating systems. The main advantage of this type of modem is simplicity of use – all that is required is a cable from the PC to the phone line and setting up the connection in the operating system. With the decline in dial-up as a means of connecting to the Internet, this type of port is of declining significance.

Memory slots

In the early days of the PC, system memory – RAM – was mounted on the motherboard as individual chips. This approach was rapidly replaced by the practice of mounting the RAM chips on printed circuit boards – Memory Modules – which fitted into slots on the motherboard. There were various systems for doing this, but current practice is dominated by variations of the Dual Inline Memory Module (DIMM).

Dual Inline Memory Modules (DIMMs)

Every motherboard has RAM slots which are compatible with a particular memory type and you can only use memory of the type supported by the motherboard. If the PC you are working on supports only (say) 168-pin DIMM modules (usually associated with a memory type known as SDRAM) then this is all you can fit into that slot. Module types have notches in their bottom edge so that only the right type of memory can be fitted the right way around. Various DIMM types are used for different RAM types. The most common slot sizes on the motherboards used in desktop machines are:

- 168-pin-DIMMs, usually used for SDRAM
- 184-pin-DIMMs, used for DDR SDRAM
- 240-pin-DIMMs, used for DDR2 SDRAM

Rambus Inline Memory Modules (RIMMs)

This is a proprietary memory type introduced in 1999. The modules are similar in appearance to DIMMs but are not compatible with them. It is more expensive than other memory types and is no longer widely used. You may still come across it in the field on legacy systems, but the cost of upgrading systems that use this type of memory is usually prohibitive.

Memory types and their characteristics are considered in more detail in Chapter 3.

Processor sockets

Just as a particular motherboard supports a particular type of memory module, with a choice of speed and capacities, it also supports a particular type of CPU chip and a range of chip speeds.

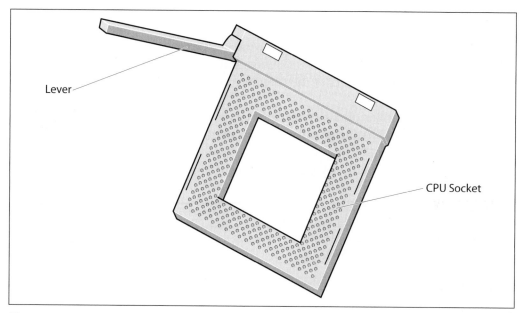

Figure 1.4

Figure 1.4 shows a typical processor socket that you might see on a modern mother-board. In order to fit the processor, raise the lever on the side of the socket, drop the processor in place, then lower the lever and clip it into place. This secures the processor. This type of socket is known as a Zero Insertion Force (ZIF) socket. The figure shows a 'generic' socket of this type – based on an Intel Socket 423, which was the early (Willamette core) Pentium 4 processor.

Note, from the figure, the arrangement of the holes, which are staggered to save space. The generic term for this is a 'staggered pin grid array' and many processors from both the major manufacturers – Intel and Advanced Micro Devices (AMD) – use a variant of it. An alternative approach is to place the pins in the motherboard socket. Instead of pins on the chip, it has pads of gold-plated copper which make contact with the pins on the motherboard. This arrangement allows higher pin densities and has been adopted by both Intel and AMD for some of their later chips.

CPU chips are discussed in detail in Chapter 2.

External cache memory

In general terms – not just chips and memory – a cache is a temporary store of data which, having been accessed once, is stored locally so that it can be accessed again quickly. Hard disks, for example, have cache memory built into them in order to speed up disk access. CPU chips have small amounts of on-the-die high-speed storage built into them for the same reason. The implementation of cache storage for a CPU chip is also extended to include not just on-the-die storage, but also external storage on-the-board. This is usually implemented as a physical module, plugged in to the board and, while it is less efficient than on-the-die cache, it can, nevertheless, improve overall performance.

Bus architecture

A bus is a physical channel which carries electrical signals – usually in parallel – across the motherboard. If you pick up a motherboard and examine it, particularly from the underside, you will see the traces of the wires that make up the various physical communications channels.

The most important bus on a motherboard is the Front Side Bus – generally abbreviated to FSB. This is the bi-directional communications channel that links the CPU and the chipset (see chipsets, below). Its speed is critical to the speed of the other components and buses on the board. A CPU, for example, will operate at a multiple of the FSB speed. Given an FSB of 133 MHz and a multiplier of 12.5, we would have a CPU speed of 1663 MHz.

In older systems, peripheral buses such as PCI and AGP ran at a fraction of the FSB speed by using a fractional multiplier. However, in modern practice, these buses may operate independently of the FSB.

Bus slots

Since the introduction of the original IBM PC – released on 12 August 1981 – it has always been an extensible system that allows additional components to be added through a variety of expansion slots. The general principle is that a bus conducts signals, power, and data across the motherboard, and an added component can access the bus simply by plugging in to it.

PCI

The Peripheral Component Interconnect (PCI) standard specifies a bus that allows for the connection of devices to it. The specification details the connections for on-board I/O devices of the type we looked at earlier as well as providing the interface for PCI expansion cards. The PCI slots shown in Figure 1.1 are the standard 32-bit slot. There is also a 64-bit variant which is physically longer. The original standard specified a 33 MHz signalling – this was doubled to 66 MHz in a later standard. PCI slots are almost invariably cream / off-white in colour and there are usually three to six of them on the motherboard according to the motherboard type. PCI and other expansion cards are considered in detail in Chapter 5.

AGP

Accelerated Graphics Port (AGP) was introduced in 1997 to provide a faster graphics interface than that delivered by PCI graphics cards. The original specification was for 66 MHz – compared with PCI's basic 33 MHz – and this has been increased several times in subsequent revisions of the standard. The AGP slot can be identified by its colour – it is nearly always brown – and the fact that it is offset from the PCI slots on the board. Unlike PCI slots, there is usually (nearly always) only one AGP slot on the board. There is more about AGP in Chapter 5.

PCI-E

PCI Express is a new standard that seems set to replace the older PCI expansion slots and cards. It has already replaced AGP for graphics cards on modern systems and a new version is scheduled for release in 2007.

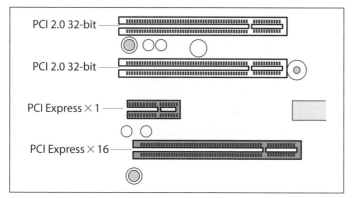

Figure 1.5

Figure 1.5 shows standard PCI slots and two different PCI-E slots. Cards that fit in the smaller (single-speed) slot can be fitted in the 16-speed slot but will only function as single-speed cards. There is more about PCI-X in Chapter 5.

(Note: do not confuse PCI-E with PCI-X. PCI-Extended (PCI-X) is a revision of the PCI standard that gives a higher performance rate than standard PCI, but has not been widely adopted and appears to have been largely superseded by PCI-E.)

AMR

The Audio Modem Riser (AMR) slot is found on older motherboards – typically from the era of Pentium III and Pentium 4 chips. It was used as an interface for analogue sound and modems. It was super-seded by the Communications Network Riser (CNR) – see next section – which has, in turn, been more or less superseded by on-board components.

The AMR slot is usually brown and is smaller than the standard PCI slot.

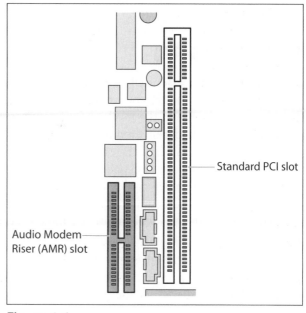

Figure 1.6

CNR

The Communications and Networking Riser (CNR) slot was a replacement for the AMR slot, found mainly on some Pentium 4-class motherboards. It is usually brown in colour and similar in appearance to the AMR slot. It supports audio, networking and modem functionality, but has largely been superseded by on-board components.

EIDE / PATA

Until relatively recently these were the standard hard disk types on nearly all desktop PCs. Enhanced Integrated Drive Electronics (EIDE) was the first hard drive type to integrate the control electronics onto the drive itself – earlier drives needed a separate expansion card – hence the Integrated in the name.

Later developments of the standard were called Advanced Technology Attachment (ATA). AT Attached Packet Interface (ATAPI) is the variant used to indicate CD-ROMs and tape drives. Other disk types such as the various specifications for Ultra Direct Memory Addressing (UDMA) use the same motherboard slots. With the advent of Serial ATA (SATA) from around 2003, ATA – which is a parallel technology – was renamed Parallel ATA (PATA) to distinguish it from the newer serial ATA technology.

Although there have been several generations of improvements in EIDE / PATA technology, the basic appearance of the motherboard slots is essentially the same. The motherboard connectors – like the drives themselves – have 40 pins and newer drives and cables are backward compatible with the older types. High-speed connectors – the type that you will find on most modern motherboards – are usually distinguished by being blue in colour to correspond with the colour coding of the 80-line / 40-pin connections used on later PATA drives. Hard disk drives are considered further in Chapter 3 and cable types are discussed in Chapter 5.

Serial ATA (SATA)

Serial ATA disks are essentially similar to their PATA counterparts, though they achieve faster data transfers though the use of serial communications. The data cable of a SATA drive has seven lines and the motherboard connectors have seven pins. The first version of the SATA standard delivered data transfers of 1.5 Gbps and this was increased to 3 Gbps in the next version of the standard. Higher speeds are planned. As with PATA, cable and connectors are designed to give backward compatibility between later specification drives and earlier cables and connectors. Figure 1.7 shows a pair of SATA connectors on a motherboard and a SATA data cable.

Modern motherboards will frequently have both PATA and SATA sockets on them and it is possible, in principle at least, to use both technologies side by side.

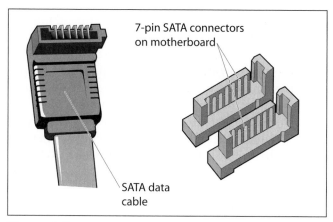

7-pin SATA connectors
on motherboard

SATA data
cable

Figure 1.7

Small Computer Systems Interface (SCSI)

Invariably pronounced as Scuzzy, the SCSI interface has been in use in various forms since before its formal definition by the American National Standards Institute (ANSI) in 1986. It has never been widely used on desktop PCs because, although it is considerably more efficient than EIDE / ATA, it is also considerably more expensive. Although you may see SCSI connectors on a motherboard, they are more commonly implemented through an expansion card and are more commonly found in server machines. Most server machines use SCSI disk sub-systems because of their speed and reliability. It is usually the technology of choice for implementing fault tolerant disk systems using a Redundant Array of Independent Disks (RAID). Surprisingly, perhaps, there are no officially defined standards for SCSI connectors.

Chipsets

The chipset is the name given to the group of chips that make a motherboard work. Although they are critical to the motherboard, they are not necessarily manufactured by the motherboard manufacturer. VIA Technologies, for example, make chipsets that are used by various motherboard manufacturers. Intel – inventors of the microchip in the first place – make both chipsets and motherboards.

Two of the most important elements of the chipset are the Northbridge and Southbridge chips. The Northbridge chip mediates directly between the CPU chip and high-speed components such as system RAM and AGP graphics. Slower components are controlled through the Southbridge, which communicates with the CPU via the Northbridge chip.

The chipset of a motherboard – the Northbridge chip in particular – determines the range of CPUs, RAM, etc. that can be used with it.

BIOS / CMOS / firmware

BIOS

The Basic Input Output System (BIOS) is implemented on a BIOS chip. This chip contains executable code – programs – that are needed to initialise the system at boot time. When the PC is powered up, the programs on the BIOS chip run routines such as the Power On Self Test (POST) which checks things like the amount of installed memory on the system. The BIOS programs have default values that they will use unless they are modified in some way. Such modifications to default behaviour are controlled by CMOS.

CMOS

Complementary Metal Oxide Semiconductor (CMOS) is a type of non-volatile memory which is used to store system settings. The CMOS is 'kept alive' by a small replaceable battery on the motherboard. Settings such as the order in which the PC examines its attached disks, for example, can be set by entering the set-up utility. This is usually accessed by holding down a particular key (the Delete key is frequently used for this) and changing the settings.

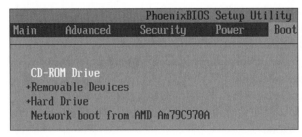

Figure 1.8

Figure 1.8 shows the boot order of a system with a Phoenix BIOS. Other BIOS manufacturers will offer the same functionality, though the user interface may be very different. If, for any reason, you cannot access the set-up utility, then as a last resort, settings can generally be taken back to factory defaults through changing a jumper on the motherboard – the position of the jumper should be documented in the motherboard manual. As a rough and ready alternative you can also remove the CMOS battery for a while so that the BIOS reverts to its default settings.

Firmware

Early BIOS chips had their programs burnt on to them permanently. This meant that if a bug was discovered or an upgrade was released then the chip had to be replaced. There were a number of developments designed to work around this limitation and the current generation of BIOS chips uses Electronically Erasable Programmable Read Only Memory (EEPROM). This technology means that a BIOS chip can be reprogrammed without removing it from the system by doing a 'flash upgrade'. This consists of flashing new programs on the BIOS chip that will modify its behaviour. Because the programs installed by this method are software embedded in hardware, the term 'firmware' was coined to describe them.

Power supplies

As noted earlier in the chapter, the Power Supply Unit (PSU) must be compatible with the motherboard type, thus an ATX board will have an ATX power connector and will require an ATX power supply. There are, of course, proprietary PSUs to match proprietary motherboards and cases.

Whatever the details of a particular PSU may be – form factor, price, etc. – its fundamental tasks are the same:

- Conversion of mains Alternating Current (AC) to Direct Current (DC)

- Reducing the mains voltage from 110 volts (USA) or 230 volts (UK)

- Supplying power to the motherboard through a connector – 20 lines in the case of an ATX PSU / board combination

- Distributing AC power to various components on lines rated at 12 volts, 5 volts or 3.3 volts.

The output of a PSU is rated in watts and most desktop PCs will have a PSU rated at 400 watts or more, though high-end machines may need more than this.

Power supplies for desktop machines are, of course, internal. Most laptop / portable machines (which are the subject of Chapter 11) use an external power supply. This delivers the same functionality as a standard desktop unit, but the voltage reduction and AC/DC conversions are done within the external unit and the reduced voltage DC power is supplied to the portable PC. This is often by way of a proprietary connector. The advantages of external PSUs of this type are space saving and heat reduction, both of which are major considerations when designing and building a laptop system.

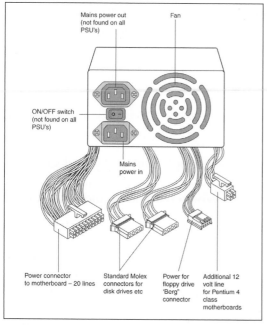

Figure 1.9

SUMMARY

This chapter has examined motherboards and their characteristics. For exam purposes – not to mention doing the job in the field or workshop – you should be able to identify a motherboard by sight or by description. You should be familiar with the various on-board ports and how to replace or upgrade them. You should also be able to identify by sight and know the characteristics of the various expansion slots and the buses to which they are connected.

We have looked at the nature and role of BIOS and CMOS and how this can be related to the installation and configuration of a motherboard. We have also looked at the characteristics of Power Supply Units (PSUs).

QUESTIONS

1　You are looking at a motherboard. It has four PCI slots, an AGP slot and a row of ports along the back including a pair of connectors that you identity as connectors for keyboard and mouse. Is this motherboard?

　　a) An NLX

　　b) An ATX

　　c) A Micro-ATX

　　d) None of the above

2　You are looking at an ATX motherboard. It has a single 40-pin connector which is blue and a pair of 7-pin connectors. What hard disk types does this motherboard support?

　　a) EIDE / PATA

　　b) SATA

　　c) SCSI

　　d) All of the above

3　You suspect that a PC has a failing power supply unit and you decide to check the output of the unit with a multimeter by probing the lines on the connector to the motherboard. Which reading would you NOT expect to see?

　　a) 12 volts

　　b) 15 volts

　　c) 3.3 volts

　　d) 5 volts

ANSWERS / EXPLANATIONS

1   You are looking at a motherboard. It has four PCI slots, an AGP slot and a row of ports along the back including a pair of connectors that you identity as connectors for keyboard and mouse. Is this motherboard?

b) An ATX

Neither an NLX nor a Micro-ATX would have that many slots and in any case, the NLX is not part of the A+ specification – it is a forerunner of the LPX form factor.

2   You are looking at an ATX motherboard. It has a single 40-pin connector which is blue and a pair of 7-pin connectors. What hard disk types does this motherboard support?

a) EIDE / PATA

b) SATA

The blue 40-pin connector would support both the original EIDE drive and the later PATA standard. The 7-pin connectors are for Serial ATA. SCSI could be supported, but only by fitting a SCSI adapter card in one of the expansion slots.

3   You suspect that a PC has a failing power supply unit and you decide to check the output of the unit with a multimeter by probing the lines on the connector to the motherboard. Which reading would you NOT expect to see?

b) 15 volts

There is no 15-volt line on a standard PC power supply.

More questions are available from www.aplusforstudents.co.uk

CHAPTER 2
CPU chips

The Central Processing Unit (CPU) chip is the component that defines what a PC is. The original IBM PC was based on the Intel 8088 chip. After the commercial success of the original PCs, variants and 'clones' from other manufacturers employed a variety of chips derived from the 8086 (a forerunner of the 8088). Successive generations of CPUs have used this '*86 architecture', though clock speeds and the number of features have increased dramatically over the years.

Exam objective 1.1 (part)
Identify the names, purposes and characteristics of processors / CPUs

> CPU chips (e.g. AMD, Intel)
> CPU technologies
> Hyperthreading
> Dual core
> Throttling
> Microcode (MMX)
> Overclocking
> Cache
> VRM
> Speed (real vs. actual)
> 32-bit vs. 64-bit

CPU chips

The microchip was invented by Intel and the first PCs from IBM were based on Intel chips. With the success of the PC, other manufacturers started to make IBM-compatible 'clones' based on the same (Intel) chips. The next development was the cloning of chips themselves and before long it was possible to buy an *86 processor from chip makers other than Intel. Some of these chips – those made by Advanced Micro Devices (AMD) – were produced under licence from Intel, and others – such as the 80286 from Cyrix – were produced independently. A lot of litigation between the companies occurred.

After the 80486 chip, Intel changed their naming conventions and what might otherwise have been the 586 was given the name Pentium®, a designation which suggested the number five without actually using it. By the time that the Pentium® brand name was established, AMD was no longer a producer of licensed clones, but an increasingly powerful rival to Intel in their own right.

The original Pentium® is, perhaps, the forerunner of all the modern CPU chips.

Table 2.1 Early Pentium-class chips.

	Intel	AMD
1993	Pentium®	K5
1995	Pentium® Pro	K6PLUS-3D
1997	Pentium® MMX	K6
1997	Pentium® II	Athlon™ K7
1999	Pentium® III	Athlon™ K75 /Thunderbird

Intel also produced a number of budget processors under the name Celeron and AMD produced rival budget chips under the Duron™ brand name.

Although you may occasionally encounter early chips in the field – there are a handful of PIIIs (and even PIIs) in use here and there – the Intel P4 is really the first modern chip which still has a significant user base.

Identifying the CPU

Where this is not indicated on the case or in the manufacturer's documentation or website you can, of course, remove the lid or side panel form the PC and look inside for the manufacturer's name and / or serial number. On a modern hot-running PC, this may require you to remove the heat sink and fan to obtain the information that you require. An easier alternative on a working machine that has an operating system is to use the System Information utility which is one of the System Tools built in to both Microsoft Windows 2000® and Microsoft Windows XP®. In addition, XP has the SYSTEMINFO command which lists the same information at a system prompt.

SYSTEMINFO [Enter] will display the information that you want at the prompt. Using the command line prompt is outlined in Chapter 8 and is covered in more depth in Working at a Command Line – a tutorial in pdf format – which you can view or download from the site at: www.aplusforstudents.co.uk.

If you want to save the system information to a file, you can do so by redirecting the output of the command to a text file, like this:

SYSTEMINFO>SYSTEMLOG.TXT [Enter]

The text file whose name you have will contain the output of the command specified can be opened on just about any system running any operating system. Figure 2.1 shows part of the output of the SYSTEMINFO command on a Microsoft Windows XP® machine as viewed with the default Notepad editor.

```
Host Name:                  BURGESS
OS Name:                    Microsoft Windows XP Professional
OS Version:                 5.1.2600 Service Pack 2 Build 2600
OS Manufacturer:            Microsoft Corporation
OS Configuration:           Standalone Workstation
OS Build Type:              Uniprocessor Free
Registered Owner:           Anthony Price
Registered Organization:    Elenmar
Product ID:                 55274-640-1597875-23070
Original Install Date:      18/11/2006, 09:20:01
System Up Time:             9 Days, 18 Hours, 59 Minutes, 57 Seconds
System Manufacturer:        System Manufacturer
System Model:               System Name
System Type:                X86-based PC
Processor(s):               1 Processor(s) Installed.
                            [01]: x86 Family 6 Model 6 Stepping 2 AuthenticAMD ~1666 Mhz
BIOS Version:               ASUS   - 42302e31
Windows Directory:          C:\WINDOWS
System Directory:           C:\WINDOWS\system32
```

Figure 2.1

The chip entry – highlighted on the figure – identifies the chip as x86 'Family 6 Model 6 Stepping 2 Authentic AMD ~1666 Mhz', and a quick search on the web identifies this as an AMD Athlon XP 2000.

Having identified the CPU, you can of course visit the manufacturer's website to find more details of the product, including information on compatibility with different motherboards along with drivers, utilities, etc.

Chip terminology

When comparing CPU chips there are three major considerations to be found from its description:

▧ Clock speed

▧ Pin count

▧ Cache size

Clock speed

CPU chips, like many components, are rated in a multiple of the standard Hertz, which is one state transition per second. Because of the high speed of even relatively slow CPUs, this is almost invariably expressed in MegaHertz (MHz) – 1,000,000 Hz – or GigaHertz – 10,000,000 Hz. These speed descriptions are widely used by manufacturers and retailers to promote their products and while they are useful as informatio,n they are by no means the only consideration when selecting a chip for a system.

Pin count

The number of pins used to connect the CPU to the motherboard socket is a frequently used descriptor of chips. Early Pentium® 4 chips came with two different pin counts, which applied to three different models. Obviously the correct pin count and layout are necessary (but by no means sufficient) for compatibility between CPU and motherboard socket.

Cache size

The CPU is the fastest component in the system and usually has a small store of high-speed cache memory that improves overall performance. All other things being equal, the greater the amount of cache memory available, the faster the performance of the chip. The type of memory used for cache – SRAM – is considered in Chapter 3 and the mechanics of how it is used in caching are outlined later in that chapter. For the time being, just be aware that, for the most part, more is better.

The processor 'generations'

The first generation of processors was, of course, the Intel 8088 and 8086, which date from the 1970s and successive developments from both Intel and their rivals such as Cyrix and AMD have been labelled as successive generations. These correspond with the digit that precedes the '86' tag in the processor name, thus the 80286 was a 'second-generation chip', and so on. The original Pentium® – released in 1992 – was the fifth generation of processors. This was succeeded by the sixth generation of processors beginning with the Pentium® Pro, which was released in November 1995. Although these sixth-generation processors are pre-modern, you may still occasionally encounter them in the field.

Table 2.2 Sixth-generation processors.

Processor	Cache
Pentium® Pro	256 KB, 512 KB or 1MB full core speed Level 2
Pentium® II	512 KB half core speed Level 2
Pentium® II Xeon	512 KB, 1MB or 2 MB full core speed Level 2
Celeron®	No Level 2 cache
Celeron® - A	128 KB full core speed Level 2 (on the die)
Pentium® III	512 KB half core speed Level 2
Pentium® III PE	256 KB full core speed Level 2
Pentium® III E	256 KB or 512 KB full core speed Level 2
Pentium® III Xeon	512 KB, 1MB or 2MB full core speed Level 2

The later sixth-generation chips incorporated a new set of microcode instructions called MMX – sometimes known as Multimedia Extensions. MMX is considered later in the chapter.

Seventh-generation processors

Intel Pentium® 4

The Pentium® 4 was introduced in November 2000.

The Willamette core was used for the original P4 processor, which ran at speeds of 1.3 to 1.5 GHz. It had 423 pins and fitted in a socket 423 on the motherboard. This was widely regarded as a stop-gap product from Intel in the face of strong competition from AMD.

The Northwood core was released in October 2001 and ran at speeds from 1.6 to 2.2 GHz. It required a new socket type – the socket 478. The Northwood core supported hyperthreading on all releases, but was disabled in all but the top of the range 3.06 GHz version, which was released in November 2002.

The Prescott core was released in February 2004 and could run at up to 3.8 GHz. Initially, it used the same socket 478 as the Northwood but overheating problems caused Intel to change this to the LGA775, which puts the pins on the board rather than on the chip. However, the move to the LGA775 socket made the thermal problems worse and the Prescott core was finally abandoned.

Other variants of the P4 include the Mobile Pentium® 4, which with lower power requirements ran cooler and was used in laptop PCs. This was superseded by the Mobile Pentium® 4 M, which was released in 2002 for use in laptop machines.

The Pentium® 4 Extreme edition was released in September 2003. It was aimed principally at gamers, but the release was timed to be just a few days earlier than a new release from AMD – the Athlon 64 and Athlon 64FX.

Power requirements for the P4

The P4 processor requires more power than its predecessors, so much so that it needs an additional power connector – the ATX12V – in addition to the standard 20-pin ATX power supply connector, which plugs into the motherboard. Most modern power supplies will have a connector of this type, but if the supply you encounter does not, then providing the power supply meets the requirement to deliver at least the 300 watts that a P4 needs, there is an adapter which can convert a standard Molex connector.

Advanced Micro Devices (AMD) processors

AMD's seventh-generation processors all used their Athlon™ brand name. Athon's first seventh-generation processor was released in October 2001 as a direct competitor to the Intel P4 range. This chip was called the Athlon™ XP and was based originally on the Palomino core. Later releases were based on the Thoroughbred, Thorton and Barton cores. In terms of performance comparisons with the rival Intel products, there has been controversy over the way in which AMD describe their chips. Whereas Intel used the raw clock speed of their processors for promotional purposes, AMD used their own Performance Rating (PR) system to describe their chips. The PR system takes into account the efficiency of the chip rather than raw speed and this is the basis for the chip names. Table 2.3 shows some of these for illustrative purposes.

Table 2.3 PR vs. clock speed.

XP 'Name'	Actual Speed	% of 'Name' Speed
1500	1333 MHz	89%
1600	1400 MHz	88%
1700	1467 MHz	86%
1800	1533 MHz	85%
1900	1600 MHz	84%
2000	1667 MHz	83%
2100	1733 MHz	83%

In addition to the range of desktop chips, there was a Mobile Athlon™-4 based on the Palomino core and an XP-M (M for mobile) based on the Thoroughbred and Barton cores. These chips are designed to run at lower voltages than their desktop counterparts and consequently they run cooler. They are sometimes deployed in desktop machines, mainly where noise from cooling systems may be a problem. They are also relatively easy to overclock and are popular with some enthusiasts for this purpose. (See page 33 for more on overclocking.)

Eighth-generation (64-bit) processors

All processors have internal storage known as registers, which are used for storing data that has been transferred from main system RAM. The original Pentium® had 32-bit internal registers but communicated with RAM over a 64-bit interface. This meant that it could process 64-bit instructions, though these were split into 32-bit operations for internal processing. This 32 / 64 arrangement was a feature of successive processors until the introduction of 'true' 64-bit processors, which are 64-bit internally and externally. The first of these eighth-generation processors – that is 64 / 64 processors – was the Intel Itanium (2001) which was followed by the Itanium 2 (2002). The Itanium 2 used 64-bit registers, but increased the memory bus width from 64 bits to 128 bits, so that this processor was 64 / 128. These were high-performance chips intended for deployment in server machines and very high-powered workstations. In 2003, AMD released their Athlon™ 64 processor for desktop PCs, followed by the Opteron processor for server machines.

The Intel Itanium chips tend to require the support of Intel chipsets, but the Athlon processors – Athlon™ 64 and Opteron – have more third-party chipset support from companies such as VIA Technologies and ATI.

The AMD Opteron processor is available in three series: the 100 series for single-processor PCs, the 200 series for dual-processor systems and the 800 for (up to) eight-processor server systems.

The AMD 64 and 64 FX are intended for single-processor desktop systems. These chips have their memory controller built into them rather than using the motherboard Northbridge or Memory Controller Chip.

Table 2.4 64-bit processors and sockets.

Processor	Socket
Itanium®	Pin Array Cartridge – PAC418
Itanium® 2	Pin Array Cartridge – PAC611
Athlon™ 64	two versions – socket 754 or socket 939
Athlon™ 64 FX	two versions – socket 939 or socket 940
Opteron™	two versions – socket 939 or socket 940
AMD Sempron™	socket 754

The AMD Sempron (Socket 754) is a budget chip intended as a low-cost alternative to the AMD 64. Some versions are 32-bit only or support 32 / 64 operations. However, because they use the same socket 754 as the Athlon™ 64, they can easily be upgraded to full 64-bit operation by replacing the processor without upgrading other components.

Dual-core processors

Modern PCs are capable of running several applications simultaneously and we all take for granted that we can, for example, run a word processor and a spreadsheet and access the Internet at the same time. However, this kind of multitasking makes high demands on the processor. One answer is, of course, to use more than one processor. Microsoft Windows® 2000 and Microsoft Windows® XP Professional (but not Microsoft Windows® XP Home) support two processors and some server operating systems support more than two. However, the hardware costs of implementing multiple processors are high and while it may be cost-effective to use two (or more) processors on a high-cost multiple socket motherboard in a server machine, this is not generally the case for desktop PCs.

Dual-core processors incorporate two separate processor cores in the same physical package. This gives nearly the same level of performance as a pair of matched processors without the cost and complexity of running two separate CPUs.

It is worth emphasising, perhaps, that while dual-core processors can deliver higher performance when multitasking by running applications in separate cores almost as if they were separate processors, the same cannot be said where the workload comes from a single very demanding application. For example, modern higher-end games in particular are demanding of processor time and power, but unless they are coded to take advantage of a dual-core processor, there is no significant advantage in deploying them on a dual-core machine. As always, you cannot assess the suitability of a hardware platform without considering the nature of the software that it will run and, ultimately, what the user of the system requires from it.

Intel Pentium® D and Pentium® Extreme

These processors were introduced in April 2005. Their pre-release codename was Smithfield but they are in fact based on the Pentium® 4 Prescott core. The two cores communicate with one another through the motherboard chipset's Northbridge chip (Memory Controller Hub). Figure 2.2 shows a schematic representation of this architecture.

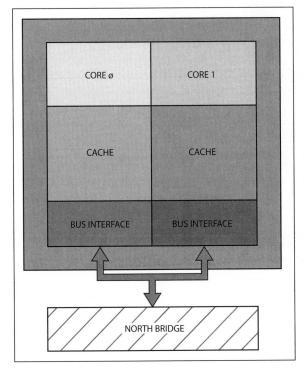

Figure 2.2

The requirement for communication through the chipset means that you may encounter compatibility problems. In particular, Intel 915 and 925 chipsets – made for the Pentium® 4 – do not support Pentium® D or Pentium® Extreme processors. The Intel 954 series and later support the dual-core chips as do some of the NVIDIA series. The working technician need not memorise the whole compatibility list, but should be aware that there may be compatibility issues with some chipsets. Obviously, when considering the deployment of a particular chip, motherboard support for it is a major consideration that needs to be researched from the manufacturer's specifications and documentation.

AMD 64 × 2 and Dual-Core Opteron

These chips were introduced in 2005 only a few weeks after the Intel chips to which they are rivals.

The 64 × 2 has two variants – the version with 1 MB of Level 2 cache (512 KB per core) is based on the Manchester core, while the version with 2 MB of Level 2 cache (1 MB per core) uses the Toledo core. Clock speeds are in the range 2.2 GHz to 2.4 GHz and it fits in a socket 939 on the motherboard.

Unlike the Intel chips discussed above, the AMD 64 × 2 and Opteron do not communicate between cores via the Northbridge chip. They use, instead, a crossbar switch that is integrated into the chip's internal structure. Figure 2.3 shows a schematic representation of this.

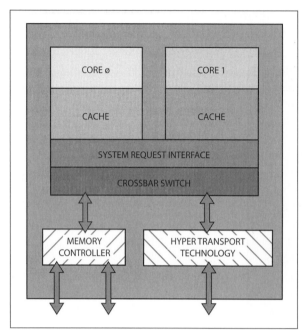

Figure 2.3

The Opteron™ Dual Core is available in the 100, 200 and 800 series with speeds in the range 1.8 GHz to 2.4 GHz and fits into a socket 940 on the motherboard.

Upgrading to AMD dual-core chips

Because the dual-core chips from AMD use the same socket 939 and socket 940 as their single-core counterparts there's a high probability that you can upgrade without replacing the motherboard. If an upgrade is proposed, you need to check that the motherboard supports the particular chip variant and that there is BIOS support for dual-core chips or a BIOS upgrade is available.

Speeds and thermal issues

Clock speeds of the AMD dual-core chips are lower than their Intel counterparts. However, it is claimed that their greater efficiency will deliver better performance than is suggested by considering raw clock speed on its own. The AMD (dual-core) chips also run somewhat cooler. For example, the hottest running 64 × 2 produces 110 watts in operation compared with 130 watts for the Pentium® D and Pentium® Extreme. Most of the AMD dual-core chips are almost as thermally efficient as their single-core counterparts.

How cache memory works

Cache is a concept rather than a technology in its own right. Wherever you have two devices – such as disk and RAM – that operate at different speeds, an intermediate store is used to smooth out the differences and improve overall performance. The CPU chip is the fastest device on the system and it needs to communicate with system RAM which is slower and, because it is based on one of the dynamic RAM types (see Chapter 3), system

RAM is not available for read / write operations during the 'Refresh Cycle'.

Although the algorithms used in the implementation of cache memory are complex (and beyond the terms of reference for an A+ working technician), the underlying concept is a straightforward one.

When the CPU requires information from main system RAM, it reads what it needs and also reads what it 'thinks' it may need soon. This information is stored in cache memory. When the processor needs further information, it first looks in cache memory to see if it is available there. Because cache is implemented in SRAM (which by its nature doesn't need refreshing), information is always available, so even if system RAM cannot be directly read because it is being

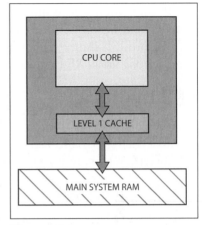

Figure 2.4

refreshed, the processor is not pushed into a wait state because of this. In practice, cache is implemented as level 1 – on the die – and levels 2 and 3, which may be on the die or on board. Different chips will have different quantities and levels of cache and not all of them (particularly level 3) are necessarily implemented. When the processor reads, it reads initially from its level 1 cache and if this is successful (a cache 'hit') it uses the information that it finds. If the read operation does not produce the required data, then the CPU works its way down the cache hierarchy until it either finds what it wants or is forced to wait.

Neither exams nor the practices of the workplace are likely to require you to know details of every configuration of cache for every chip. What you need is the ability to read a specification and to make a decision based on your understanding of the concept in order to compare competing products.

Hyperthreading

Hyperthreading is a technology that was developed by Intel, and Hyper-Threading Technology (HTT) is their trademark. In effect, although there is only a single processor, if it is HTT enabled then the operating system will 'see' two processors and distribute tasks between them. Obviously, the operating system has to support multiple processors – whether physical processors as in a multi-processor machine, multiple cores on the same die, or the 'virtual processors' which it 'sees' as a result of running on a HTT enabled chip. Any operating system which supports Symmetric Multiprocessing – more than one physical processor – will also work with virtual processors of a HTT chip. Microsoft Windows

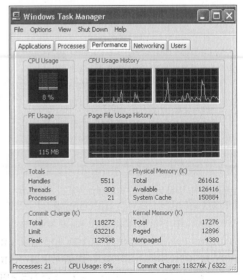

Figure 2.5

2000® and Microsoft Windows XP Professional® (but not Microsoft Windows XP Home®) and nearly all Linux distributions support multiple chips, whether virtual or real. Figure 2.5 shows the output of the Microsoft Windows® Task Manager on a Microsoft Windows XP Professional®system with two processors.

CPU throttling

Throttling is a generic term for restricting the CPU resources for a particular thread or process. The term is also used in connection with processor management as part of the Advanced Configuration and Power Interface (ACPI).

Multiple processes

Where many processes – possibly from many users on a server machine – appear to be running simultaneously they are, in fact, taking it in turn to use the CPU for a while, then relinquishing the CPU resources to another process. The working of this time-slicing can, in some conditions, result in some processes having an 'unfair' time slice or even locking out other processes (and the users who own them) altogether. Throttling – which is implemented through the operating system – controls the allocation of resources between competing processes and users. This is an advanced server management topic and is unlikely to be the concern of the A+ certified working technician.

Power management

CPU throttling as part of power management is more likely to be the concern of the A+ technician than server management. CPUs use more power when they are working at full speed than when they are not, and – power consumption apart – they also generate a lot more heat. Both power consumption and heat are important considerations for all PCs, but are particularly significant in laptop / portable systems. 'Throttling down' the speed of a processor to a fraction of what is required for a full workload is a means of saving power and reducing the overall temperature of the system. Two commonly encountered proprietary technologies used to achieve this are Intel's Speedstep®, which can reduce CPU clock speed and voltage, and AMD's Power Now! ™, which provides similar functionality for their chips.

Where there are power management problems, the settings can be changed through the Windows interface. The Power Options applet in the Control Panel (Microsoft Windows 2000® and Microsoft Windows XP®) gives you control over the power management features and you can adjust the settings to suit the user's needs or the requirements of the system. In a particular instance you could, for example, disable power management through the Control Panel as a quick fix, then research the specific problem further. There is, for example, a known problem with Microsoft Windows XP Media Center 2005® affecting dual-core processors. The fix is a Registry tweak which is detailed on the Microsoft support site. Obviously, this type of detailed knowledge isn't required for the exam, but the approach – looking it up on the web – is part of your standard troubleshooting procedures.

Microcode (MMX)

MMX is popularly believed to be the initial letters of Multi Media Extensions and this describes the function of the MMX microcode which was first incorporated into Intel's Pentium® MMX processor in 1997. However, MMX is Intel's registered trademark and the company have stated that it is not an abbreviation of anything – it is, they say, a three-letter trademark that is not an abbreviation or an acronym. This position, of course, gives Intel legal protection for their trademark and prevents rivals (such as AMD) from using it to describe their products, which may deliver similar functionality.

MMX is a specialised example of microcode, that is an instruction set integrated into the chip that operates at a very low level. In effect, a single instruction from an application is broken down into a series of microcode instructions – an example of a technique known as Single Instruction Multiple Data (SIMD), which was originally developed for large-scale supercomputers. The details of the operation of MMX involve the liaising of existing registers within the chip. This may be of interest to programmers and chip designers, but is far beyond anything which will affect the working A+ technician. From a practical point of view, you merely need to be aware that chips that incorporate MMX can be expected to outperform similar chips that do not have this functionality.

Overclocking

When a batch of chips is produced, there are variations in quality and manufacturers test the chips and allocate a speed rating for each chip. The chips are then badged and sold as performing at a given clock speed. However, the clock speed of a chip isn't something that is built into a chip, it is a setting that can be changed through hardware, firmware or software. The manufacturer's speed rating indicates a recommended speed that should guarantee stable and reliable operation. The manufacturer's rating has a margin built into it, so the chip can often be pushed a bit faster than its intended (recommended) speed by tweaking system settings. Increasing clock speeds in excess of the manufacturer's rating is known – unsurprisingly, perhaps – as overclocking. It has a number of implications:

Cooling. An overclocked chip will run hotter than intended, so you may experience thermal problems. These can be offset by improving the cooling system – bigger heat sink, more powerful fan on the heat sink, additional case fans, or even liquid cooling solutions.

Stability. Pushing a chip faster than intended can cause stability problems. There are various diagnostic programs to test for stable and accurate operation, but these may not provide a full or accurate picture of the chip's functioning and they cannot predict how the overclocked chip will perform as its age increases.

Warranty. Overclocking a chip will almost certainly invalidate any warranty or guarantee from the manufacturer or the vendor. Many modern chips from both Intel and AMD are 'locked' to prevent overclocking, so unlocking them in order to overclock them is easily detected and will invalidate any warranty.

Most overclocking is done by enthusiasts who, presumably, accept the risks involved. However, unscrupulous system builders may overclock a chip and pass it off as being a faster (and therefore more expensive) chip than it, in fact, is. This is simply fraud. As a working technician, you are not concerned with law enforcement, but you should be able to detect an overclocked chip and to advise your customer accordingly.

Although it is not the concern of this chapter, it is worth noting that overclocking is not restricted to CPU chips but can be done with other components such as graphics cards, chipsets or RAM. The implications for cooling systems, stability and warranties are, of course, similar.

Voltage Regulator Module (VRM)

Different chips have different power requirements – core voltages in particular have dropped considerably over the years and the trend seems set to continue. A Voltage Regulator Module (VRM) may be soldered on to the motherboard or it may be an installable device. Either way, its function is to provide the correct voltage for the installed chip. At boot time, the VRM receives a signal from the CPU which indicates the required voltages and adjusts its output to meet these requirements. This means, for example, that if you are asked to upgrade a CPU chip, then provided that it has motherboard and chipset support, you need not be concerned with the details of its voltage requirements.

SUMMARY

In this chapter, we have considered briefly the history of the CPU as pioneered by Intel and developed by them and others. We have looked at the more modern sixth-, seventh- and eighth-generation processors in a little more detail. We have looked at some of the technologies used in CPUs such as hyperthreading, cache levels and microcode. The requirements of the Essentials exam as described in this chapter are by no means a complete treatment of a very complex subject and if you are interested in the technology or if you intend to do the 604 (Depot Technician) exam as your elective exam you will need to look at CPUs in rather more depth. The material for the 604 (Depot Technician) exam is presented in A+ for Students: Electives.

QUESTIONS

1 You have been asked to upgrade the CPU on a working system that is currently running Microsoft Windows 2000®. You suspect that the badge on the case is wrong and need to identify the CPU type. Which of the following methods will produce the required information?

a) Use the System Information utility from the System Tools menu

b) Run the SYSTEMINFO command from a prompt

c) Examine the CPU in situ

d) Any of the above

2 Which of the following processors will fit in a socket 478?

a) P4 Willamette core

b) AMD Opteron™

c) P4 Prescott core

d) Itanium® 2

3 You have been asked to advise on upgrading a system that is used primarily for high-end games. The system has 1 GB of RAM with two spare slots and a socket 940 single-core processor. What do you recommend?

a) More RAM

b) Upgrade to a dual-core processor

c) Fit a faster hard disk

d) None of the above

4 You have been asked to upgrade the operating system on a dual-processor PC that is currently running Microsoft Windows 2000®. Which of the following are valid choices for the new operating system?

a) Microsoft Windows® XP Professional

b) Microsoft Windows® XP Home

c) Linux

d) Microsoft Windows® XP Media Center

5 What are the principal disadvantages of overclocking a CPU?

a) Thermal problems

b) Invalidating the warranty

c) System instability

d) Any or all of the above

ANSWERS / EXPLANATIONS

1 You have been asked to upgrade the CPU on a working system that is currently running Microsoft Windows 2000®. You suspect that the badge on the case is wrong and need to identify the CPU type. Which of the following methods will produce the required information?

a) Use the System Information utility from the System Tools menu

c) Examine the CPU in situ

Option B applies only to Microsoft Windows® XP.

2 Which of the following processors will fit in a socket 478?

c) P4 Prescott core

The P4 Northwood also uses socket 478.

3 You have been asked to advise on upgrading a system that is used primarily for high-end games. The system has 1 GB of RAM with two spare slots and a socket 940 single-core processor. What do you recommend?

a) More RAM

b) Upgrade to a dual-core processor

c) Fit a faster hard disk

Answer a is the most effective upgrade.

Answer b may be feasible but would need more particulars of the chip involved and would, if implemented, have only a limited impact on a PC used mainly for running a single application.

Answer c is worth considering. A faster hard disk could improve performance, not least because it will probably have a larger cache.

4 You have been asked to upgrade the operating system on a dual-processor PC that is currently running Microsoft Windows 2000®. Which of the following are valid choices for the new operating system?

a) Microsoft Windows® XP Professional

c) Linux

d) Microsoft Windows® XP Media Center

XP Home does not support more than one processor.

5 What are the principal disadvantages of overclocking a CPU?

d) Any or all of the above

CHAPTER 3
Storage – memory and disks

Although the CPU does the 'real work' in a PC – calculations, comparisons of values and so forth – it needs temporary (volatile) storage for data, running programs, and intermediate results. This is implemented in Random Access Memory (RAM). However, this type of storage loses its contents when the PC is turned off, so everything needs to be written – 'saved' – to non-volatile storage, usually in the form of some type of magnetic or optical disk. This chapter considers both RAM and disk storage.

Exam objective 1.1 (part)
Identify the names, purposes and characteristics of memory.

> Types of memory (e.g. DRAM, SRAM, SDRAM, DDR / DDR2, RAMBUS)
> Operational characteristics
> Memory chips (8, 16, 32)
> Parity vs. non-parity
> ECC vs. non-ECC
> Single-sided vs. double-sided

Identify the names, purposes and characteristics of storage devices

> FDD
> HDD
> CD / DVD / RW (e.g. drive speeds, media types)
> Removable storage (e.g. tape drive, solid state such as thumb drive, flash and SD cards, USB, external CD-RW and hard drive)

Types of Random Access Memory (RAM)

DRAM and SRAM – the basic difference

These are the two fundamental types of RAM that you will find in a PC.

Dynamic Random Access Memory (DRAM) is widely used for main system memory because it is relatively cheap. Its main disadvantage is that it loses its information content unless it is 'refreshed' every couple of milliseconds. Static Random Access Memory (SRAM) is more expensive, but does not need to be refreshed, that is it retains its contents until the PC is turned off.

How DRAM works

All of the information held in memory is in the form of electrical charges. These represent the zeroes and ones that are the fundamental language of computer operations. The difference between a one and a zero at a particular memory location depends on the difference in charge. If the charge is eroded or decays, then the information is lost. In order to counter this, a refresh logic circuit reads the contents of each address in memory, then rewrites it to the same location every two milliseconds. This is the 'refresh cycle', and while it is happening no other part of the system can read or write to RAM. This means, for example, that the CPU may need read / write access to RAM but is effectively blocked and put into a 'wait state' by the refresh process. For this reason SRAM (see below) is used as an always-available cache to avoid wait states and to improve CPU performance.

How SRAM works

Static RAM is several times more expensive (byte-for-byte) than its dynamic counterpart. Its defining characteristic is that it does not need to be refreshed so, as long as it has power, its contents can be accessed at any time. Because of the expense of using it, it is generally used in small quantities – as a cache – where the need for DRAM to be refreshed would otherwise cause a bottleneck. As already noted, SRAM may be used as a processor cache, but it is not restricted to this. It is also used for high-speed always-available storage, particularly on disk drives. The working of processor cache memory is described in Chapter 2.

There are a number of variants on SRAM: Asynchronous SRAM (the standard SRAM) and higher-performance variants such as Synchronous SRAM, Pipeline SRAM and Burst-mode SRAM. Detailed knowledge of the differences between SRAM types is less important than the distinction between SRAM and DRAM.

DRAM types

Synchronous DRAM (SDRAM)

This is the oldest of the DRAM types that you will encounter in day-to-day work as well as being the oldest type listed by the A+ exam specification. The term synchronous indicates that its read / write operations are *synchronised* with the PC's system bus and, consequently, its CPU.

SDRAM was introduced in 1996 and is packaged as a Dual Inline Memory Module (DIMM) in which a number of RAM chips are mounted on a printed circuit board, which fits into a slot on the motherboard. The original SDRAM modules were rated at 100 MHz and soon after their introduction, Intel published the PC100 standard, which defined the characteristics required for 100 MHz SDRAM, and the PC prefix to describe RAM modules was widely adopted. SDRAM modules have 168 pins and obviously the motherboard slot has to be of this type. SDRAM is no longer used in the production of PCs, having been superseded by other RAM types.

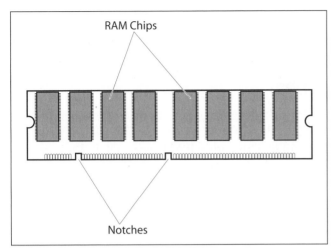

Figure 3.1

Double Data Rate (DDR) RAM

Double Data Rate (DDR) RAM is a development of the standard SDRAM in which data transfers take place on both the rising and falling edge of the PC's clock signal, thus nearly doubling the performance compared with SDRAM. As both of these memory types are synchronised with the Front Side Bus speed standard, SDRAM has been retrospectively designated as Single Data Rate (SDR) SDRAM, to distinguish it from Double Data Rate (DDR) SDRAM.

The DDR module is longer than its SDRAM counterpart, has one notch on the bottom edge and 184 pins.

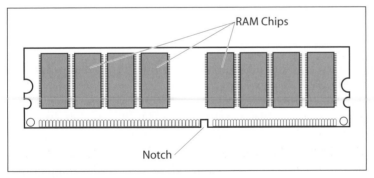

Figure 3.2

The Joint Electronic Devices Engineering Council (JEDEC) specifies the standards for DDR SDRAM for both chips and modules. A chip that runs at an underlying speed of 100 MHz before it has been doubled is therefore designated as a DDR 200 chip. Since data is transferred eight bytes at a time, we can calculate the data transfer rate for the module by multiplying the bus speed by two (because it is doubled by making a transfer on both the rising and falling edge of the clock tick) and multiplying by eight (the number of bytes). For 100 MHz chips mounted on a 200 MHz RAM stick with a 100 MHz bus speed, the calculation will be:

$100 \times 2 \times 8 = 1600$ and the RAM stick will be designated as PC-1600. Other published ratings by JEDEC are for PC-2100, PC-2700 and PC-3200. Intermediate values are manufacturers' or vendors' approximations.

Double Data Rate-2 RAM (DDR2)

A further development of DDR RAM makes higher operating speeds possible. DDR-2 Modules are currently rated at PC-3200, PC-4200, PC-4300 and PC-5400. They have 240 pins and are not backwards compatible with earlier RAM types. DDR-3 is currently under development.

Table 3.1 DIMM types.

RAM	Pins	Voltage
SDRAM	168	3.3 v
DDR	184	2.5 v
DDR-2	240	1.8 v

In addition to these DIMM types, there are specialised packages for portable systems:

▦   Small Outline DIMMs (SODIMM) are used in laptop / notebook machines. These come in 144-pin and 200-pin packages.

▦   MicroDIMMs – these are even smaller than the standard SODIMM and are also used in notebook systems. They have 144 pins and are generally almost square – 38 mm in width and 25 mm in height, though heights vary between manufacturers.

RAMBUS

Rambus memory is a proprietary type manufactured under licence from the Rambus Corporation. It is a form of SDRAM. It was introduced in 1999 as a rival to the then dominant PC 133 SDRAM. It has not been widely adopted by PC manufacturers and is seldom used in new PCs. It is fitted in a 184-pin DIMM-type slot known as a Rambus Inline Memory Module (RIMM). Unlike SDRAM and DDR, RIMM modules have to be fitted in pairs and slots cannot be left empty. Where a module is not fitted, the slot has to be filled with a 'continuity module'. RIMMs also have the disadvantage of high operating temperatures, so the modules have a heat sink built in to them.

Operational characteristics of RAM types

Memory chips (8, 16, 32)

Although RAM is fitted in modules that plug into the motherboard, the modules are made up of chips mounted on a printed circuit board. Early DRAM chips had a single data in / out (I/O) pin so that memory could only be addressed one bit at a time. Because

PCs use their data in bytes (or multiples of bytes known as 'words'), it was necessary for the memory controller chip to make the data appear to the system as 8-bit (byte) units. Modern DRAM chips have additional I/O pins and are made with widths of 8-bit, 16-bit or 32-bit that can be directly addressed. This gives a level of flexibility in the design and manufacture of RAM modules.

Single-sided vs. double-sided

A single physical module can be divided into logical banks that make the single module appear to the system as a bank of separate modules. This gives some flexibility to the memory designer in terms of the chips used, and the system accesses the banks as if they were physically discrete modules. Accessing the modules in this way allows interleaving of read / write access and enhances performance.

Do not confuse 'dual-banked' memory with 'double-sided' memory. Double-sided refers to the physical construction of the memory module – dual-banked refers to the electrical separation of a single physical module into two discrete parts.

Parity vs. non-parity

Parity checking is a fairly basic means of checking that data has not been corrupted during transmission. For each word of data, there is an additional parity bit. The parity bit is added to the total number of bits in the data to make an even number (if you are using even parity) or an odd number (odd parity). When a chunk of data is checked and found to have the wrong parity, then a parity error is reported. Although this prevents corrupted data from being used, there are no mechanisms for correcting the error. Obviously this parity checking uses resources and, as most errors on a desktop machine are not mission critical, parity memory tends not to be extensively used.

ECC vs. non-ECC

Error Correction Code (ECC) is a more sophisticated method of detecting errors. It can detect and fix single-bit errors and can detect and report more serious errors up to 4 bits. Any form of RAM that does not implement this is described as non-ECC.

The majority of systems that you will work on as a PC technician will use non-parity, non-ECC RAM types. In general, when you are adding or replacing memory on a system, it is usual to replace like with like. A rule of thumb is to count the number of individual chips on the RAM module. If this is exactly divisible by three or five, then it has some form of error-checking built in to it.

Where to find more information

The major RAM manufacturers are a useful source of information. The Crucial web site has a downloadable utility that will probe the target system and report the installed memory type. Kingston provide (as a free download in Portable Document Format) The Ultimate Memory Guide http://www.kingston.com/tools/umg/default.asp. This runs over 100 pages and examines memory to a depth well beyond the requirements of the working technician or the A+ examination.

Disk storage

Floppy disk drives

The floppy disk drive – in various formats – has been part of the PC since the 1980s, although modern systems are sometimes built without a floppy drive. Storage capacities increased over the years and the dominant physical format moved from 5.25 in to 3.5 in. The present-day floppy disk is 3.5 in, with a rigid outer case and a storage capacity of 1.44 MB. This format / capacity has replaced all earlier types and you will seldom encounter any other floppy type. Nearly all motherboards and cases support the fitting of an internal 3.5 in FDD and its 34-line cable even where it is not part of the original hardware build. Most BIOSs support the standard 1.44 MB type by default, though other sizes can usually be set up by using the set-up utility. When physically installing a floppy drive, the data cable needs to be properly oriented. A pink line on the cable identifies line one and this has to correspond with pin one on the motherboard. Connectors are sometimes keyed to ensure correct orientation. There are usually two connectors at the drive end of the cable, separated by a twist in the cable. This is a leftover from the days of twin-floppy PCs and is rarely used. To ensure that the floppy drive is identified as drive A by the operating system, it should be attached to the connector after the twist in the cable.

A popular alternative is to use an external floppy attached through a USB port. Where the target PC supports booting to a USB device, this means that the floppy drive can still be used to boot a machine to a diagnostic disk for troubleshooting purposes or even to prepare a hard disk for use.

How floppies store data

If you break open a floppy disk case, you will see that inside the rigid outer cover there is a black, circular disk which is – literally – floppy. This inner disk – the real disk as it were – is covered in magnetic compounds that are capable of storing electronic zeroes and ones as magnetic fields. Although you cannot see it, a formatted floppy disk is divided into tracks and sectors that constitute the file system.

Each side of the disk is divided into concentric rings known as tracks, and the tracks are divided into storage units known as sectors. Each sector on a floppy disk can hold 512 bytes of data. Each sector is numbered and can be referenced by the File Allocation Table (FAT), which acts rather like the index of a book. When you write a file to disk, an entry in the File Allocation Table records the sector on which it starts. If the file is larger than the storage unit (a 512-byte sector), then the last couple of bytes of that sector contain the address of the next sector containing that file. This means that a file need not necessarily be stored in the same area of the disk – it can be daisy-chained across it.

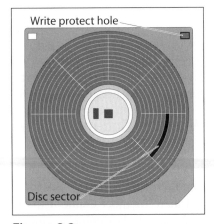

Figure 3.3

The FAT file system was also used for hard disk drives in earlier versions of Microsoft Windows® up to and including Millennium Edition. Although modern systems use a more sophisticated system (NTFS), the FAT model used on floppies can be a good way of understanding the principles involved in disk storage: the disk rotates and a read / write head is positioned over a storage area and data is read from or written to the storage area. Details of the locations are held in the File Allocation Table or, in later Microsoft Windows® versions, the Master File Table of the NT File System (NTFS). File systems are considered further in Chapter 8.

Hard disk drives

Although there are different interfaces for connecting hard disk drives – Parallel ATA, Serial ATA, SCSI and ports to external drives (USB or FireWire), the storage mechanisms and structures on the drives are fundamentally similar. In order to provide greater storage capacity, a hard drive is better engineered. It has multiple rigid platters and each side of each platter has its own read / write head. The rotation speed of the spindle has increased over time and, on desktop machines, 7200 rpm has more or less superseded the 5400 rpm speed of earlier EIDE / PATA disks. Some SATA disks can work at 10,000 rpm and some top-of-the-range SCSI drives can work at 15,000 rpm. The smaller disks used in portable systems tend to be slower.

Figure 3.4 shows a read / write head as it passes across the top platter of a hard disk that has been opened.

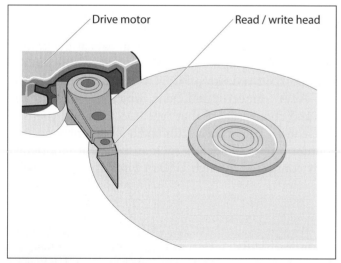

Drive motor   Read / write head

Figure 3.4

If you break open an old hard disk to take a look for yourself, you will see something very like what is shown in the figure. However, be aware that the drive will be a write-off as a result.

Drive capacities

Early hard drives measured their capacity in megabytes (MB) but today's larger disks are rated in gigabytes (GB). There is sometimes confusion about the reported sizes of disk drives because of the different definitions of the units of measurement. A kilobyte is 2^{10} (1024 bytes) but this is often rounded to 1000 bytes. At this level, the difference is small. However, if we derive measurements based on it by successively multiplying or dividing by 1000 instead of 1024, the differences soon become significant. Thus, a drive described by the manufacturer as 30 GB will contain 30,000,000,000 bytes because the calculation is based on 1000 bytes to the kilobyte. If however, we adopt the (technically correct) definition of 1024 and divide successively by that, then our 30 GB drive will only weigh in at 27.9 GB. Various standards bodies have attempted to resolve the confusion in the units of measurement but none have found universal acceptance. As a working technician, you need to be prepared to see apparently contradictory reports of disk sizes.

Figure 3.5 XP reporting the size of an '80 GB' drive.

Optical drives

Floppy and hard disk types encode zeroes and ones on magnetic surfaces. CD and DVD drives use laser light to encode the data and are therefore known collectively as *optical drives*. Most optical drives are fitted internally in the standard 5.25" in bays at the front of the case. (The 5.25" in bay size is, of course, a legacy from the days when this was the standard for the early floppy drive types). On a desktop PC, connection is nearly always through a standard 40-pin EIDE / ATA connector and cable, which is similar to and compatible with hard drive cables and connectors of that type. Occasionally, you may encounter SCSI optical drives. These use a 50-pin connector and a 50-line ribbon cable. Very occasionally, you may encounter other connectors such as SATA or proprietary interfaces. External drives – usually connected through USB or FireWire – are considered further later in the chapter.

CD drives and disks

The original *compact disk* was used for recording music and its speed is still the basis for speed ratings for data disks and drives. A single-speed CD spins at 500 rpm and delivers a data transfer rate of 150 kilobytes per second. Other CD drives work at a multiple of this speed. Calculating the speed of a given drive is, then, a simple exercise in multiplication:

Table 3.2 CD data transfer speeds.

Data transfer speed	Kilobytes per second
1 ×	150
2 ×	300
4 ×	600
8 ×	1200
10 ×	1500
12 ×	1800
20 ×	3000
32 ×	4800
36 ×	5400
40 ×	6000
48 ×	7200
50 ×	7500
52 ×	7800

Although a CD was originally a read-only medium, there are writable media too. CD/R indicates a recordable CD that can be written to once but read many times (sometimes known as WORM). CD/RW indicates a disk type that can be written to and read from several times. As you might expect, the data transfer rate is different according to the type of operation, and rewritable CD drives are usually described with three different speeds – for write once, rewrite and read only operations, usually in that order. Thus a drive described as a 12× / 10× / 32× is capable of a 12-speed write to a recordable disk, a 10-speed write to a rewritable disk and of reading a read-only disk at 32 speed (4800 KB per second).

Disk sizes

A standard CD is 120 mm in diameter and can hold 650–700 MB of data. Stripped of layout information and illustrations, the text of this book would fit on a standard CD around 500 times – more if the data was compressed before recording. There are also mini-CDs – 80 mm in diameter – with a correspondingly smaller storage capacity (around 190 MB). Because CDs start reading from the centre of the disk and work outwards towards the edge, it is possible, in principle at least, to manufacture a CD of any capacity.

DVD drives and disks

DVD is the subject of the DVD forum which includes major industry participants such as Sony, Toshiba and Mitsubishi. Officially at least, the forum has decided that DVD does not actually stand for anything, although most people regard it as an abbreviation of either Digital Versatile Disk or Digital Video Disk.

Physical disk sizes for DVDs are the same as CDs but they hold considerably more data. A single-sided single-layered DVD disk holds 4.7 GB of data. Dual-layer and double-layer formats increase this to 8.5 GB.

Like CD, DVD was originally a read-only format DVD-ROM, but now there are also writable and re-writable formats.

Table 3.3 DVD formats and capacities.

DVD Format	Capacity
DVD-ROM	Read only 4.7 GB or 8.5 GB depending on the number of sides and recording layers
DVD-R	Write once 4.7 GB
DVD-RW	Rewritable 4.7 GB
DVD-R DL	Dual layer – write once 8.5 GB
DVD-RAM	4.7 GB (single sided) or 9.4 GB (double sided) – needs a special drive.
DVD+R	Write once 4.7GB up to16 speed
DVD+RW	Rewritable 4.7 GB up to16 speed
DVD+R DL	Dual layer – write once 8.5 GB upto16 speed

Note: the + in these format names is a 'plus' but the – is a dash, not a minus.

Many modern DVD recorders / drives support several of the popular formats.

Removable storage

Removable storage devices can be used to provide additional storage to a system without opening the case and may also be used for backing up and transporting data.

Tape drives

Tape drives are commonly used for back-ups, particularly for server machines. The drives are usually internal – connected to ATA or SCSI interfaces – but the tapes themselves are removable. An important characteristic of tape drives is that they only offer sequential access, i.e. you have to wind the tape to find the information you want. They are used almost exclusively for backing up large quantities of data – usually as an overnight job. The common tape types are:

Table 3.4 Common tape sizes.

Drive Type	Size	Storage Capacity
DAT (digital audio tape) cartridge	4 mm	1 GB–20 GB
DLT (digital linear tape)	0.5 in	10 GB–50 GB
Exabyte	8 mm	2.5 GB–60 GB
QIC (quarter inch cartridge)	0.25 in	40 MB–20 GB
Redwood	0.5 in	10 GB–50 GB

DAT and DLT are the most common types on desktop systems; the others are more commonly used on servers.

The tapes themselves should be safely stored away from temperature extremes or strong magnetic fields such as those produced by CRT monitors or Uninterruptible Power Supplies.

Solid state drives

A solid state drive is based on non-volatile memory rather than the spinning platter and mechanical read / write head found in conventional disks. Figure 3.6 shows a comparison of a solid state drive and its mechanical counterpart.

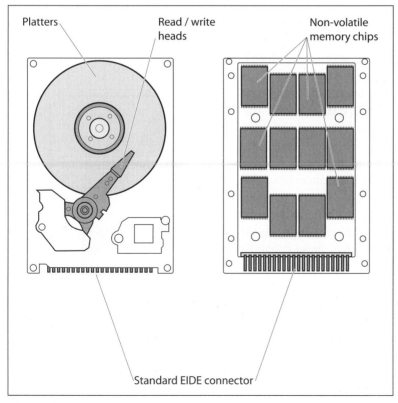

Figure 3.6

As you can see from the figure, the solid state drive has an EIDE / PATA interface. This means that it can simply be dropped into place unlike its conventional counterpart. These devices are often referred to as solid state disks because, although they have no platters and are not strictly speaking disks, they offer an alternative to conventional disk drives and are thus disk-like.

Solide state drives have been in use since their introduction in 1995 and in spite of being expensive in comparison with conventional hard disks, they are faster run cooler and offer a mean time between failure up to ten times that of conventional disks. They have been used in military and aerospace applications because of their speed, reliability and the fact that they weigh less than conventional drives. However, technical progress and the familiar downward trend in hardware prices means that solid state storage has been adopted for use in other, consumer-level devices such as 'thumb drives'.

Thumb drives

These drives – also known as 'pen drives' or 'gizmo sticks' are familiar as a means of storing and transporting data. They usually plug into a USB port and are recognised by Microsoft Windows® as a disk drive that needs no further configuration or drivers. They use the FAT or FAT32 file system, so they are portable across most operating systems. When not in use, they have a removable cap to protect the connector which fits in the USB port. Figure 3.7 shows a typical thumb drive.

Flash and SD cards

Non-volatile memory is commonly used in a variety of storage applications: PCMCIA cards for use with laptop systems, storage for digital cameras and phones, and Secure Digital cards (SD cards). SD cards are technically similar to other forms of flash memory storage and the term 'Secure' is mainly of historical interest. When these cards were first developed (by Toshiba) it was a development of earlier card types and, mainly to meet the concerns of the music industry about piracy of content, the new cards incorporated an improved encryption technology to help the enforcement of digital rights management. In practice, these capabilities are seldom used.

Many devices such as printers have ports for one or more of the memory card types so that images can be transferred and printed without going through a host PC.

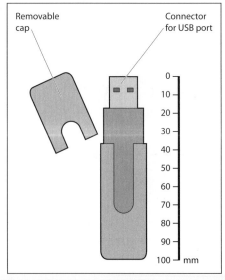

Figure 3.7

USB

The Universal Serial Bus (USB) is used to connect both USB sticks (see page 48) and other external devices such as external CD / DVD drives and hard drives. Firewire / IEEE 1394 is used similarly as an interface for connecting external storage. Once an external drive is attached through a USB or FireWire port, it is identical in its operation to an internal drive and considerations such as jumper settings, formatting and so forth are much the same. The various drive types are considered at some length in Chapter 6.

SUMMARY

In this chapter we have considered various types of storage: memory (RAM) – static and dynamic – and various forms of disk storage. We have looked at magnetic storage – from floppies to multiple-plattered hard disks – and their optical equivalents, CD and DVD, in read-only and read / write versions. In the final section of the chapter, we considered the use of non-volatile memory for disk-like storage, which may be implemented as EIDE-connected 'disks' or the more familiar 'thumb drives', and various cards that use flash memory storage for a variety of applications.

QUESTIONS

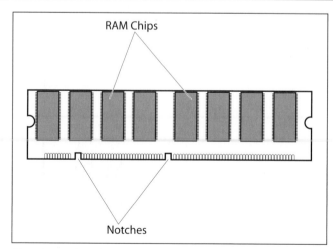

RAM Chips

Notches

Figure 3.8

1   What type of memory module is shown in the figure:

   a) Rambus

   b) SDRAM

   c) DDR RAM

   d) SODIMM

2   Which of the following are typical uses of SRAM?

   a) Processor cache

   b) Disk cache

   c) Internet browser cache

   d) All of the above

3   What type of memory module requires a continuity module in unused slots on the motherboard?

   a) DDR-2

   b) Rambus

   c) ECC

   d) SDRAM

4   Which of the following is not a connection type for internal hard drives?

   a) SATA

   b) PATA

   c) ECC

   d) SCSI

5   Which of the following file systems are used by thumb drives?

   a) NTFS

   b) FAT

   c) FAT 32

   d) Reiser FS

ANSWERS / EXPLANATIONS

1   What type of memory module is shown in the figure?

  b) SDRAM

2   Which of the following are typical uses of SRAM?

  a) Processor cache

  b) Disk cache

  The browser cache is a disk file.

3   What type of memory module requires a continuity module in unused slots on the motherboard?

  b) Rambus

4   Which of the following is not a connection type for internal hard drives?

  c) ECC

  ECC is a memory type.

5   Which of the following file systems are used by thumb drives?

  b) FAT

  c) FAT 32

CHAPTER 4
Video and I/O devices

This chapter looks at how a PC displays information to the user through video outputs and how information is input by various means such as keyboards, mice, cameras, etc. It also considers the connector types used to connect the various input and output (I/O) devices to the PC.

Exam objective 1.1 (part)
Identify the names, purposes and characteristics of display devices, for example: projectors, CRT and LCD

   Connector types (e.g. VGA, DVI / HDMi, S-Video, Component / RGB)
   Settings (e.g. V-hold, refresh rate, resolution)

Identify the names, purposes and characteristics of input devices, for example: mouse, keyboard, bar code reader, multimedia (e.g. web and digital cameras, MIDI, microphones), biometric devices, touch screen

Display devices

Monitors

Monitors and their associated cards and drivers are one of the most complex (and expensive) peripheral devices attached to the PC. They are also the most straightforward to install. It is usually just a case of attaching to the appropriate video port, powering up, and letting Microsoft Windows® get on with the business of detecting the type and installing any necessary drivers. Microsoft Windows XP® in particular is well provided with drivers that will work out of the box, although you may have to provide drivers from the monitor vendor's installation CD or download them from the appropriate site. However, most of the technician's work is concerned with adjusting the installed monitor to suit the end-user's requirements.

Monitor settings

Irrespective of the monitor or connector type, there are some basic settings that you need to be able to adjust to set the monitor up for safe and effective use. These can be adjusted through the Microsoft Windows® interface.

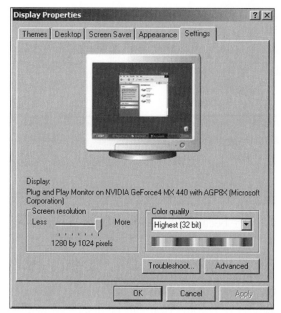

Figure 4.1

Figure 4.1 shows the Display Properties panel in Microsoft Windows® XP. To access this – in XP or 2000 – right-click on an empty area of the desktop and select **Properties** or click on the **Display** applet in **Control Panel**. Note the **Advanced** button which gives you access to further settings including the monitor's refresh rate.

In addition to the software controls, there are, of course, hardware controls on the monitor itself that can be used to control the vertical and horizontal positioning of the image, brightness, contrast, etc. These will be product-specific and you will need to consult the vendor's documentation or be prepared to experiment.

REFRESH RATE

The refresh rate is a measurement (expressed in Hertz – Hz) of the speed at which the screen is repainted from top to bottom by the CRT's electron beam. Low refresh rates can cause eye strain and pushing a monitor beyond the refresh rate it can support can cause permanent damage to the hardware. To change the refresh rate, click on the **Advanced** button (as in Figure 4.1) and select the **Monitor** tab.

If necessary, check the box marked **Hide modes that this monitor cannot display**. Then choose a known safe setting from those displayed in the drop-down list.

The minimum refresh rate for a Super Video Graphics Array (SVGA) monitor is in the range 70–75 Hz. This standard is laid down by the Video Electronics Standards Association (VESA).

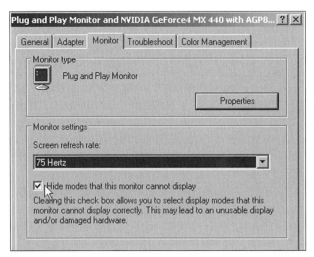

Figure 4.2

COLOUR DEPTH

The colour depth is also known as the 'bit depth' because the colour depth is expressed as the number of bits required to display it.

The colour depth is the number of individual colours that a single pixel can display. The number of bits in the colour depth determines the number of colours available. For example, 8-bit colour can represent 256 colours because an 8-bit number can express the range 0–255 (256) values. Generally, the number of colours that can be displayed will be given by the binary value +1.

Twenty-four-bit colour gives 16.7 million colours which is slightly more that the human eye can distinguish between. Twenty-four-bit or higher colour is usually designated as 'true colour'.

Cathode Ray Tube (CRT) monitors

This is an old technology, similar to that used in television sets, which was the standard display device for the very earliest PCs. They are rapidly being replaced by flat panel monitors that use Liquid Crystal Display (LCD) technology, which is familiar from its use in laptop / notebook PCs. The internal workings of a CCRT monitor are not examined by the A+ tests. A monitor is a Field Replaceable Unit, which may need to be adjusted, configured, tweaked or replaced. Internally, a CRT monitor contains sufficient voltage to kill (even when it is turned off) and it should never be opened in the field.

Liquid Crystal Display (LCD) monitors

LCD monitors are small and lightweight and have become increasingly popular as replacements for the older CRT monitors in recent years. At the lower end of the market, they still use a standard VGA connector to attach to the PC, whereas more expensive models use one of the Digital Video Interface (DVI) connectors (see page 56 for more on connectors). Image quality depends to a great extent on whether the LCD monitor is constructed using passive or active matrix technology.

Passive matrix screens use two rows of transistors – one along the top of the display and one down the side – so a particular pixel can be addressed through its x,y co-ordinates. This is a slow way of addressing a pixel and the result is a rather sluggish display.

Active matrix screens have a transistor for each pixel. This results in a faster responding, clearer display at the expense of power consumption. While this is not particularly significant on a mains-powered desktop PC, it places a strain on the battery capacity of a laptop / notebook machine.

Projectors

These are stand-alone devices that may be connected to a PC through one of the standard video interfaces in order to display the screen output on (say) an interactive whiteboard for making presentations to groups such as student classes or seminars. Care of the projector itself will require you to be familiar with the manufacturer's documentation and is not part of the A+ specification.

Video adapter standards

The earliest PCs were designed to use a standard (US) television set for video output. The first dedicated adapter (from IBM) was the Monochrome Display Adapter (MDA). It was text only, which was fine in the days of black and white text-based DOS systems. Other early adapters were the Hercules Graphics Adapter (HGA), the Colour Graphics Adapter (CGA) and the Enhanced Graphics Adapter (EGA). All of these are now obsolete.

Modern standards begin with the Video Graphics Array (VGA) and the current standard is Super VGA (SVGA). These two standards dominate the industry and you should be familiar with the capabilities of VGA and SVGA standards for exam purposes.

Table 4.1 VGA / SVGA standards.

Video Standard	Resolution	Colours
VGA (Video Graphics Array)	640 × 480	16
	320 × 200	256
SVGA (Super VGA)	800 × 600	16
	1024 × 768	256
	1280 × 1024	256
	1600 × 1200	256

Resolution is the number of pixels used to display the image on the screen. The more pixels used, the better and clearer the image will be, and the greater the amount of video RAM necessary to support it.

Screen resolutions are expressed as the number of pixels in a row and the number of rows on the display. Thus, for example, an 800 × 600 resolution consists of an 800 pixel row and 600 of these 'lines' are used to fill the screen.

Because resolution, colour depth and refresh rates are all controllable through Microsoft Windows®, these are part of a technician's everyday work as well as being sources of A+ exam questions.

Extended Graphics Array (XGA)

This is an old standard from IBM that could support a resolution of 1024 × 768 with 256 colours or, by reducing the resolution to 800 × 600, it could deliver 65,536 colours. Although this is an outmoded system, it is used as the basis for comparison for later systems.

Later standards

These are usually extensions of either SVGA or XGA and are indicated by a letter prefix so, for example, the letter W indicates a wide screen variant and Q indicates a quadruple variant in which the pixel count for both horizontal and vertical dimensions are double that of the reference standard.

Connector types

VGA

The VGA connector is still the most commonly used connector for video output, though newer connectors are gaining in popularity. The VGA connector is male with 15 pins in 3 rows in a D sub-form factor. The connector on the PC – which may be on-board or the interface to a graphics card – is female.

Figure 4.3 VGA Port

Digital Video Interface (DVI)

DVI provides a digital interface that can outperform the older (analogue) VGA system in terms of both quality and speed. It is widely used to connect flat panel monitors and projectors.

There are three main categories of DVI connector:

▨ DVI-D (digital) the most common of the DVI types

▨ DVI-A (analogue)

▨ DVI-I (integrated) supports both digital and analogue connections.

Within those categories, there are single-link and dual-link variants on DVI-D and DVI-I. The dual-link versions have more pins and support higher resolutions.

High Definition Multimedia Interface (HDMI)

HDMI is an all-digital technology designed to outperform DVI in terms of data transfer rates and resolution. It carries both visual and audio signals and can be used to connect any compatible audiovisual device such as a DVD player or a set-top box for a TV set as well as high-end PC monitors.

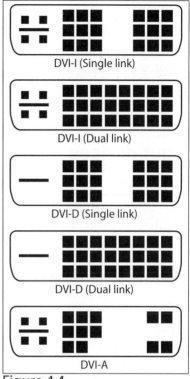

DVI-I (Single link)

DVI-I (Dual link)

DVI-D (Single link)

DVI-D (Dual link)

DVI-A

Figure 4.4

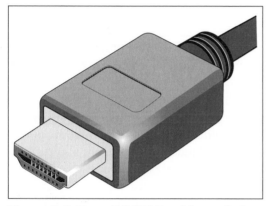

Figure 3.5 Type 'A' HDMI cable and plug.

The type 'A' plug has 19 pins. There is also a newer type 'B' connector with 29 pins, designed to achieve even higher levels of performance.

Component video /RGB

This is an analogue technology that delivers better quality video by splitting the red, green and blue components of the signal at source but delivering them as a non-colour – luminence – signal and two colour signals known as chrominance signals. There are a number of variants on this but they are at a level of detail which need not concern the A+ technician.

This type of plug is often colour coded.

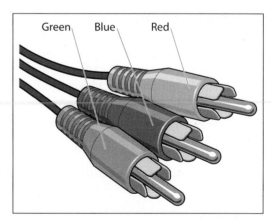

Green   Blue   Red

Figure 4.6 Component video plugs.

S-video

S-video is a type of (analogue) component video that delivers slightly lower performance than 'true" component video. It uses either a 7-pin or a 4-pin mini-din port. The mini-din port is 9.5 mm in diameter and there are various types for different uses. The most familiar of these is probably the standard mouse port on an ATX system.

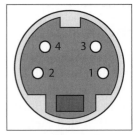

Figure 4.7 4-pin
S-Video port.

Input devices

Keyboard

The keyboard is arguably the most important input device in computing. A PC without a keyboard would be all but unusable and keyboard problems can cause severe operational problems.

The standard QWERTY keyboard follows the layout of the typewriter, although it has additional keys – function keys, arrow keys and (usually) a separate numeric keypad. There are other layouts, such as the Dvorak Simplified Keyboard, which are supported by the major operating systems including Microsoft Windows®. There are also regional variations in layouts. However, the overwhelming majority of keyboards that you will deal with as a technician will be the QWERTY layout.

Problems with keyboards may be physical. Keyboards accumulate dirt and dust and can benefit from the occasional clean with a brush and / or a blow through with canned air. Other problems with keyboards arise from incorrect settings and these can be fixed through the Microsoft Windows® Control Panel. There is a Keyboard applet in both Microsoft Windows® 2000 and XP that gives you access to keyboard settings. You should also check the Regional and Language applet (Microsoft Windows® XP) and the Regional Options applet in Microsoft Windows® 2000. There are differences in how the keyboard / language settings are split across the applets in Microsoft Windows® 2000 and XP and these may be worth exploring as a practical exercise.

Keyboard connectors can also cause problems if they are not fully engaged with ports on the PC or they have bent pins. Always check them if a keyboard fails to respond and, of course, a reboot of the affected PC may help. The main connector for keyboards on the modern PC is a 6-pin mini-din known as a PS/2 because it was released (in 1977) with the IBM Personal System/2 PCs. These days, it is almost invariably colour-coded green, though this is a convention, not an official standard.

Earlier systems with the AT motherboard form factor used a larger 5-pin DIN connector. Both PS/2 and DIN connectors are male on the keyboard end and plug into a female port on the PC. Keyboards that connect through the Universal Serial Bus (USB) interface are commonly used on modern systems. There are various adaptors that allow you to plug a keyboard into a different port – a DIN to PS/2 for example – and while these generally work well enough, they can be yet another source of bad physical connections.

Mouse

Next to the keyboard, the mouse is probably the most frequently used input device on a PC. Early mice detected motion though a ball in the base of the device. This moved two rollers, which in turn translated the motion of the mouse into onscreen movements of the cursor. These ball mice are still widely used and the main problem with them is the build-up of dirt on the ball and the rollers. They need to be cleaned from time to time, usually by physically scraping the dirt from the rollers with something like a toothpick.

More modern mice are optical. The ball and roller mechanism has been replaced by light reflected from the surface – such as a mouse pad – underneath it. The number of buttons on a mouse varies with the manufacturer and model, and a scroll wheel that sometimes doubles up as a middle button is frequently used. Mice connect though a PS/2 connector – usually colour-coded purple – on modern systems. Older mice frequently used the standard 9-pin serial port (also known as an RS232 port) with a female connector on the mouse end to match the male port on the PC. USB mice are also available.

Variants on the standard mouse include: trackballs, tablets, touchpads and other pointing devices. In terms of connectors, they are the same as mice and software adjustments are made through the Mouse applet in the Control Panel of both Microsoft Windows® 2000 and XP.

A note on PS/2 connectors – these are not intended to be hot-swappable. Unlike a serial connector, which can be connected after boot time, you should power down before attaching a keyboard or a mouse to a PS/2 port. In practice, if you hot-swap a PS/2 device, you will probably get away with it, but you are risking damage to the system if you do this.

Bar code readers

These are specialised input devices that read a bar code – typically on a product label – which contains information about the product such as stock control information, the unit price, and so on. This type of reader is familiar to most of us through their use in supermarket checkouts and other specialist systems. From the point of view of a PC technician, connection to a PC is through one of the standard ports such as PS/2 or RS232. Wireless, infra-red and Bluetooth are also possible connection technologies for these devices.

Multimedia devices

This category includes both audio and visual input devices.

Microphones are by their nature analogue devices and they deliver an audio signal to the PC which needs to be digitised. Connection is usually to a jack on the PC's soundcard.

Musical Instrument Digital Interface (MIDI) devices don't use an audio signal as such but send MIDI channel messages from a MIDI musical instrument to the PC. These are then translated into actual sounds. The standard MIDI connector is a 5-pin mini-din, but the connection at the PC end may be through a 15-pin game port or USB.

Cameras

Various camera types – stills, movies, webcams, etc. – can all be connected to a PC through one of the standard ports. Movie cameras, where there are both audio and visual components, may attach through a FireWire (IEEE 1394) port because this technology supports simultaneous transmission of both data types. This is known as isochronous data transfer.

Biometric devices

These are devices that read physical characteristics and encode them for processing by the PC. This may be fingerprint scanning, retinal pattern scanning, voice or face recognition. From the point of view of the working PC technician, they are simply peripheral devices that connect through a port. Problems arise from the operation of the device itself (check the manufacturer's documentation) or from poor physical connections or software configuration.

Touch screens

There are several underlying technologies – Resistive, Capacitative, Acoustic Pulse Recognition – which are the basis of touch screens. Regardless of the underlying technology, a touch screen is a device that converts mechanical energy, such as touching the screen with a finger or using a stylus on a Personal Digital Assistant (PDA), into electrical signals that can be processed by a computer. Touch screens are often found as commercial point-of-sale devices, such as a store catalogue where a keyboard and mouse would be less intuitive for the user. From the point of view of a working technician, the problems are the familiar ones of physical connections and / or software configuration. Connections are usually though one of the standard ports.

SUMMARY

In this chapter we have looked at the various forms of video output used by PCs to display information. We have looked at the principal monitor types, how to configure them and adjust their key settings through hardware, and the utilities built into Microsoft Windows®. We have also considered other video output devices such as projectors. For exam purposes in particular, you should know the main VGA / SVGA standards, resolutions and colour depths, and how these base standards relate to later ones. In terms of connector types, we have looked at the most commonly encountered means of attaching video output devices to a PC.

In terms of input devices, we have looked at the fundamental devices of keyboard and mouse and noted the connector types used to attach them to a system. We have also considered mouse variants such as the trackball, as well as more specialised input devices such as bar code readers, cameras and touch screens.

QUESTIONS

1 You attach a new CRT monitor to a PC which is running Microsoft Windows® 2000. The display is clear enough but the user complains that it causes eye strain after a few minutes of working with it. Which settings would you change as a first step to rectify the problem?

   a) Refresh rate

   b) Colour depth

   c) Resolution

   d) Contrast settings in hardware

2 You attach a new LCD monitor to a PC running Microsoft Windows® 2000. When the machine reboots, the display is set at 800 × 600 and you are unable to change this through the operating system. What is the most likely cause of the problem?

   a) Wrong video connector

   b) Wrong hardware settings

   c) Wrong drivers

   d) None of the above

3 You have reinstalled Microsoft Windows® XP on a PC and all appears to be well until you use the keyboard. The letter keys all work satisfactorily but other keys do not. For example, pressing the £ key outputs a # symbol to the screen. What do you do next?

   a) Replace the keyboard

   b) Adjust settings through the Keyboard applet in Control Panel

   c) Adjust settings through the Regional and Language applet

   d) Adjust settings through the Regional Options applet

4 A user reports that a mouse attached to a PC has stopped working. You discover that it has somehow become unplugged. The mouse connector and the port on the PC are both colour-coded green. Do you?

   a) Reconnect the mouse and test it

   b) Connect the mouse to the port and reboot the PC

   c) Power down, reconnect the mouse, then reboot

   d) Replace the mouse

▶

5   A user reports that a touch screen attached to an in-store catalogue no longer responds to user input. The computer to which it is attached has been rebooted, but this has made no difference. What is the most likely cause of the problem?

    a) Device drivers

    b) Physical connection

    c) Hardware failure

    d) A virus

ANSWERS / EXPLANATIONS

1   You attach a new CRT monitor to a PC that is running Microsoft Windows® 2000. The display is clear enough but the user complains that it causes eye strain after a few minutes of working with it. Which settings would you change as a first step to rectify the problem?

    a) Refresh rate

    b) Colour depth

    c) Resolution

    d) Contrast settings in hardware

    Any or all of these factors may contribute to the problem, though option a – refresh rate – is the most likely.

2   You attach a new LCD monitor to a PC running Microsoft Windows® 2000. When the machine reboots, the display is set at 800 × 600 and you are unable to change this through the operating system. What is the most likely cause of the problem?

    c) Wrong drivers

    If you don't have an installation disk from the manufacturer, go to their website and download the latest version.

3   You have reinstalled Microsoft Windows® XP on a PC and all appears to be well until you use the keyboard. The letter keys all work satisfactorily but other keys do not. For example, pressing the £ key outputs a # symbol to the screen. What do you do next?

    c) Adjust settings through the Regional and Language applet

▶

The symptom reported suggests that you have the default US keyboard installed. This can be changed through the Regional and Language applet in XP. Answer d would be correct for Microsoft Windows® 2000.

4   A user reports that a mouse attached to a PC has stopped working. You discover that it has somehow become unplugged. The mouse connector and the port on the PC are both colour-coded green. Do you?

c) Power down, reconnect the mouse, then reboot

The colour coding indicates that this is a PS/2 mouse and these are not hot-swappable.

5   A user reports that a touch screen attached to an in-store catalogue no longer responds to user input. The computer to which it is attached has been rebooted, but this has made no difference. What is the most likely cause of the problem?

b) Physical connection

Power down. Check the connector for bent pins. Reconnect and reboot.

CHAPTER 5
Adapter cards, ports, cables and cooling systems

This chapter looks at adapter / expansion cards that can be fitted to a standard PC and the cabling and ports associated with them. It also looks at cooling systems for both components, such as the CPU and for systems as a whole.

Exam objective 1.1 (part)
Identify the names, purposes and characteristics of adapter cards.

Video including PCI / PCI-E and AGP

Multimedia

I/O (SCSI, serial, USB, parallel)

Communications including network and modem

Identify the names, purposes and characteristics of ports and cables, for example: USB 1.1 and 2.0, parallel, serial, IEEE 1394 / FireWire, RJ45 and RJ11, PS2 / mini-din, Centronics (e.g. mini, 36) multimedia (e.g. 1/8 connector, MIDSI COAX, SPDIF)

Identify the names, purposes and characteristics of cooling systems, for example: heat sinks, CPU and case fans, liquid cooling systems, thermal compound

Adapter cards

Much of the flexibility of the PC is the result of the ability to connect an adapter card to one of the standard PC buses through one of the standard expansion slots on the motherboard. Provided that the adapter card matches the slot type, you can attach almost anything to your PC. For example, PCs built before the introduction of the Universal Serial Bus (USB) can be upgraded by attaching the correct expansion card for the purpose.

Slot and card types

Adapter (or expansion) cards exist for various purposes – graphics adapters, network cards, modems, and so on. Regardless of the purpose of the card, it must fit into one of the standard slots on the motherboard. Common types are:

- **Industry Standard Architecture (ISA)** – an old slot type not always found on newer motherboards

- **Peripheral Component Interconnect (PCI)** – commonly used for various expansion cards (see page 14)

- **Peripheral Component Interconnect Express (PCI-E)** – a newer high-speed PCI slot commonly used for graphics cards and high speed network cards

- **Accelerated Graphics Port (AGP)** – a dedicated high-speed graphics port (see page 14).

These slot types are illustrated in Figure 1.1 (see page 7) as part of the discussion of motherboards, with the exception of the PCI-E slot type which is shown – with a standard PCI slot for comparison – in Figure 5.1.

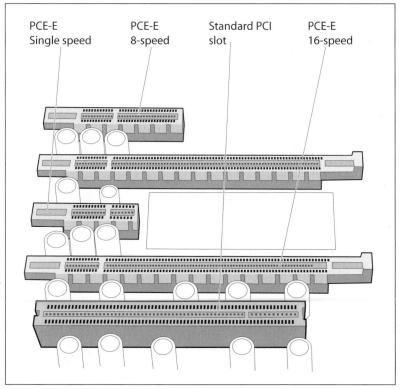

Figure 5.1

Video cards

Early video cards

Early video adapters could be fitted in ISA slots, although these are rarely seen on modern machines. The PCI slot was popular for VGA and SVGA cards until late 1997, by which time the technology was seen to be too slow for the needs of many users.

Accelerated Graphics Port (AGP)

The next development was the Accelerated Graphics Port (AGP). This was introduced as a single dedicated slot or as an on-board port which operated – in single-speed mode – at twice the rate of the PCI cards, that is a single-speed AGP card ran at 66 MHz compared with 33 MHz for the PCI bus. Subsequent developments led to two-speed, four-speed and eight-speed AGP cards. AGP 1 and 2 used a signalling voltage of 3.3 volts and this was reduced to 1.5 volts for the four-speed and eight-speed cards. Both cards and slots are keyed to prevent using the wrong card – see Figure 5.2 below.

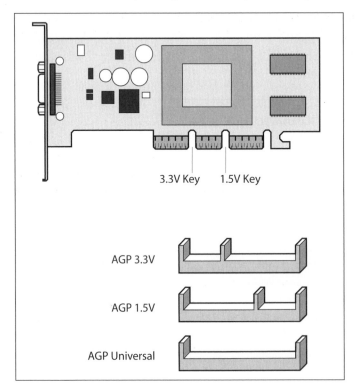

Figure 5.2

You may occasionally encounter a 'universal' slot or even an incorrectly keyed older AGP card. These can lead to damaged components if they are fitted incorrectly.

There are also some proprietary variants on AGP and an 'AGP Express', which is not a true AGP but a means of connecting to a specially adapted PCI slot known as 'AGP Express'.

PCI Express (PCI-E)

The PCI-E interface is rapidly becoming the technology of choice for graphics (and other) cards. Many new motherboards use PCI-E and don't have an AGP slot at all. Slot sizes (see Figure 5.1) ensure that a single-speed device can be fitted into a four- or eight-speed slot (where it will operate as a single-speed device) but that faster devices cannot be fitted into a slower (smaller) slot. PCI-E is software-compatible with PCI. PCI-E supports full duplex operation, so an eight-speed card in full duplex mode can deliver a data transfer rate of 16 GB per second.

Multimedia cards (MMC)

These are flash memory cards, typically used for storage in portable devices such as phones or cameras. The MMC card can then be removed from the portable device and attached (directly or through a standard interface such as USB) to a PC. They are manufactured to an open standard controlled by the MultiMedia Card Association (MMCA). News and developments can be seen on their website at www.mmca.org.

Input / output (I/O) cards

Input / output cards are available for standard expansion slots on the PC motherboard and can be used to extend the I/O capabilities of the system. Any port that you may encounter as an on-board feature, such as USB, FireWire / IEEE 1394, serial or parallel ports can be added to a system through a card fitted in the appropriate slot and – where necessary – provided with the correct drivers.

The Small Computer Systems Interface (SCSI) is not usually implemented as an on-board feature and is almost invariably installed as a PCI / PCI-E expansion card. SCSI is not often used on desktop PCs but tends to be used on server machines, which can benefit from its high speeds of operation. SCSI devices are implemented as a 'chain' in which each device has a unique identity in the form of a decimal number. The SCSI card is allocated the highest number in the chain, thus a 16-device chain will be numbered 0–15 and the card will be given the ID of 15.

Communications cards

Network cards are available for ISA, PCI and PCI-E slots. They need to be physically installed and configured for use. For Ethernet cards, speed can range from 10 Mbps for an old ISA card to 100 Mbps or 1000 Mbps in the more modern slots.

Modems may fit in one of the standard motherboard slots or they may use the dedicated Audio Modem Riser (AMR) slot or the later variant on this, the Communications Network Riser (CNR) slot.

Ports and cables

Figure 5.3 shows the back of a typical ATX machine and some of the ports that you would expect to find. A similar range of ports may be present on the back of an older AT-style machine, though most of these would probably be fitted through expansion cards rather than on-board.

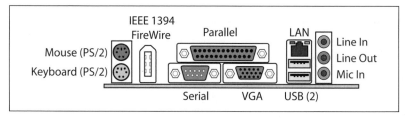

Figure 5.3

The ports and associated connectors you need to know are:

Table 5.1 Common ports and connectors.

Port	Connector	Common Uses	Comment
PS/2 or mini-DIN	Round in section – 6 pins	Keyboard or mouse connector	Sometimes colour-coded – purple for keyboard, green for mouse
DIN	Round – 5 pins	AT keyboard connector	Not shown in the figure
USB	Rectangular in section – type 'A' and / or square in section – type 'B' (See USB cable type, below)	Connector for many peripherals such as cameras, printers – anything with a USB interface	A high-speed serial interface. Version 2 is backward-compatible with earlier versions
IEEE 1394 – FireWire	Almost rectangular in section	High-speed connections of compatible devices. Rival to USB	Frequently used for transferring multimedia and video data
Serial	'D' shaped in section 9 or 25 pins	One of the original PC ports. Slow by today's standards. Often used for external modems	Usually a 9–pin connector, occasionally 25 pins. Always male
Parallel	'D' shaped in section 25 connectors – female	One of the original PC ports. Generally used for printers	Sometimes used for data transfers via 'Laplink' style cable
VGA Graphics	'D' shaped in section Female – 15 connectors in 3 rows	Still the most common video connector	Alternatives are various Digital Video Interfaces (DVI) not shown in the figure
Game Port and Audio Jacks	Game port is female – 'D' shaped in section 15 connectors in 2 rows	One of the original PC ports. Used for games joysticks, etc.	Originally an IBM proprietary standard
Modem	RJ11 rectangular in section	Connector for internal modem	RJ = 'Registered Jack' Same size as a US telephone connector
LAN RJ 45	RJ45 rectangular in section	Ethernet LAN connector	Similar to RJ11 in appearance but bigger
LAN BNC	Round in section	Thinnet LAN connector	Bayonet Neill Concellman connector. Pre-dates the PC

▶

Port	Connector	Common Uses	Comment
Centronics	Not actually a PC port, but found on printers	Standard (DB 25) connector at the printer end of a parallel printer cable	A 'D' shaped connector with a central block of flat edge connectors. It has 36 'pins'. There is also a 'mini Centronics' which is smaller but has the same pin count

Characteristics of ports

Serial and parallel devices

- Serial data transmitted one bit at a time.

- Parallel data transmitted in 8-bit (byte) units or in multiples of bytes (words).

To transmit an 8-bit byte, then, requires eight separate bits (and control bits) on a serial connection, whereas the same byte can be sent as a single unit over a parallel connection.

Serial ports

USB and FireWire are, strictly speaking, serial communications ports, but the term serial ports is generally taken to mean the standard 9- (and occasionally 25-) pin male ports on the back of the box.

Serial communications

A serial transmission moves less data than a parallel transmission but can do so faster and over a greater cable length. A serial cable can be up to 50 feet long, whereas the limit for a parallel cable is 15 feet.

Most serial devices are external and plug into the serial port on the computer. These are usually 9-pin (occasionally 25-pin) ports with the D-type connector and they are invariably male. They are also referred to as COM ports or RS-232 ports. RS-232 refers to the Electronic Industries Association (EIA) Reference Standard number 232 Serial ports may be any of the following:

- Added to the PC via an expansion board

- A port that is connected to pins on the motherboard

- Built in to the motherboard.

The list above is in historical order, though additional or replacement ports may be fitted through expansion cards even on modern machines.

Serial ports are referred to as DB (Data Bus)-9 or DB-25. This indicates their shape and the number of pins. Not all pins are used.

Most PCs use 9-pin ports for serial communications, though the DB-25 is still found on some older machines and it is still used by some modems. When serial ports are added to a computer through expansion cards, the DB-9 connector is usually attached as COM 1 and the DB-25 as COM 2. This is, however, a convention rather than a standard.

Parallel ports and devices

▦ Parallel data is transmitted 8 bits (1 byte) at a time.

▦ The maximum cable length is 15 feet.

▦ The standard for parallel ports is IEEE 1284

The IEEE 1284 standard

The IEEE 1284 standard incorporated and formalised earlier parallel port protocols and includes:

▦ **Standard Parallel Port (SPP)** – allows data to travel from computer to printer, that is, one direction only.

▦ **Enhanced Parallel Port (EPP)** – allows data flows in either direction, though not simultaneously. This means, for example, that a printer can signal back to the computer that it is out of paper, or ink, or whatever.

▦ **Enhanced Capabilities Port (ECP)** – allows simultaneous bi-directional communications (i.e. full duplex) over a special parallel cable. Not all bi-directional cables support this mode of operation, that is, they may support EPP but not ECP.

High-speed serial ports (USB and FireWire)

The growth in popularity of external devices for PCs meant that there was a need for more and faster communications ports for devices such as: cameras, scanners, external storage drives, etc. This led to the development of Small Computer System Interface (SCSI), but this is an expensive technology and lack of standardisation in the early days worked against its widespread acceptance. What was required, then, was a relatively simple high-speed serial interface. In response to this demand, two new serial connection standards emerged, Universal Serial Bus (USB) and IEEE 1394 (FireWire).

Universal Serial Bus (USB)

This supports low-speed devices such as mice and keyboards as well as faster devices such as scanners and cameras. USB supports transfer rates of:

▦ 12 Mbps for 'fast' devices

▦ 1.5 Mbps though a sub-channel for 'slow' devices

▦ 480 Mbps – introduced with USB 2.0.

USB uses a pair of connectors and ports known as type A and type B. The type A connector is flat and rectangular in section and the type B is almost square in section. Type A connectors are usually at the computer or hub end of the connection and type B is used at the device end.

The USB interface supports up to 127 devices connected directly to the PC or through one or more hubs. Each port carries 0.5 amps of power, which is sufficient for lower power devices such as keyboards, mice, etc. USB devices such as printers usually have their own AC adapters.

IEEE 1394 – FireWire

An alternative to USB is defined by the standard IEEE 1394. There are several proprietary implementations of the 1394 standard:

- FireWire – owned by Apple Computing

- i.Link® – owned by Sony

- Lynx – owned by Texas Instruments

The generic version of the standard is called High Performance Serial Bus (HPSB). IEEE 1394 provides:

- Transfer speeds of 100 Mbps up to 4000 Mbps

- Supports up to 63 external devices

- Peer-to-peer interface (does not require a host system)

Higher data transfer rates (800 Mbps up to 1.6 Gbps) are planned. Like USB, IEEE 1394 is a developing standard and has a website at www.1394ta.org. The 'ta' stands for 'trade association'.

The 1394 connector is larger than those used by USB and is nearly square in shape. The standard connector has 6 pins; there is also a 4-pin connector (on some Sony devices) where the connected device has its own power supply.

The main differences between 1394 and USB are:

- 1394 is faster (and more expensive).

- 1394 supports isochronous data transfers – that is real-time transfers, so it can, for example, be used to transfer audio and video data at the same time.

- 1394 does not require a host. It is capable of managing data transfers between attached devices without any of them being attached to a PC (or other host computer).

Both Microsoft Windows® 2000 and XP have support for IEEE 1394, which is also referred to (sometimes) as 'Serial SCSI'.

Multimedia ports

Sony / Phillips Digital Interface Format (SPDIF)

This is a standard that specifies hardware and protocols for carrying digital audio signals between devices. It can be implemented using either coaxial cable or fibre optic. When using coaxial cable the connector is the RCA jack (developed in the 1940s by the Radio Corporation of America). The optical version gives a choice of two connector types: TosLink, which is rectangular in section; or the mini-optical which is a 3.5 mm jack.

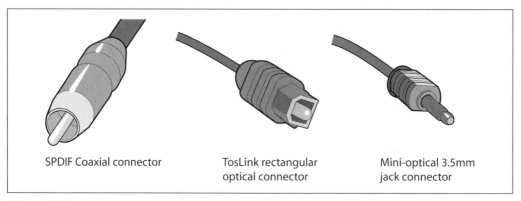

SPDIF Coaxial connector   TosLink rectangular   Mini-optical 3.5mm
                                 optical connector   jack connector

Figure 5.4

The 1/8 inch connector (not shown in the figure) is a stereo audio plug similar in appearance to – but slightly smaller than – the mini-optical connector. It is typically used for connecting stereo headphones to an audio output. There are various converters and gender changers available for most connectors and ports.

Cooling systems

As PCs have developed over the years, the speed of components has increased considerably and this has generated a need for more efficient cooling methods.

The ATX motherboard form factor rearranged the layout of the internal components to improve the airflow throughout the case, and the now familiar heat sink or heat sink and fan combination was introduced to meet the increased operating temperatures of the Pentium chip.

Heat sinks

The heat sink is the simplest cooling device. A passive heat sink has a surface that is in contact with the component needing to be cooled and also with an array of fins, which allow heat to be dissipated. In order to improve heat conduction from the component surface to the underside of the heat sink, it is common to use a smear of thermal compound (aka 'thermal gunk') between the two surfaces. Figure 5.5 shows a passive heat sink.

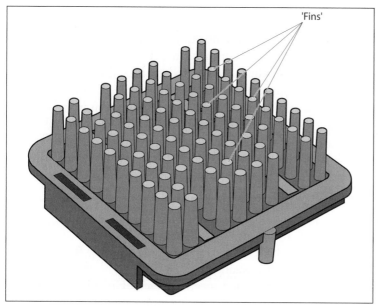

Figure 5.5

Passive heat sinks are used on many components: motherboard components, graphics cards and, of course, CPUs. However, modern components – particularly CPUs – generate considerable heat, so it is often necessary to attach a fan to the heat sink in order to increase the airflow across the fins to improve cooling performance. Figure 5.6 shows a typical heat sink and fan arrangement for a CPU.

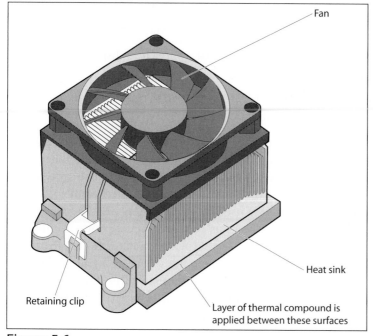

Figure 5.6

The heat sink / fan combination is also referred to as an active heat sink.

Fans

Fans may be attached to any hot-running component in the system, such as the mother-board chipset or the video card chipset or even a hard drive. There are also heat spreaders available for memory (RAM) modules. Most modern PCs also have case fans, front and rear, to draw a continuous supply of air across all components in addition to their own heat sink / fan arrangements. These case fans are supplementary to the fan, which is part of every Power Supply Unit (PSU). Ever since the ATX motherboard replaced the older AT specification, the planned airflow though the case has been an important element in overall cooling. Because of this, the slot covers at the back of the case are regarded as part of the cooling system. A missing slot cover can disrupt the engineered air flow through the case and cause overheating.

Liquid cooling systems

Liquid cooling is not yet considered to be a mainstream option for PCs, though it has been used on mainframes for many years. It is mainly used by people who tweak a processor – overclock it – to run faster than its intended speed. Overclocking places increased demands on the cooling system and one solution is to use a liquid cooling system to deal with this. (See page 33 for more on overclocking.)

The principle of a water-cooled system is similar to that used in a car. Water is circulated though a closed system in order to conduct heat away from the heat source to a radiator, which disperses it to the atmosphere.

A water-cooled system has four essential components:

- A water reservoir tank

- A water pump that circulates water through the system – these are generally adaptations of aquarium pumps and need an external mains power supply

- A condenser coil / radiator with fans that cool the water and disperse heat to the atmosphere

- A CPU cooling block connected to the CPU in order to extract heat to the cooling system. This block is 'wrapped' in a 'water jacket'.

The water pump operates from inside the reservoir and pushes the water around the system. It passes over the CPU cooling block and absorbs heat from the CPU. It passes through the radiator at the back of the system case, and a fan disperses the heat from the liquid to the atmosphere. The cooled liquid is recirculated through the system.

Although water cooling systems are mainly used by overclockers and knowledgeable enthusiasts, they may become more mainstream as processor speeds increase further. Certainly, Pentium 4 and later motherboards are sold with standard hole patterns to allow for the easy connection of such devices. The main advantage of liquid cooling systems is their efficiency. Because a water-cooled system requires fewer case and component fans, it tends to run more quietly than an air-cooled system. The obvious disadvantage is the additional cost.

SUMMARY

In this chapter we have looked at adapter cards, their types and characteristics and the motherboard slots that accommodate them. We have considered the standard ports on a modern PC – most of which can be added by way of expansion cards – and the cables and connectors associated with the standard port types. Finally, we have looked at cooling systems – passive, active and liquid.

QUESTIONS

1   You have been given a USB 2.0 device, but the PC has only USB 1.1 ports. Which of the following statements applies in this scenario?

   a) It won't work

   b) Plug it in. It will work but only at USB 1.1 speed

   c) You need to fit a USB 2.0 upgrade card in a spare PCI slot

   d) You need to download additional drivers

2   You have been asked to buy and connect a second local printer to a PC that already has a printer connected to the parallel port. Which of the following statements applies in this scenario?

   a) It can't be done

   b) You can fit a second parallel port in an expansion slot

   c) You can attach a USB printer through a USB port

   d) You can attach a serial printer to a serial port

3   Which of the following cannot be added to a PC by way of a PCI slot?

   a) FireWire ports

   b) USB ports

   c) CNR modem card

   d) Gigabit Ethernet adapter

4   A PC that you maintain shows signs of overheating after prolonged use. It has an active heat sink on the CPU and a rear case fan. Which of the following would improve the efficiency of the cooling system?

   a) Fit an additional case fan

   b) Remove a couple of slot covers to increase the airflow through the case

   c) Clean the heat sink on the CPU

   d) Any of the above

▶

5   A user reports that a PC is excessively noisy in normal operation. You examine the machine and it is a high-specification hardware build with several fans. What do you recommend?

     a) Remove one or more of the fans to reduce the noise

     b) Replace the Power Supply Unit (PSU)

     c) Install a liquid cooling system

     d) Replace existing fans with quieter ones

ANSWERS / EXPLANATIONS

1   You have been given a USB 2.0 device, but the PC has only USB 1.1 ports. Which of the following statements applies in this scenario?

     b) Plug it in. It will work but only at USB 1.1 speed

     Option c would be a good solution, but you do not need to do it in order to use the device.

2   You have been asked to buy and connect a second local printer to a PC that already has a printer connected to the parallel port. Which of the following statements applies in this scenario?

     b) You can fit a second parallel port in an expansion slot

     c) You can attach a USB printer through a USB port

     d) You can attach a serial printer to a serial port

     Option d is feasible, but serial printers are not commonly used. Answers b and c would probably be preferable in practice.

3   Which of the following cannot be added to a PC by way of a PCI slot?

     c) CNR modem card

     This requires a dedicated CNR slot.

4   A PC that you maintain shows signs of overheating after prolonged use. It has an active heat sink on the CPU and a rear case fan. Which of the following would improve the efficiency of the cooling system?

     a) Fit an additional case fan

     c) Clean the heat sink on the CPU

     Option b would make things worse!

▶

5   A user reports that a PC is excessively noisy in normal operation. You examine the machine and it is a high-specification hardware build with several fans. What do you recommend?

b) Replace the Power Supply Unit (PSU)

c) Install a liquid cooling system

d) Replace existing fans with quieter ones

Answer a would help the noise problem but could cause overheating. Answers b and d would probably lead to some improvement. Answer c – liquid cooling – would be technically efficient but expensive.

CHAPTER 6
Installing and upgrading components

One of the most important tasks that you need to carry out as a working technician is the installation and upgrading of PC components. In this chapter we will look at various internal and external storage devices – mainly hard disk drives – as well as techniques for drive imaging.

Exam objective 1.2
Install, configure, optimise and upgrade personal computer components.

Add, remove and configure internal and external storage devices
Drive preparation of internal storage devices including format / file systems and imaging technology
Install display devices
Add, remove and configure basic input and multimedia devices

Add, remove and configure storage devices

The most important storage devices on the modern PC are hard disk drives. There are three basic types:

  Enhanced Integrated Drive Electronics (EIDE) / ATA

  Serial ATA (SATA)

  Small Computer Systems Interface (SCSI)

We will consider each of these in turn.

Enhanced Integrated Drive Electronics (EIDE)

Early hard disks were attached to PCs through expansion cards with the necessary chips and circuits built on to them. Each drive had its own card. The next development was to build the electronics into the drive – Integrated Drive Electronics (IDE). This was later improved and was called Enhanced Integrated Drive Electronics (EIDE). There have been subsequent improvements and specification changes for hard drives, but the terms IDE and EIDE are still commonly used to indicate (non-SCSI, non-SATA) drives with

40-pin connectors. With the advent of serial ATA (SATA) disks, EIDE / ATA is often designated as Parallel ATA (PATA).

Cable types

All EIDE / ATA cables have a 40-line connector to 40 pins on both the motherboard and the device end of the cable. Later specification cables (see page 80) have 80 lines but still connect to 40-pin connectors at each end. The higher-specification cables (ATA / 66 and later) usually have colour-coded connectors and use 'cable select' rather than jumpers to set the master / slave distinction of the drives. On this type of cable, the blue connector attaches to the motherboard, the grey connector to the 'slave' device and the black connector to the 'master' device.

Usually, (E)IDE cables have a single pink or grey stripe down one side to indicate line one and this should be attached to pin one on both motherboard and device. Many modern cables are 'keyed' to make cable orientation easy.

EIDE / ATA cables are usually flat ribbon cables, but there are also cables that are round in section. These are functionally identical to their ribbon style counterparts; the round section just helps the airflow in the computer case.

EIDE / ATA key facts

The EIDE interface is defined by the ATA standards (for AT attachment) and the standard for CD-ROM, DVD and tape drives is ATAPI (ATA Packet Interface).

- IDE – and later EIDE – replaced earlier hard drive technologies called ST506 and ESDI (Enhanced Small Drive Interface); these technologies are no longer in use. They required low-level formatting as a matter of routine before use.

- EIDE drives only require a high-level format (FORMAT.COM) to create the track structure and File Allocation Table / Master File Table on a disk that has been partitioned with FDISK, DISKPART or a similar utility.

- EIDE devices attach to either the motherboard or to an expansion card with a 40-pin ribbon cable that has a maximum length of 18 inches.

- ATA / 66 (and later) drives require an 80-line / 40-pin data cable. However, you can use a standard 40-pin EIDE cable but the data transfer speed will be limited by the cable type.

- EIDE hard drives receive a low-level format at the factory and A+ is only concerned with partitioning and high-level formatting (DISKPART and FORMAT.COM), which are part of a technician's normal work.

Configuring EIDE drives

Most motherboards provide two EIDE / ATA controllers. These are designated as primary and secondary. Each controller – or channel – supports two devices and these are designated as master and slave. This is actually rather misleading terminology as neither drive has any sort of priority over the other, they merely share a cable and a channel. A drive is set to be either master or slave by setting jumpers either on the end or the under-side of the drive.

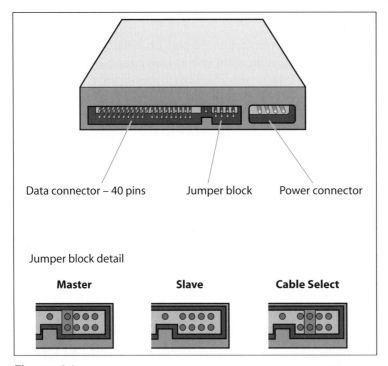

Figure 6.1

Figure 6.1 shows the connectors at the back of a typical Parallel ATA / EIDE drive. The detail at the bottom of the figure shows the jumper settings for master / slave / cable select for that particular drive.

The jumper settings are usually labelled somewhere on the drive. As a minimum you would expect three sets of pins for master, slave and cable select. There may be other pairs of pins for other configuration options such as drive size. There is no set standard for drive jumpers – look at the drive or the manufacturer's website if in doubt.

ATAPI devices – CD / DVD and tape drives – set their master / slave options in the same way as EIDE / ATA hard drives.

The cable select option means that the drive ID is determined by its place on the cable. The cable positions are colour-coded on the newer 80-line / 40-pin cables. The blue connector is attached to the motherboard, the grey connector – which is part-way along the cable – to the 'slave' device and the black connector – on the end of the cable – to the 'master' device. You can, however, use standard master and slave jumper settings on this type of drive and cable if you wish.

Installing a PATA / EIDE drive

This is a routine task for the working technician.

1   Set master / slave / cable select jumpers.

2   Physically install the drive in the PC.

3   Connect the power supply.

4   Connect the ribbon cable to the drive and to the controller.

5   Check that the drive is correctly identified in CMOS / BIOS – they usually auto-detect on modern systems.

6   Partition and format the drive using operating-system or third-party tools.

The EIDE / ATA standards

All drives – hard disks, CD-ROMs, tape drives, etc. – that have the drive electronics built into the drive are known generically as EIDE or ATA. Like most technologies, ATA has developed through time and there are, at present, eight standards. The first three of these (ATA-1, ATA-2 and ATA-3) are considered to be obsolete by the American National Standards Institute (ANSI).

ATA-4 or Ultra ATA/33 (1998) introduced a new technology known as Ultra Direct Memory Access (Ultra-DMA), which supported a maximum data transfer rate of 33 megabytes (MB) per second. It also introduced support for Attached Packet Interface (ATAPI) drives such as CD-ROM and tape drives.

ATA-5 or Ultra ATA/66 (2000) supports transfer modes of up to 66 MB per second. This requires an 80-line / 40-pin cable and motherboard / IDE controller support. ATA-5 drives are backward-compatible with earlier cables and controllers but can only deliver data transfer rates normally associated with these earlier technologies.

ATA-6 or Ultra ATA/100 (2002) supports data transfers of up to100 MB per second.

ATA-7 or Ultra ATA/133 or SATA 150 (2005) supports data transfers of up to150 MB per second and introduces support for Serial ATA (SATA).

ATA-8 is currently under development.

Serial ATA (SATA)

SATA offers a high-speed alternative to the older Parallel ATA technology. The original release (2003) delivered a maximum data transfer rate of 1.5 GB per second and is known as SATA/150. A later development of the specification increased the maximum data transfer rate to 3.0 GB per second and is known as SATA/300. SATA/300 is often referred to as SATA 2 (or SATA II), although this is not endorsed by the standards body, The Serial ATA International Organisation. An increase in transfer rates to 6.0 GB per second is planned. As with nearly all specifications in computing, the quoted data transfer rates for all SATA drives are theoretical maxima and are unlikely to be achieved in practice.

SATA cables

Unlike the earlier PATA technology, SATA connects only one device per cable and the difference between PATA and SATA cables is one of the most easily identifiable differences when you work with them. Figure 6.2 shows typical SATA and PATA cables and connectors for comparison.

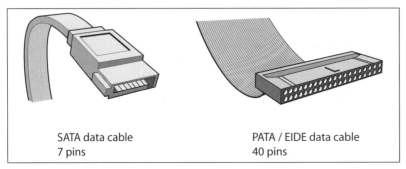

SATA data cable   PATA / EIDE data cable
7 pins   40 pins

Figure 6.2

Parallel ATA cables have 40 pins and either 40 or 80 data lines. The maximum cable length is specified as 46 cm (18 in). SATA cables have a maximum length approximately double this: 1 metre (39 in).

The power cables for the two drive types are equally distinctive, as shown in Figure 6.3.

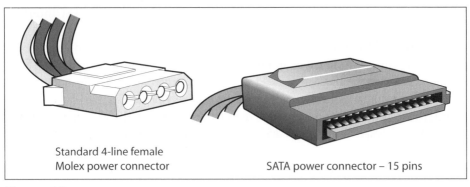

Standard 4-line female
Molex power connector   SATA power connector – 15 pins

Figure 6.3

External drives PATA / SATA / SCSI

All drive types can be connected as external drives. Parallel ATA / EIDE drives don't do this natively, but they can be mounted in caddy-style external drive housings that connect to the host PC through USB or FireWire interfaces. The main drawback to this approach is that the external housing requires a bridge chip to convert ATA signals to USB / FireWire format and this reduces data transfer rates substantially. There is an external SATA type, eSATA – standardised in 2004 – which supports external drives without the USB/FireWire conversion overhead. This can be implemented where there is an eSATA controller on the motherboard or by using an expansion card. In this respect, eSATA resembles the Small Computer Systems Interface (SCSI), which supports both internal and external devices.

Small Computer Systems Interface (SCSI)

SCSI – Scuzzy – dates back to 1986 when the American National Standards Institute (ANSI) formalised the Shugart Associates System Interface (SASI) specification. This specification is known as SCSI 1 and there have been many enhancements since then. SCSI 2 and SCSI 3 developed the SCSI 1 standard in the 1980s and 1990s.

Ultra 2 SCSI (1997) introduced Low Voltage Differential SCSI and is also known as LVD SCSI. Ultra 2 increased cable length from 6 metres to 12 metres and brought data transfer rates up to 80 Mbps. This specification was rapidly superseded by Ultra 3 SCSI (1999), which doubled the data transfer rate to 160 Mbps. Ultra 320 (2002) increased the data transfer rate to 320 Mbps and this is the most widely used SCSI specification of current equipment, although further developments are planned.

SCSI is not usually found on desktop PCs. Its expense and relative complexity means that it is usually reserved for very high-end workstations and server machines.

SCSI implementations

SCSI is a collection of standards that allows for the connection of a variety of devices on a SCSI bus or chain. Each device on the chain requires a unique SCSI ID and this is usually set by jumpers or switches on the device. Some BIOSs support SCSI Configured Automatically (SCAM), though for this to work, both the SCSI adapter and the device must also support it. SCSI chains have to be terminated at both ends.

A+ test questions on SCSI generally fall into one of three areas:

- The various SCSI standards

- Assigning device IDs

- Problems with termination of chains.

SCSI is implemented as a SCSI chain – a series of SCSI devices attached to a host adapter. The adapter is usually a PCI device, but other slot types (such as ISA) are supported. The adapter card has an external connector and an internal connector. Because it is part of the SCSI chain, it, too, has a unique SCSI ID and, by convention, this is set as the highest available number in the chain. On an eight-device chain, then, the adapter (numbering from 0) will have the SCSI ID of 7. A boot drive may need to be set as device 0 in order to be allocated the drive letter C: on a Microsoft Windows® system. Other device IDs are not generally important so long as they are unique within the chain, that is a 'missing' ID is acceptable (but a duplicate is not).

Internal SCSI chains

These attach to the adapter through a ribbon cable, which looks rather like an EIDE / ATA cable with additional connectors, and the device IDs are set through jumpers or switches that resemble the jumpers on an IDE device, though the IDs are set by using simple binary arithmetic rather than the pre-configured settings familiar from IDE.

External SCSI chains

These attach to the adapter through its external connection. The first device attaches directly to the adapter and subsequent devices daisy-chain by each device providing a connector for the next in the chain.

Assigning Device IDs

Device IDs are assigned by setting jumpers or switches, or through software. Each device must have a unique number. Three jumper pairs (or switches) are sufficient to set IDs 0-7 and four pairs (or switches) are necessary for a 16-device chain. This is simple binary arithmetic:

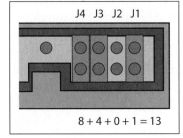

$8 + 4 + 0 + 1 = 13$

Figure 6.4

To set the device number to 13 would require jumpers 4, 3 and 1 to be set and jumper 2 to be clear. This could also be done with DIP switches. The jumpers / switches may be numbered from left to right or right to left (experiment or read the manual for the product).

Resolving ID conflicts

Each SCSI device on a chain must have a unique identity. If two devices have the same ID, at least one of them will be invisible. Except where IDs are configured automatically, the only way to resolve a conflict is by manual inspection of the jumpers and switches and making incremental changes until the problem is solved.

SCSI cables and connectors

There are no official standards for SCSI cables and connectors. However, the commonly encountered types are:

▦   Type A – 50 lines / pins commonly used on internal chains, similar in appearance to an EIDE / PATA cable.

▦   Type P – 68 lines / pins commonly used on internal chains on 16-bit SCSI 2 or later.

In addition, some SCSI 3 adapters and devices use an 80-pin D-type connector – the SCA 80 – which supports hot-swapping of devices. Typically, these drives will work with 68-pin cables, providing that the hot-swapping capability is not required.

External connectors

All external connectors are female on devices.

▦   50-pin Centronics – obsolete SCSI 1

▦   50-pin HD DB – SCSI 2

▦   68-pin HD DB – wide SCSI 2 and SCSI 3

▦   25-pin D-type (looks like a parallel port) SCSI 2 Macs and Zip drives

Termination

One of the most common causes of problems on a SCSI chain – and a favourite source of exam questions – is the failure of proper termination of the chain. Symptoms of improper termination may include:

- Boot-time failures
- Hard-drive crashes
- Random system failures.

Older SCSI types use *passive termination*, usually a resistor block on the bus which is sufficient to prevent noise from the cable end being reflected back onto the bus.

Newer (and faster) SCSI types require *active termination* in which voltage regulators are added to the resistors used for passive termination. This gives more consistent termination to the bus and is required as a minimum for anything later than SCSI 1.

Forced perfect termination is an even more sophisticated variant on active termination and is the best form of termination for a high-specification SCSI chain.

Drive preparation

Irrespective of the physical characteristics of the drive type – PATA, SATA, or SCSI – or how it is connected – internal or external, on its own cable type or connected through USB or Firewire – it needs to be partitioned and formatted before it can be used. Even a USB 'thumb' or 'pen' drive needs a file system before it can be used.

Partitioning

A file system – such as NTFS or FAT 32 (see page 119) – is a data structure that is applied to one or more partitions on a physical disk. These partitions are logical divisions of the physical disk and may be *primary* or *logical*. Logical partitions are created and formatted as logical drives within an extended partition. A physical disk may have up to four primary partitions, or it may consist of a primary partition and a single extended partition, which can contain several logical drives. Figure 6.5 shows such an arrangement.

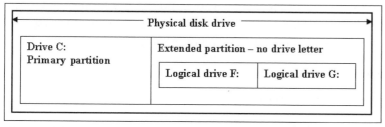

Figure 6.5

If you are installing an operating system on a new disk, the installer will present you with various partitioning and formatting options and these are considered in Chapter 9, which looks at the installation process in some detail. In particular, see the section on disk preparation in that chapter. However, a common task for the working technician is to install and prepare a disk for use as additional storage on a running system. This is most easily achieved by physically connecting the new disk and then using the partitioning and formatting tools that are part of Microsoft Windows® 2000 and XP. In order to access these tools, navigate to: **Control Panel** | **Administrative Tools** | **Computer management** | **Disk management**.

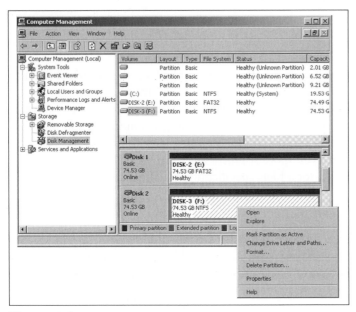

Figure 6.6

Figure 6.6 shows disks E: and F: on a Windows XP system. In this instance, Disk-3 (F:) is selected and the context menu shows the options available. Because there is an existing partition, you have the opportunity to remove it (as a first step in re-partitioning) and / or formatting the partition. If you intend to do this as a practical exercise, note that either of these options will destroy all data on the disk.

In addition to the 'easy' options outlined here, it is also possible to boot to a Microsoft Windows® installation disk, to start a recovery console and use the DISKPART command from the command line. There are also third-party disk preparation tools such as Norton Partition Magic or Paragon Hard Disk Manager, which provide the same functionality and some additional features. The A+ exam does not require you to know the details of how these third-party products work.

Formatting

All modern drives receive a low-level format at the time of manufacture and this does not need to be repeated. However, a high-level format of a partition is necessary before it can be used for storage. As with partitioning, the need for formatting and the tools used to do it apply equally to PATA, SATA and SCSI drives and regardless of the means of physical connection.

Like partitioning, formatting can be done as part of the installation process or, in the case of an additional disk, through the disk management tools that we considered earlier.

You can also boot to an installation CD and use the FORMAT command from a recovery console. Whichever method you use, you will have to select either the FAT 32 or the NTFS file system for the partition. Unless there are compelling reasons to do otherwise, you should use the default NTFS file system because this is the basis of many of the security features of Microsoft Windows® 2000 and XP that distinguishes them from earlier 'home user' operating systems such as Microsoft Windows® 9.x or Millennium.

Formatting a partition consists of creating the structure necessary to save and retrieve data. The main structures are tracks and sectors, as shown in Figure 6.7.

In practice, the operating system combines sectors into clusters (also known as allocation units) as the basic unit of storage. When a file is written to disk, it is stored in one or more clusters and the start address of the file on disk is recorded in the File Allocation Table (on FAT 32 systems) or the Master File Table (on NTFS systems). In effect, these structures act like an index that enables the system to keep track of its files.

When you are formatting a partition through a GUI, you can choose the file system type – FAT 32 or NTFS – through the menu system. When formatting from a command line, you need to specify the file system

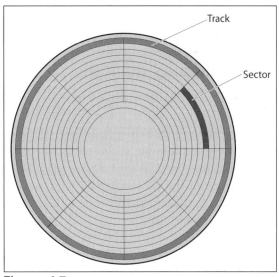

Figure 6.7

type as one of the command line arguments. For example, to format the partition on drive Q: with the NTFS file system you would use: FORMAT Q: /FS:NTFS.

Quick formatting

Regardless of the formatting tool that you are using – Installer, GUI or command line – you may be offered the option of performing a quick format. This is only possible where the disk has been previously formatted and you wish to keep the same file system. If you choose this option, the existing track / cluster structure is left in place and the File Allocation Table / Master File Table is blanked and all storage areas are marked as available for use. This has the advantage of being quicker than a full format, but there is no check of the disk's physical structure so it should only be used where you are confident of the drive's integrity. A further disadvantage is that until the clusters that are marked as 'free' are overwritten, the original data may be recoverable by anyone with the necessary software tools.

Drive imaging

As we have seen, the contents of a partition consist not just of data, but also of control structures – metadata – such as the Partition Table and the Master File Table. By using appropriate software such as Norton Ghost™ or Acronis True Image, it is possible to 'clone' all of the contents of a partition by making a sector by sector copy of data and metadata – control structures, installed programs and user data – in a single image file. This saved image can then be 'restored', that is copied sector by sector to a new partition. This technique is used widely by large-scale system builders and companies who are rolling out large numbers of machines with identical (or near identical) hardware. Because the software packages used to do imaging are proprietary, you are not required to know in detail how they work for examination purposes. You should, however, have an understanding of how imaging works and why it is used. Drive imaging is discussed in Chapter 9 and there is a detailed examination of the techniques necessary to prepare a Microsoft Windows® 2000 or XP drive for imaging in order to avoid problems with the security identifiers used in NT-based operating systems (see page 138).

Install display devices

Most aspects of installing display devices have been covered in Chapter 4. For the most part, installing a monitor or a projector consists of physically connecting the device and providing any required drivers. It may, of course, be prudent to visit the manufacturer's website to obtain the latest drivers for the device and to check for any known compatibility problems. Physical connection will be through one of the standard ports – probably VGA or one of the DVI variants – and, after physical connections and AC power have been checked, the most likely source of operational problems will be drivers and settings. Chapter 4 considers key settings such as refresh rate and colour depth, both of which are important considerations from the point of view of the end user (see page 53). Finally, from the health and safety point of view, remember that a Cathode Ray Tube (CRT) monitor may contain potentially lethal voltages even after it has been disconnected for several days. Never open or attempt to adjust the internal components of a CRT monitor it is a Field Replaceable Unit that you may adjust or configure to meet user needs. If it requires attention at the hardware level, then it should be returned to a base workshop or repair centre for specialist attention.

Input and multimedia devices

Input devices – from the basics like mice and keyboards to touch screens, bar code readers and so on – all need to be upgraded or replaced as a result of normal wear and tear in use or technological progress. As with most components, the most common problems arise from poor physical connections or wrong or out-of-date device drivers. Input and multimedia devices are considered at length in Chapter 4 (see pages 58–60).

Removing components

For the most part, removing a component consists of physically removing the device from the system and removing any unwanted drivers or associated software through Device Manager and / or the Control Panel. Where disk storage is concerned, you need to bear in mind the destination and future use of the removed drive as it may contain data remnants that could be recovered by using the necessary software tools. Chapters 16 and 17 examine this from a security perspective.

SUMMARY

In this chapter we have looked at how to add, configure and remove both internal and external storage devices. We have considered the main disk storage types – PATA, SATA and SCSI – and compared their characteristics. We have looked at the file systems – FAT 32 and NTFS – used on modern PCs and how to create and format disk partitions using these file systems. We have also looked at how to install, configure and remove input / output, multimedia and display devices.

QUESTIONS

1 You install a new PATA disk as a second drive on a Microsoft Windows® 2000 system as drive Q:. You have been asked to format it with the FAT 32 file system. In order to do this, you go to a command prompt and issue the command FORMAT Q: /FS:FAT32. You receive an error message: 'Specified drive does not exist'. The drive is correctly connected to the motherboard and has been recognised at boot time by the BIOS. What is the most likely cause of this message?

a) Wrong disk type

b) You can't have a FAT 32 partition on Windows 2000

c) Wrong command syntax

d) The disk has not been partitioned

2 You have been asked to install a new SCSI disk on a newly built PC and to install an operating system on it. The maximum length of the SCSI chain on this system is eight attached devices. What device number would you assign to the new drive?

a) 0

b) 8

c) 7

d) It doesn't matter

3 You attach an ATA / 100 drive to a blue controller on the motherboard of a PC as a replacement for an older unit and reuse the EIDE ribbon cable. The new drive is recognised at boot time by the BIOS but you receive an error message indicating that the drive will work but with reduced functionality. What is the most likely cause of this problem?

a) The BIOS is out of date

b) Wrong motherboard controller type

c) Wrong cable type

d) Incorrect jumper settings

▶

4   You have been asked to fit an external Serial ATA (SATA) disk to a PC but, on examination of the system, it proves not to have an external SATA port. Your customer wants the additional storage in place as soon as possible. What do you suggest?

   a) Buy an expansion card to provide the external port

   b) Replace the motherboard

   c) Fit the drive internally

   d) None of the above

5   You have spent some time adjusting settings on an ageing CRT monitor, but the customer is still not satisfied with the display. What do you do next?

   a) Disconnect the monitor, open the case and realign the gun at the back of the tube

   b) Disconnect the monitor, open the case and check for loose components

   c) Recommend that the monitor be sent to an approved disposal site and be replaced with a new one

   d) Any of the above

ANSWERS / EXPLANATIONS

1   You install a new PATA disk as a second drive on a Microsoft Windows® 2000 system as drive Q:. You have been asked to format it with the FAT 32 file system. In order to do this, you go to a command prompt and issue the command FORMAT Q: /FS:FAT32. You receive an error message: 'Specified drive does not exist'. The drive is correctly connected to the motherboard and has been recognised at boot time by the BIOS. What is the most likely cause of this?

   d) The disk has not been partitioned

   Although we all refer to 'formatting a disk', you in fact format a partition on a disk. In this example you have failed to create a partition.

2   You have been asked to install a new SCSI disk on a newly built PC and to install an operating system on it. The maximum length of the SCSI chain on this system is eight attached devices. What device number would you assign to the new drive?

   a) 0

   Device number 7 would be the SCSI adapter card and 8 doesn't exist because the chain is numbered from 0–7 to accommodate eight devices.

▶

3   You attach an ATA / 100 drive to a blue controller on the motherboard of a PC as a replacement for an older unit and reuse the EIDE ribbon cable. The new drive is recognised at boot time by the BIOS but you receive an error message indicating that the drive will work but with reduced functionality. What is the most likely cause of this problem?

c) Wrong cable type

ATA / 66 or later drives require an 80-line / 40-pin cable to work at full efficiency.

4   You have been asked to fit an external Serial ATA (SATA) disk to a PC but, on examination of the system, it proves not to have an external SATA port. Your customer wants the additional storage in place as soon as possible. What do you suggest?

a) Buy an expansion card to provide the external port.

Option b would be feasible but expensive. Option c would not work because the connectors are incompatible.

5   You have spent some time adjusting settings on an ageing CRT monitor, but the customer is still not satisfied with the display. What do you do next?

c) Recommend that the monitor be sent to an approved disposal site and be replaced with a new one

Options a and b could kill you! Disposal of a monitor has health and safety considerations which are considered in Chapter 18 (see pages 287–288).

CHAPTER 7
Troubleshooting hardware and preventive maintenance

Modern hardware is usually fairly robust and reliable but when it fails, the PC technician needs to know how to go about the business of tracking down and fixing the fault in a systematic way that meets the customer's need for a working system with the minimum of disruption and cost. Preventive maintenance – tedious though it may be – helps to reduce the amount of time spent troubleshooting. It is also a source of questions for the Essentials exam.

Exam objectives 1.3 and 1.4
1.3 Identify tools, diagnostic procedures and troubleshooting techniques for personal computer components.

Recognise the basic aspects of troubleshooting theory, for example:

Perform back-ups before making changes
Assess a problem systematically and divide large problems into smaller components to be analysed individually
Verify even the obvious, determine whether the problem is something simple and make no assumptions
Research ideas and establish priorities
Document findings, actions and outcomes

Identify and apply basic diagnostic procedures and troubleshooting techniques, for example:

Identify the problem, including questioning user and identifying user changes to computer
Analyse the problem, including potential causes and make an initial determination of software and / or hardware problems
Test related components including inspection, connections, hardware / software configurations, device manager, and consult vendor documentation
Evaluate results and take additional steps if needed, such as consultation, use of alternate resources, manuals
Document activities and outcomes
Recognise and isolate issues with display, power, basic input devices, storage, memory, thermal, POST errors (e.g. BIOS, hardware)

Apply basic troubleshooting techniques to check for problems (e.g. thermal issues, error codes, power, connections including cables and / or pins, compatibility, functionality, software / drivers) with components, for example:

Motherboards
Power supply
Processor / CPUs
Memory
Display devices
Input devices
Adapter cards

Recognise the names, purposes, characteristics and appropriate application of tools for example: BIOS, self-test, hard drive self-test and software diagnostics test

1.4 Perform preventative maintenance on personal computer components

Identify and apply basic aspects of preventative maintenance theory, for example:

Visual / audio inspection
Driver / firmware updates
Scheduling preventative maintenance
Use of appropriate repair tools and cleaning materials
Ensuring proper environment

Identify and apply common preventative maintenance techniques for devices such as input devices and batteries.

Aspects of troubleshooting theory

No matter how complex the problems presented by a malfunctioning (or even non-functioning) PC, there are only a finite number of things that can be wrong with it. Admittedly, when you are sitting at a desk or standing at a workbench examining a difficult case, the number of possibilities can seem overwhelming. However, the fact is that 'when you have eliminated the impossible, whatever remains, no matter how improbable, must be the truth.' The key, then, to successful troubleshooting is a calm systematic approach. The basics are so simple that they are easily forgotten:

- **Back up the user's data before you start**. Where data is stored on the local hard drive, you need to back it up before making any changes to the system. You can replace hardware, you can reinstall the operating system or the applications programs, but data, once gone, is gone for good. Even on a network site where data is stored on a file server, there may be some files that have been stored locally, so it is generally worth taking a look at the local hard drive for word-processor files and the like.

- **Assess the problem systematically**. Without prejudging anything, you need to form a first working impression of the nature of the problem. For example, ask yourself whether the symptoms you are looking at are caused by hardware, software, network problems or a virus. Having divided the problem into separate areas, you can now investigate each in turn. The real trick at this stage of the process is not to become attached to some 'pet theory'. Leave your ego at home – you find a problem on a PC by proving yourself wrong several times until, in the end, you get it right!

- **Do not forget to check for the obvious**. There is little point in removing the cover of a PC and checking the Power Supply Unit (PSU) with a multimeter if the PC isn't connected to the mains power or the fuse on the wall plug has blown.

- **Research ideas and establish priorities**. While many problems are soluble from your own stock of knowledge and experience, you may also need to supplement these by referring to manuals, product documentation and, of course, the resources of the Internet. In terms of priorities, your main concern must be a satisfied customer. If necessary, escalate the enquiry to second-line support or arrange a swap out of the defective PC – that is, put a replacement box on the user's desk, configure it and check that it meets their immediate needs. The defective box can then go to a base workshop, be repaired, refurbished and placed back in working stock.

- **Document findings, actions and outcomes**. If you are part of the technical support team in a large organisation, there will probably be reporting and recording procedures for every call out. Through time and with proper organisation, these can be built into a comprehensive knowledge base which will be of benefit to everyone. Even where systematic reporting and documentation are not a formal job requirement, it is useful to make notes on what you did and why and the outcome. Apart from being useful to others who may face the same problem in the future, you are building your own knowledge base, which will make your job easier and quite possibly enhance your career prospects.

Diagnostic procedures and troubleshooting techniques

Troubleshooting – hardware or software – requires an approach rather than a set of predefined answers. Whatever the problem, the approach is always:

- Gather the facts. Observe, use diagnostic utilities, ask the user.

- Make a list of the possibilities.

- Work through the list carefully and methodically, testing and noting results until a solution is found.

Obviously there are times when the 'list' is just couple of items in your head and the process of 'working through it' is brief and informal. At other times, you may have to adopt a more formal approach, making written notes and recording test results.

Ask the user

Most technical support call-outs are the result of a user making a support call because they are experiencing some sort of difficulty. An obvious first step, then, is to ask the customer what the problem is. It is also worth asking whether anyone else uses the PC that you are examining. This may be particularly important if you are working on a family PC where children may have access to it.

This first step in the troubleshooting process is definitely more art than science. It is easy to forget that most users are not familiar with the terminology of computing and may, for example, confuse memory with disk storage or not even know what version of Microsoft Windows® they are running. They certainly can't be expected to know, down to the last mouse click, what other users have been doing.

This initial investigation of a problem will require you to exercise all of the communication and professionalism skills that are discussed in Chapter 19.

The initial problem is, as often as not, described along the lines of, 'When I click on so-and-so nothing happens'. The next step, then, is to ask the user to reproduce the problem.

Reproducing the problem

Having listened to the user's description of the problem, simply ask them to show you the steps which lead to the error they reported. Note exactly what they do and the error messages (if any) that the system puts out. At this stage, the problem and its solution may become apparent. Frequently, it is something simple like a missing desktop shortcut or a wrongly mapped drive and this can be fixed there and then.

Before proceeding further, you should always reboot the machine. There are often one-off failures caused by memory allocation failures and the like, and these can be 'fixed' by rebooting. A fault isn't really a fault unless it happens more than once.

Identifying changes

Systems that have had hardware or software changes are more likely to exhibit faults. Ask for, and note, information about recent changes: hardware upgrades, new software installation, operating system updates or service packs from disk or over the Internet. It may be possible to track down and fix the problem from this information or even to restore the system to its earlier state and start again.

Microsoft Windows® can also be useful in tracking down changes. System Information – one of the System Tools – summarises the current configuration and the XP version has the facility to look at changes made after a date you specify. The Add / Remove programs applet in Microsoft Windows®2000 and XP can also be a useful source of information, particularly about automatic updates that may have been installed without the user's knowledge.

Beware, though, of giving too much credibility to recent changes. The fault may have arisen through other causes. For example, if a machine boots fine after a memory upgrade but crashes after a few minutes' operation, this is probably not a memory fault. The crash-after-five-minutes symptom is typical of an overheating CPU – possibly the CPU fan became disconnected in the course of the memory upgrade.

Analysing the problem

Isolating the symptom

Given the complexity of a modern multimedia PC, it is necessary to try at least to narrow the search for the cause of the problem. When diagnosing hardware, this usually means removing suspect parts systematically, one at a time until the problem rights itself. Using this approach, the last piece of hardware removed is a strong candidate for the defective part.

In software, this means removing any background programs (typically TSRs such as quick launchers for applications) until only the suspect program is running.

Separating hardware from software

It is often difficult to know whether a problem is caused by a software or hardware fault. The following are all worth trying:

- **Known good hardware**. The best way to separate hardware from software in diagnosing a problem is to replace the hardware with a known good component. For example, a reported memory fault may be caused by a software fault or a defective stick of RAM. If replacing the RAM cures the problem, then it was a hardware fault. If not, it is probably a software problem, though it would be as well to consider the possibility that it was both.

- **Uninstall / Reinstall**. Uninstalling and reinstalling suspect software often provides a quick fix.

- **Patching / Upgrading**. A frequent cause of problems is incompatibility between hardware and the associated software drivers. Download patches or upgrades where these are available, especially if the hardware and the drivers are more than two years different in age.

- **Virus check**. At some point in the investigation, a virus check with an up-to-date scanner is a necessity. Where a system has sufficient functionality, it may be a good idea to check for viruses at the start.

- **Common sense**. No set of rules or guidelines or procedures can provide a substitute for common sense. Think carefully about what the user reports, note symptoms and make written notes if necessary. Assume nothing and always look for the obvious: if the fuse in the plug on the wall has blown, there is not much point in testing the power supply in the computer.

Testing related components and connections

Sometimes the easiest way of tracking down a problem is to strip the PC down to its constituent parts and rebuild it, carrying out testing from time to time. There are many connections in the PC and one poorly seated component can be sufficient to cause a failure. The key to this process – like all troubleshooting – is being systematic. Rebuild and test with the minimum hardware necessary to boot (motherboard, RAM, CPU and power) – then add components and test from time to time. Once you have a working

GUI, you can also check in Device Manager. For example, a poorly seated expansion card – sound card, modem, etc. – may not even show up in Device Manager, whereas a card that appears but reports a fault may simply have a driver problem. Also worth checking is the vendor's website for a particular suspect component. There are occasionally 'known issues' with components and these are often documented either in product documentation or on the website. There may also be user forums where you can find any workarounds that other users may have found for your problem.

Evaluate results

Troubleshooting is an iterative process. Go through the steps, making notes where necessary; evaluate your results in the light of your experiences, information gained from product manuals and websites. Then step through the process again until you find a solution.

Document activities and outcomes

Once you have found your solution, write it down. Describe the problem, the symptoms, the methods of investigation and the outcome. This need not be long or complex documentation – indeed the shorter the better. All that is required is that when you, or anyone else, encounter a similar problem in the future, there are some clear notes on the problem, the methods of investigation and the solution.

Recognise and isolate issues with hardware

A complex system such as a PC consists of a number of sub-systems: display, power, input devices, storage (disks) and memory (RAM). Usually, it is a fairly straightforward job to determine which of the sub-systems is the probable source of the reported operational problems. For example, failure to display the desktop is a display problem. Its cause is probably a bad connection between the monitor and system box (this, along with 'is it plugged in and does it have power?' is in the 'obvious' category mentioned earlier). Failing that, you may have a defective graphics card. Similarly, complete failure to boot may indicate a power problem, which may arise from the system not being connected to the mains or a blown fuse in the wall plug (the 'obvious' category again), or it may indicate a failed Power Supply Unit (PSU). The most common cause of failure of any component is poor quality of connection. Before starting a detailed examination of the system, a good first approach is to reseat any connections, check cables for orientation and look for bent pins. Then reboot the system. This basic approach, along with the exercise of common sense and experience, will cure many a problem before you have even reached for the toolkit.

Power On Self Test (POST)

When you boot a PC, its Basic Input Output System (BIOS) runs some diagnostic routines. The BIOS reports any errors that it encounters by one of two methods:

■ **Beep codes.** The system speaker emits a series of short and long beep codes to indicate problems in a system component during the hardware phase of the boot sequence. For example, an AMI BIOS which emits one long beep, followed by three short beeps, followed by a further long beep (–-–-–) indicates a bad or missing graphics adapter. Because there is no visual output at this stage of the start-up process we have to rely on beep codes or employ a POST card (see page 99).

▨ **Error messages**. Once the monitor is working, the BIOS can output text error messages and / or codes to indicate a problem that has shown itself in the later stages of the boot process.

Unfortunately each BIOS manufacturer uses a different set of beep codes to indicate errors so you will need some form of documentation (or a reference book) to decode them. The A+ examinations will not assume or require a detailed knowledge of the various manufacturer-specific codes.

Although the beep codes used by a particular BIOS are specific to that manufacturer, it is almost always the case that a single beep indicates that the system is OK. Any other number of beeps indicates a problem. A common scenario is the PC that starts to boot, outputs a series of beeps, then hangs. You may be able to diagnose the problem on the basis of the beep codes, but a useful alternative is to use a Power On Self Test (POST) card that displays BIOS error outputs as hexadecimal numbers on a seven-segment display. Figure 7.1 shows a POST card that has edge connectors for both PCI and the older ISA motherboard slots. Many of the newer ones only have a PCI connector.

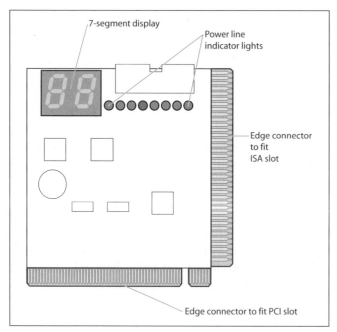

7-segment display

Power line indicator lights

Edge connector to fit ISA slot

Edge connector to fit PCI slot

Figure 7.1

USING A POST CARD

1 Power down the PC and remove its cover or side panel.

2 Using standard anti-static precautions, fit the POST card in an expansion slot. Take care if you are using the ISA slot as the card can be fitted back to front if you are not careful. There should be an orientation mark somewhere on the card.

3 Reboot the PC. The power line indicators will flash and the seven-segment display will output hexa-decimal codes that correspond to the beep codes output to the system speaker.

4 When the system stops, note the HEX code on the seven-segment display and consult the POST card's manual for the code's meaning.

A POST card does not fix anything, but it gives a quick diagnostic answer. Even if it indicates a fatal fault that requires a motherboard replacement to fix it, at least you have an answer quickly.

BIOS

The Basic Input Output System (BIOS) is a set of start-up routines on the BIOS chip. They run as the system starts up and use either default values or those provided by the values held in CMOS. Chapter 1 examines the role of BIOS and its relationship to CMOS (see page 17).

The most likely cause of boot-time problems associated with BIOS is one or more wrong settings in CMOS. Before doing anything else, check the CMOS settings and check that the CMOS battery is still delivering sufficient voltage to maintain the settings while the PC is turned off. If – and only if – you have established that the problem is with the BIOS chip itself rather than settings, then you may have to update the BIOS. This is a non-trivial undertaking.

Modern BIOS chips are based on a technology known as Electronically Erasable Programmable Read Only Memory (EEPROM). This means that the chip can be erased and reprogrammed without removing it from the system. This is frequently known as a 'flash upgrade'. In order to update a BIOS, you need to download an update program from the manufacturer's web-site and run it on the target system. Often, this will require you to put the upgrade program on a bootable floppy disk, boot to it, and run it from the A: drive. The key thing to remember is that an upgrade of this sort is an all-or-nothing undertaking. It only takes a couple of seconds, but if it is interrupted you may end up with a damaged system that will not boot at all. Similarly, if you use the wrong flash upgrade, you may damage the BIOS beyond use. If this happens, you will need to replace the BIOS altogether and in practice this may mean buying and installing a new motherboard. In general, you should only upgrade a BIOS in response to a known problem and double check that you are using the right utility.

Motherboards

It is not always easy to tell if the failure of a PC is caused by a motherboard fault or some other cause. A PC that just 'sits there' may have a defective motherboard, defective RAM or a dud CPU. It could be that the power supply has failed. As with any PC problem, check the obvious first – make sure that the system has mains power, reseat components and check for bent pins. Check that the PSU is delivering adequate voltage on all its output lines. Power down and investigate with a POST card. You may also want to boot to one of the industry-standard diagnostic utilities such as Eurosoft's PC Check®. This boots to its own proprietary operating system and allows you to run diagnostic tests on all hardware components.

If the target PC simply will not boot in spite of a known good power supply, you may have to swap out RAM and / or the CPU for known good components in order to isolate the problem. Once you have established that the motherboard is faulty, there is little on it that can be repaired, so you will need to replace it.

Power supply

A failed power supply is easy to diagnose. When connected to a mains source, it fails to deliver any power on its Direct Current (DC) lines to the motherboard and attached drives. The solution is to replace it. A more difficult problem, and one you will encounter more frequently in practice, is that of a failing power supply. Typical symptoms of a failing power supply is a PC that displays boot-time failures but which, if it boots at the third or fourth attempt, works properly until the next start-up. The solution is to check the DC output lines with a multimeter and if any of them fails to deliver the correct voltage, replace the PSU. A voltage shortfall of as little as one tenth of a volt can cause boot-time problems.

Processor / CPU

The CPU is another component that, for the most part, either works or does not. The majority of CPU problems are in fact thermal problems. Modern chips run hot and the failure of a cooling fan can cause overheating and a complete system lockup in a few seconds. If you have a CPU lockup, the first thing to do is to check that the CPU fan is working. If it is not, power down IMMEDIATELY and fix the fan. A couple of minutes without cooling is enough to render the CPU useless – it will simply burn out. Where the problem is not one of overheating, check that it is properly seated in its socket and if the PC is capable of booting even with reduced functionality, run some diagnostics such as Eurosoft's PC Check®.

Memory (RAM)

Memory problems can be difficult to identify and are frequently the cause of apparently random failures, which may even be reported as something else. For example, a defective memory location in RAM may cause a disk write to fail and the system may report this as a disk error. Because there are often several RAM sticks in the PC, it may be possible to remove them one at a time and if removing a particular stick cures the problem, replace it. You may also be able to borrow some known good RAM from a similar PC and test with that. You can also, of course, boot to a suitable diagnostic utility and test system RAM with that. You can download a free memory diagnostic program from the Microsoft web-site, although many technicians prefer one of the commercially available test suites.

Display devices

A display device such as a monitor displaying no output at all almost always indicates a hardware failure somewhere on the system. The first step is to check the obvious: does it have power, is it connected to the PC, are the brightness and contrast controls turned up on the unit itself? It is easy, particularly after cleaning a monitor, to accidentally change the hardware controls and lose the output as a result. Having checked the obvious, the next thing to check is the quality of the connection to the port on the PC. Disconnect the monitor and look for any bent pins on the connection. If this does not show any problems, then connect the monitor to a known working PC. If it does not work on the new system either, then from the point of view of the A+ service technician, it is simply 'dead' and, as a Field Replaceable Unit, it should be replaced and sent for further specialist attention at a base workshop or disposed of in line with the health and safety laws which apply in your country or state. Chapter 18 looks at safety and environmental issues.

Where a monitor fails to work on one machine, but works fine on another, the obvious candidate is the graphics card on the original PC. As with any problem with an adapter card (see page 102 for more on this), the first thing to do is to power down the PC and reseat the card. If this does not work, replace the card and if that does not work, you will need to start a thorough examination of all the hardware: power supply, CPU and motherboard in particular.

A more common problem with display devices is a poor-quality image and this is nearly always the result of wrong settings or wrong drivers. If, in the case of a Windows PC, you have sufficient display to see what you are doing, the first two checks are in Device Manager and the Display settings, which can be reached either through the **Display** Applet in the Microsoft Windows® **Control Panel** or by right-clicking on an empty part of the desktop and selecting **Properties** from the context menu. Where the display is too distorted for this to be feasible, you can boot into Safe Mode to carry out these checks.

Uninstalling and reinstalling or upgrading the video drivers is the obvious next step to cure the problem. Particularly where you are dealing with a display device other than a standard monitor, you may need to consult the manufacturer's documentation for the product and visit their website for updates for news of 'known issues'.

Input devices

Apart from bad connections and bent pins, the majority of problems with input devices – particularly mice and keyboards – is the build-up of dirt. Grease from fingers and dust attracted by static electricity forms a patina of muck that is familiar to most of us. The cure is simply to clean the input device, though where standard keyboards and mice are concerned it may be cheaper to replace them than to carry out extensive maintenance work. Where maintenance work is likely to be cost-effective, a keyboard can be cleaned with a proprietary cleaner and a blow through with canned air. Some technicians remove a couple of keyboard caps to aid the flow of the air through the keyboard housing. The older style 'ball' mice and trackballs can be cleaned by removing the build-up of dirt on the rollers and the ball itself with something like a toothpick, which will not damage the surfaces to which it is applied. While alcohol is a useful cleaner for many parts on the PC, it can damage mice balls and should not be used on them. Where you are dealing with less common (and more expensive) input devices such as touch screens, scanners or bar code readers, you will need to consult the manufacturer's documentation and / or website for product-specific information.

Adapter cards

Problems with adapter cards in general are the familiar ones: poor connections, bent pins and software drivers, and as a rule they are best approached in that order. Whether you are investigating a non-functioning modem card, a network adapter or a custom-built expansion card to control a machine tool, the first thing to check is that the device that it controls is properly connected and has power. If you have a working display on the PC, have a look in Device Manager to see the status of the card. Where the card is not shown at all, it is either dead, or not properly seated in its expansion slot. Where it is present in the Device Manager list, you probably have a problem with drivers. In the case of a completely non-functioning device, you may also want to connect the device to a similar PC to see whether it is the device or the card that has failed. If this is not possible, or you have done it and the device is OK, power down the problem PC and reseat the card. If the reseated card is still not visible in Device Manager, it is probably in need of replacement. If it is visible but not working, then you have problems with drivers. This can probably be fixed by reinstalling drivers or obtaining new drivers from the manufacturer's website. Once you have working hardware and correct drivers in place, any remaining problems are almost certainly configuration problems. For a network card, for example, you would need to look at various network settings such as correctly installed protocols, IP addressing, etc.

Tools and techniques

Multimeters

Apart from the basic hardware tools – screwdrivers, pliers, etc. – one of the most useful hardware tools is a multimeter. Figure 7.2 shows a typical digital multimeter.

The multimeter – as the name suggests – has many uses, but the three that you will need as a working technician are:

- Measuring AC mains voltage

- Measuring DC voltage – mainly from batteries or the output lines of Power Supply Units (PSUs)

- Measuring resistance – usually to check for a broken wire or a blown fuse.

Measuring AC mains voltage requires you to set the function selector to measure (AC) volts. Some meters – typically the cheaper or older ones – will also require you to select the expected voltage range and, if you get this wrong, you will probably burn out the meter. Having selected your voltage, apply the probes to the circuit to be tested. As often as not, in the field, you will use this to test the 'kettle lead' that provides mains power to the PSU. For alternating current, it doesn't matter which probe goes into which connector. Providing you have set the meter properly, you should see the standard mains voltage for your location. A zero reading indicates lack of mains power, usually the result of a blown fuse.

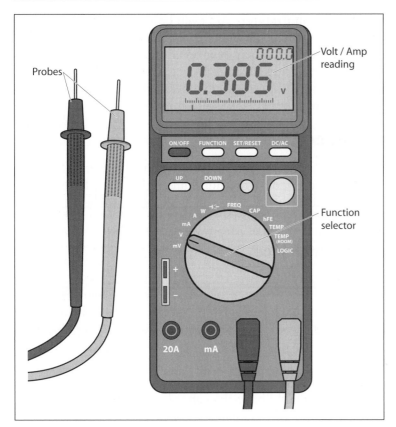

Figure 7.2

Measuring DC voltage requires that you set the meter to measure (DC) volts and possibly to set the range of the expected voltage. Use the red (positive) probe for the positive connector to be tested and the black (negative) probe for the negative connector to be tested. Read the voltage from the digital display.

Measuring resistance requires that you select the function to measure ohms – the symbol for this is the upper-case Greek letter Omega Ω. This symbol is frequently used on multimeters. The most common use for this function is to check for a blown fuse. Set the meter as required and place the fuse to be tested between the two probes. If the fuse has blown, then the resistance in the completed circuit will be infinite. A reading of 'normal' resistance indicates that the fuse is okay. Obviously, the same logic applies to any other circuit which you decide to test for continuity.

Different manufacturers' meters will vary somewhat in the functions that they provide and the detailed means of operation so consult the manufacturer's documentation if you have any doubt about a particular function.

Self tests

Apart from the BIOS / POST tests outlined above, hard drives can be configured to self test. Most modern hard disks incorporate a technology called Self Monitoring Analysis and Reporting Technology (SMART) and it has been estimated that this can predict around 30 per cent of hard disk failures before they happen. The criteria used to predict failures by SMART vary between manufacturers and even between products from the same manufacturer. Although most modern BIOSs support SMART, it is frequently disabled by default because – valuable though it may be in some circumstances – it imposes an overhead on the system where it is implemented. In practice, if you have a suspect hard disk, your best bet is to back up the data stored on it before it fails entirely, then run some software diagnostics such as Eurosoft's PC Check®.

Preventive maintenance

Preventive maintenance can be a cost-effective means of extending the working life of a system. If it is properly organised, it can reduce downtime and productivity losses by carrying out work according to a schedule, predicting and avoiding probable failures and dealing with them before problems arise.

Scheduling preventive maintenance

Obviously not every aspect of preventive maintenance needs to be carried out with the same frequency. For example, a disk needs to be defragmented more frequently than you would strip down and reseat internal components. No two companies or individuals will have the same needs or priorities for preventive maintenance tasks, but a possible schedule might be:

DAILY

- **Virus scan.** Your virus scanner should have the capability of running at a pre-set time each day. If you leave your system permanently on, you can schedule this for the small hours of the morning. Don't forget that the scanner needs to update its 'definitions' files, so schedule the update to run just before the scan.

- **Spyware scan.** This complements the virus scan and ideally it should be done immediately before or after the virus scan.

- **Back-up.** It is prudent to back up your data daily. The minimum you should do is to back-up data that has been modified (a differential backup) with a full data back-up once a week.

WEEKLY

- **Full data back-up.** Make a full data back-up, preferably to a rotating disk (or tape) set.

- **Defragment the hard disk.**

- **Run the Disk Cleanup Wizard.**

MONTHLY

- **Clean optical drives** – CDROM / DVD – with a 'cleaner' disk.

- **Archive back-up of data.** Store this away from the PC.

- **Clean the mouse.** If you are still using a 'ball' mouse, clean the rollers by scraping gently with a toothpick or similar.

- **Clean the monitor**. Power down and clean the screen with a soft cloth or an anti-static wipe.

- **Clean the keyboard**. Check the keyboard for sticky keys – clean with canned air if necessary.

ON FAILURE

- **Clean the floppy disk drive**. The cleaning disk that you can use for cleaning floppy drives is mildly abrasive, so it should only be used sparingly to avoid long-term cumulative damage to the drive.

YEARLY

- **Case**. Open the case. Remove dust deposits by brushing gently with a natural bristle brush, then blow out with canned air, or use a special PC vacuum cleaner.

- **Adapter cards, cables and removable components**. Clean contacts and reseat.

ONGOING / AS REQUIRED

- **CMOS**. Record and / or back-up CMOS settings.

- **System**. Maintain a record of hardware, software and settings of the system. Note all changes in a 'system notebook' or other written record and store this away from the system concerned.

Use of appropriate repair tools and cleaning materials

Commonly used products and tools include:

- **Canned air**. Use this for blowing dust from awkward corners. Most PC shops sell it.

- **Natural fibre brushes**. A small paint brush or a pastry brush is ideal. Make sure, though, that it has natural bristles as some man-made fibres can generate static electricity, which can damage components.

- **Antistatic wipes**. These are usually individually wrapped. They can be bought from most PC shops.

- **Denatured alcohol**. This can simply be a bottle of methylated or surgical spirit, which you can buy from a hardware shop or pharmacy. Alcohol cuts through grease very effectively and evaporates quickly

- **Mild detergent solution**. Tap water with a squirt of washing-up liquid is a very good cleaning solution, especially for the outside of the case, etc. Of course, it needs to be used with care; water and electricity can be a hazardous combination. Don't apply the solution directly, but use a dampened cloth and use sparingly.

- **Cleaning disks**. The disks that you use on a floppy drive are mildly abrasive and should be used with restraint. The cleaning disks / kits you can use for CD or DVD drives are not generally abrasive and can be used as necessary or monthly as a routine preventive measure.

▧ **Cotton Buds**. These are useful for general-purpose cleaning. They can be used in conjunction with canned air and a natural bristle brush for mechanical removal of dirt and debris from awkward corners. They can also be dipped in alcohol for liquid cleaning where necessary.

▧ **Non-static vacuum cleaners**. These are small cleaners – often 'pistol grip' in shape – and are intended for use with PCs. They need to be used with care as there is the possibility of them damaging or dislodging components.

Safety note:

Before using any product on any PC, you should check that it is suitable for the intended use. For instance, if you plan on cleaning the case with a detergent solution or alcohol, apply it to a small area that is usually out of sight just to check that it is okay. In terms of health and safety law in the UK, there are regulations under the Control of Substances Hazardous to Health (COSHH) regulations, and in the USA all such products have a Material Safety Data Sheet (MSDS). You can check the nature of any product you plan to use by searching on the Internet.

Cleaning the outside of the case

Power down and 'wash' the outside of the case with a cloth dipped in mild detergent solution and wrung out. Allow the cleaned surfaces to dry fully before reconnecting the power. For a really good job, you can follow detergent cleaning with a rub down with a cloth moistened with alcohol. Again, allow the cleaned surface to dry fully before reconnecting the power.

Cleaning monitors

LCD – flat panel – monitors can be cleaned with a glass cleaner and a lint-free cloth. Don't spray the cleaner directly on to the screen; apply a small amount to the cloth, then wipe the surface with it. LCD screens are easily scratched, so work gently. Be careful not to leave any excess on the screen and allow half an hour or so before powering up again.

Cathode Ray Tube (CRT) monitors – the ones that look like a television set – need to be treated with care. Even when they are turned off they contain very high voltages. Always disconnect the monitor before working on it and never wear a wrist strap or even metal jewellery that could come into contact with it.

A simple soap-and-water solution can be used for cleaning the outside of the case and the screen itself. Don't use excessive amounts of the solution; dip the cleaning cloth in it, then wring out until it is damp but has no excess moisture. Clean the monitor and dry it with a clean cloth before powering up. Don't use commercial cleaners or aerosol sprays other than those specifically designed for use with monitors.

With either type of monitor, power up when you have finished and the screen is dry, then check that any controls for brightness, alignment, etc. are okay. It is quite easy to knock a control accidentally during cleaning and to lose the 'picture' as a result.

Cleaning inside the case

Dust is an ever-present problem with computer systems. The components generate static charges as a by-product of their operation, and the various cooling fans draw air (and dust) into the case. Over time, the accumulation of dust can be sufficient to cause over-heating, so an annual 'spring clean' of the interior of the case can be a useful investment of your time. As with all work on the inside of the system box, power down and discon-nect from the mains before removing the covers or side panels.

The first line of defence against accumulated dust is a small paint brush, or a pastry brush, with natural bristles that will not induce static in the components to which they are applied. Simply use the brush to dislodge accumulated dust – particularly on the CPU heat sink / fan assembly and the power supply fan. Blow the loosened dust away using canned air or remove it with a non-static vacuum cleaner. (Either of these tools can be used equally well to clean a keyboard, by the way.)

While you have the case open, check that all of the fans rotate freely and are properly connected to the power connectors on the motherboard – it's quite easy to dislodge a connection during the cleaning process. This is also a good time to replace any missing covers from unused expansion slots. This will help to optimise the airflow in the case and to keep atmospheric dust out.

Before replacing the cover or side panel, connect the machine to the mains and power up. Check that all fans – particularly the CPU fan – are working. A non-functioning CPU fan will cause the chip to overheat and the system will lock up in under a minute. Longer than a minute is sufficient to cause permanent damage so this is a check worth making.

Cleaning contacts and connections

This is not really necessary if a system is functioning properly, but some people like to clean and reseat internal components as part of their annual maintenance. If components have been handled and fitted properly – that is, contacts and edge connectors have never been touched by hand – then there is not likely to be any corrosion or oxidation to the surface.

If you do find it necessary to clean edge connectors on expansion cards or memory modules, then remove the module and use a very fine emery cloth or a specialist electri-cal contact cleaner spray. The easiest method is to use a pencil eraser to brush the contacts. When doing this, always work from the inner to the outer edge of the module to avoid peeling back the edge connectors.

Other internal components that fit into slots or sockets on the motherboard may work themselves loose over time. The repeated cycle of heating and cooling causes repeated expansions and contractions of the components and this can cause components to work loose in their sockets – a phenomenon known as 'chip creep'. As a preventive measure, it is prudent to remove and reseat any such components to establish a fresh electrical contact.

Cleaning removable media devices

Removable drives such as tape drives, floppy drives, CDs, DVDs, etc. are open to the air, and the media themselves are physically handled. This means that they can collect dust and finger grease that can be transferred from the disk to the drive heads. An indirect form of preventive maintenance, then, is to exercise care when handling removable media.

Magnetic media, floppy disks and tapes, etc., can easily be corrupted if they are stored close to strong magnetic fields, so you should avoid storing them near anything with an electric motor – like a vacuum cleaner – or anything with strong electro-magnetic fields such as CRT monitors or speakers.

When it comes to cleaning drives themselves, there are two approaches: removal and manual cleaning or using cleaning tapes or disks. Generally speaking, floppy drives are now so cheap that it may be cost-effective to replace them rather than spend time on cleaning them, though cleaning kits are available.

Optical drives – CD and DVD – as well as tape drives may be removed, stripped down and cleaned with alcohol and a lint-free cloth. A cotton bud dipped in alcohol is an easy way to clean a lens. As an alternative, there are cleaning disks and kits available for most drive types. Optical media are mechanically 'swept' clean by brush heads mounted on a cleaning disk passing over the laser lens. This is a non-destructive process. Cleaners for magnetic media are generally mildly abrasive so, while they are effective at removing the build-up of contaminants on the drive heads, excessive use can shorten the life of the drive.

Visual / audio inspection

In the course of working with a PC, there are many auditory and visual clues that indicate its state. Some of these, such as the beep codes that are used by the Power On Self Test (POST) routines are formal and documented. Others, the sound of a disk drive as it spins up, the fans of the cooling system, and the power supply, can all be indicators of whether or not a particular sub-system is working. Similarly, there are many visual clues: error messages, activity lights on a network card, the lights on a disk drive, even the pattern of the dust inside the case, can all help in identifying problems.

Driver / firmware updates

Out-of-date or corrupt drivers are always a possible cause of problems. In general, if you suspect a problem with a device, you will update any necessary drivers after downloading them from the manufacturer's website. Similarly, many devices such as CD-ROMs have firmware built into them and this may need to be upgraded from time to time or in response to operational problems. Earlier in the chapter, we considered BIOS flash upgrades, and the process is similar for the firmware that is built into other components using EEPROM chips. As with a BIOS upgrade, a firmware upgrade needs to be approached with care and attention to detail.

Ensuring proper environment

Generally speaking, PCs work best in the same sort of conditions as humans: not too hot, not too cold, moderate humidity and no sources of dust. In most office environments 'standard' conditions will be acceptable, though in industrial applications it may be necessary to regulate temperature and humidity through heating and / or air conditioning systems. These environmental considerations can be particularly important where laptop PCs are used because these systems are as prone to the build-up of dust (for example) as their desktop counterparts, but are considerably more troublesome to clean.

Input devices and batteries

The useful working life of input devices can be increased by routine cleaning and maintenance: keyboards, for example, can be cleaned with a brush or even a couple of key caps removed and blown through with canned air. Mice and trackballs can be cleaned by using a toothpick to remove accumulated dirt without scratching the rollers. Any and every device can be inspected for bent pins, cracked insulation and so on. Some battery types – notably nickel cadmium – that are used on laptop systems display a 'memory effect', which means that they will lose capacity if they are recharged before they are fully discharged. Battery life, for this type of battery, can be extended by allowing them to fully discharge from time to time before needing to recharge them fully. This type of battery is rapidly being replaced by more modern technologies. The main problem that you will face with batteries is that of safe and legal disposal. This is discussed in Chapter 18 (see page 287). Other batteries, such as those used to maintain the CMOS settings, are cheap and can be treated as consumables to be replaced and the old ones disposed of safely.

SUMMARY

In this chapter we have considered the process of troubleshooting with regard to hardware components. We have considered some of the specifics as they are applied to particular components – such as PSUs and expansion cards – which you will need to diagnose in the field and which may be the subject of exam questions. We have noted the need for a systematic customer-focused approach and the need to document problems and their solutions for future reference. The preventive maintenance section of the chapter has considered the ways in which the working life of some components can be increased by carrying out planned maintenance work at both component and system level.

QUESTIONS

1   A user reports intermittent boot-time failures. You inspect the PC, reboot it and it starts to boot, then fails. Which of the following is a likely cause of this problem?

a) Failing PSU

b) Boot sector virus

c) Defective RAM stick

d) Motherboard fault

2   A user reports that a PC regularly shows the wrong time of day. Putting the clock right fixes the problem for a while, but it always recurs the next day. You suspect a BIOS problem. What do you do first?

a) Reboot and check the CMOS settings through the set-up utility

b) Replace the CMOS battery

c) Connect to an Internet Time Server

d) Flash upgrade the BIOS

3   A system that was working suddenly stops and refuses to boot at all. You check the PSU with a multimeter and all voltages are OK. What is your next step? (Choose two options.)

a) Reseat RAM modules

b) Reseat CPU

c) Swap the RAM modules for known good ones from another PC

d) Replace the motherboard

4   A user reports that some of the keys on a PC are displaying the wrong characters on screen – the £ symbol is replaced by #, and so on. You test the system and the report appears to be correct. What do you do next?

a) Check for bent pins in the keyboard connector

b) Replace the keyboard

c) Run a virus check

d) Check the Regional Options through Control Panel

5   A user reports difficulty in 'saving' files. After an initial assessment of the system, you suspect that the hard disk is failing. What do you do next?

a) Run some diagnostic utilities to track down the problem

b) Replace the disk

c) Back up the data

d) Run the Disk Cleanup Wizard

ANSWERS / EXPLANATIONS

1 A user reports intermittent boottime failures. You inspect the PC, reboot it and it starts to boot, then fails. Which of the following is a likely cause of this problem?

a) Failing PSU

b) Boot sector virus

c) Defective RAM stick

d) Motherboard fault

Any of these could be the fault. The answers listed would, perhaps, be your initial list of things to investigate.

2 A user reports that a PC regularly shows the wrong time of day. Putting the clock right fixes the problem for a while, but it always recurs next day. You suspect a BIOS problem. What do you do first?

a) Reboot and check the CMOS settings through the set-up utility

Check the settings first. After that, you may want to check the CMOS battery with a multimeter and replace it if it does not deliver the correct voltage. Answer c is irrelevant and answer d is – at this stage – overkill.

3 A system that was working suddenly stops and refuses to boot at all. You check the PSU with a multimeter and all voltages are OK. What is your next step?

a) Reseat RAM modules

b) Reseat CPU

Answers a and b (in either order) would be a good next step.

4 A user reports that some of the keys on a PC are displaying the wrong characters on screen – the £ symbol is replaced by #, and so on. You test the system and the report appears to be correct. What do you do next?

d) Check the Regional Options through Control Panel.

Where possible, before checking the hardware, take a look at operating system settings.

5 A user reports difficulty in 'saving' files. After an initial assessment of the system, you suspect that the hard disk is failing. What do you do next?

c) Back up the data

CHAPTER 8
Operating system fundamentals

Two versions of the Microsoft Windows® operating system – Windows 2000 and Windows XP – are central to the operating systems domain of the Essentials exam. The material covered in this chapter and in Chapters 9 and 10 accounts for 21 per cent of the marks available for the exam as a whole.

Exam objective 3.1
3.1 Identify the fundamentals of using operating systems.

Identify differences between operating systems (e.g. Apple Mac®, Microsoft Windows®, Linux®) and describe operating system revision levels, including GUI, system requirements, application and hardware compatibility.

Identify names, purposes and characteristics of the primary operating system components, including registry, virtual memory and file system.

Describe features of operating system interfaces, for example:

> Windows Explorer
> My Computer
> Control Panel
> Command Prompt
> My Network Places
> Task bar / systray
> Start Menu

Identify the names, locations, purposes and characteristics of operating system files, for example:

> BOOT.INI
> NTLDR
> NTDETECT.COM
> NTBOOTDD.SYS
> Registry data files

▶

Identify concepts and procedures for creating, viewing, managing disks, directories and files in operating systems, for example:

Disks (e.g. active, primary, extended and logical partitions)
File systems (e.g. FAT 32, NTFS)
Directory structures (e.g. create folders, navigate directory structures)
Files (e.g. creation, extensions, attributes, permissions)

Operating systems

Operating system software – typically a version of Microsoft Windows® – is the collection of programs that make the computer work. For example, when you save a word-processor document, the content of the document in memory (system RAM) is written to disk, and the Master File Table on the disk is updated with details of the edited file. In order to do this, the word-processor program (an application) uses the services of the operating system.

When you quit the word processor (or other application), the operating system releases the memory it has been using so that it is available for other uses, then it redraws your desktop and displays menus, icons, etc. – the familiar Microsoft Windows® Graphical User Interface (GUI).

To be a bit more formal about it, an operating system has four basic functions:

- It communicates between the application programs and the hardware: disk access, reading from the keyboard and mouse, sending data to the monitor, etc.

- It provides a User Interface – usually, these days, a Graphical User Interface – so that the user can see an understandable representation of the system.

- The operating system – through the user interface – provides tools for the user to view, add, or remove applications and add support for new hardware.

- The operating system also provides tools to manage data: add and remove files, create folders (directories), manage disk storage with utilities such as 'Defrag' and tools to shut the system down.

The A+ Essentials exam is primarily concerned with how Microsoft Windows® 2000 and XP implement these features.

Differences between operating systems

Although the exam is concerned with the modern Microsoft Windows® versions, you are also required to know, at a more general level, the characteristics of other operating systems. As far as earlier Microsoft Windows® versions such as NT 4 or the 9.x family are concerned, all you need to know is the upgrade paths from them to the modern versions. Chapter 9 looks at upgrade requirements.

You are also required to be able to identify and know the basic characteristics of other operating systems such as Linux and Mac OS®.

Linux

Linux (it is pronounced with a short i, by the way) was developed by Linus Torvalds as a student at the University of Helsinki in 1991. It started as a student project that he described as: 'just a hobby [that] won't be big and professional'. The aim was to produce a free Unix-like operating system as an alternative to commercial releases of Unix, which would run on the same sorts of PCs dominated by Microsoft Windows®. The official Linux mascot – proposed by Linus and originally drawn by Larry Ewing – appears on most Linux products.

Thanks to the appeal of Tux the Penguin, not to mention the Internet, the ever-increasing power and decreasing cost of hardware and licensing that ensures that it is free and will remain free, Linux grew from a small private project to the fastest developing operating system ever. Worldwide, there are tens of millions of Linux installations and it is particularly significant in the operation of the Internet. The chances are somewhat better then 50 / 50 that, when you log on to a website, it will be running on a Linux server. Unlike Microsoft Windows®, Linux is available on CPU chips other than Intel and its functional clones.

The main disadvantage of Linux is that its power comes at the cost of complexity and this many users find off-putting. Its relatively small user base – particularly on desktop machines –

Figure 8.1 Tux

also means that there are fewer end-user applications available, though developments such as the cross-platform Open Office suite are beginning to close the gap.

MAC OS®

The Apple Mac was the first affordable desktop computer to run a Graphical User Interface (GUI). Macs run on their own proprietary hardware and the modern version of the operating system is MAC OS X® (the X is the Roman numeral for 'ten' and is generally pronounced as such). MAC OS X has a sophisticated GUI, which means that a user seldom – if ever – needs to access a system prompt. However, the operating system is based on BSD Unix, so the full range of Unix commands are available and the sheer power and stability of the system means that it has an enthusiastic user base. MAC OS® is particularly widely used in graphic design and publishing environments, though for general desktop home or office use, Microsoft Windows® is still the dominant operating system – hence its importance to the A+ technician.

Revision levels

All operating systems have some means of distinguishing between them on the basis of version numbers. On a Microsoft Windows® system, typing the command VER at a system prompt will show the version number. This has three parts: a major version number, a minor version number and a build number.

```
C:\>VER

Microsoft Windows XP [Version 5.1.2600]
```

Figure 8.2

The first digit – 5 – tells us that this is major version number 5. The second digit is the minor version number – in this case 1 – and the final number is the 'build' number used mainly in the development process to distinguish the various compilations of the source code. Running the VER command at a prompt in Microsoft Windows® 2000 will show a major version number of 5 and a minor version of 00. On the basis of this information, we can conclude that Microsoft Windows® XP is the first revision of version 5 – that is, XP is an update of 2000 rather than an entirely new release. If you check a Microsoft Windows® Vista machine, you will see that the major version number is 6 – that is, a completely new Microsoft Windows® release. Note that knowledge of Vista is NOT required for any of the A+ exams.

System requirements and hardware compatibility

Any operating system will have minimum requirements – CPU speed, total RAM, etc. – necessary for it to be installed and to run. These are examined in Chapter 9. Hardware compatibility is another consideration, particularly in the early phase of an operating system release. Most installation disks will have a Hardware Compatibility List in a text file and most will have some sort of hardware checking routine available as part of the installation program. Websites also have information on hardware compatibility and – for the forthcoming release of Microsoft Windows® Vista at least – you can download a compatibility testing program ahead of the actual operating system release date.

Applications compatibility

Most applications which will run under Microsoft Windows® 2000 will also run under XP. Older applications – dating from as far back as Microsoft Windows® 95 – may be useable by tweaking the compatibility mode in XP. In order to do this, right-click on the program's desktop icon, select Properties from the context menu and select the compatibility tab. You will be presented with the choices shown in Figure 8.3.

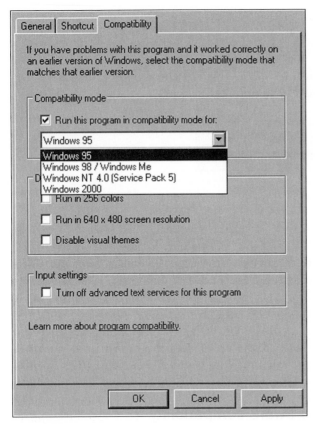

Figure 8.3

This facility is not available in Microsoft Windows® 2000.

Primary operating system components

The registry

All versions of Microsoft Windows® from 95 onwards keep a hierarchical database of information about themselves: settings, user information, etc. Every time you change just about anything on the system, it is recorded in the Registry. Information held in the Registry is the key to how Windows 'knows' which program to use when you open a file, the size and position of a window, the registered owner of the operating system etc. The Registry entries are kept in disk files and / or memory and are presented to the user in an Explorer-style tree structure.

Registry values can be examine or edited by using the Registry editor REGEDIT.EXE. Typing REGEDIT at a command prompt or in a 'Run' box on a Microsoft Windows® 2000 or Windows XP machine will access the Registry editor. Figure 8.4 shows the Registry editor in Microsoft Windows XP® Professional.

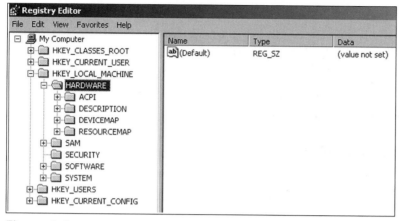

Figure 8.4

Changes made to the Registry are instant in their effect – you do not have to save them to disk – and if you make a mistake, the consequences can destabilise or damage the system. Use the Registry editor with care.

Microsoft Windows® 2000 has a second Registry editing tool – REGEDT32.EXE. This presents Registry information is a slightly different way – each top-level key is presented in its own window – and it also offers a read-only mode which is ideal for exploring values without the risk of accidentally changing them. The command REGEDT32 is also present in Microsoft Windows® XP, but it is not the same editor as in 2000. In XP, REGEDT32 merely starts the standard REGEDIT.EXE editor. Differences between the Microsoft Windows® versions of this type are little more than incidental annoyances when working in the field, but are possible sources of exam questions for A+.

Virtual memory

Modern multi-tasking operating systems are very demanding in terms of system RAM, so they use a disk file to extend the amount of memory that appears to be available to the system by swapping the contents of RAM in and out of a disk file as required. Information not immediately required is written to a file in order to free real system RAM for immediate use. Because the additional working memory gained by this only appears to be RAM, it is known as virtual memory. Both Microsoft Windows® 2000 and XP use a file called PAGEFILE.SYS for virtual memory and this is stored in the root directory of the system partition (usually C:). Because this is a hidden system file it cannot be seen unless Microsoft Windows® is set up to show these types of file (which it is not, by default) or you use the ATTRIB command at a system prompt in the root directory of the system partition.

The size of the PAGEFILE.SYS virtual memory store is determined by Microsoft Windows®, though its size can be altered manually if necessary. In order to see / change virtual memory settings in Microsoft Windows®XP:

1   Right-click on the **My Computer** icon on the desktop and select the **Properties** entry in the context menu.

2   Click on the **Advanced** tab.

3   Click on the **Settings** button in the **Performance** section to bring up another properties sheet.

4   Click on the **Advanced** tab in the properties sheet. You will see something like Figure 8.5.

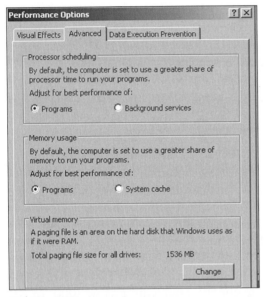

Performance Options

Visual Effects | Advanced | Data Execution Prevention

Processor scheduling

By default, the computer is set to use a greater share of processor time to run your programs.

Adjust for best performance of:

◉ Programs   ○ Background services

Memory usage

By default, the computer is set to use a greater share of memory to run your programs.

Adjust for best performance of:

◉ Programs   ○ System cache

Virtual memory

A paging file is an area on the hard disk that Windows uses as if it were RAM.

Total paging file size for all drives: 1536 MB

Change

Figure 8.5

The Virtual memory panel at the bottom of the figure shows the amount of virtual memory – the size of the swap file. Clicking on the **Change** button will bring up the dialogue that allows you to change the virtual memory settings for the system.

Virtual Memory

Drive [Volume Label]   Paging File Size (MB)

C: 1536 - 3072
E: [DISK-3]
F: [DISK-2]
Q: [Partition-2]

Paging file size for selected drive

Drive: C:
Space available: 2683 MB
◉ Custom size:
Initial size (MB):   1536
Maximum size (MB):   3072
○ System managed size
○ No paging file   Set

Total paging file size for all drives

Minimum allowed: 2 MB
Recommended: 3070 MB
Currently allocated: 1536 MB

OK   Cancel

Figure 8.6

Note: you will need administrator privileges to do this and the PC will need to be rebooted in order for them to take effect. The means of changing these settings in Microsoft Windows® 2000 is all but identical.

File system

The file system is the means by which the operating system keeps track of the various files on the disk – rather like an index in a book. When you create a new file and save it to disk, it is allocated disk storage and the address of the start of the file on disk is recorded. Earlier Microsoft Windows® versions used the File Allocation Table (FAT) to do this. Modern Microsoft Windows® versions such as 2000 and XP use the more sophisticated Master File Table system to achieve the same thing.

By default, 2000 / XP systems use the NTFS 5 file system because of its superior security and stability. However, the modern Microsoft Windows® versions also support the older NTFS 4 and FAT file systems where necessary, so you need to know their basic characteristics for exam purposes. These are summarised in Table 9.1.

Table 9.1

Windows Version	FAT 16	FAT 32	NTFS 4	NTFS 5
NT 4.0	Yes	No	Yes	No
98 / Me	Yes	Yes	No	No
2000	Yes	Yes	No – can convert	Yes
XP	Yes	Yes	No – can convert	Yes

Generally speaking, each release of Microsoft Windows® is backward-compatible with earlier versions of the file system – for example, the old FAT 16, which goes back to the original DOS operating system, can be accessed by all later versions of Microsoft Windows®. There are also conversion utilities built into modern operating systems that enable you to upgrade from an older file system such as FAT 32 to a modern one such as NTFS. Trivially, perhaps, floppy disks have always used the FAT 12 system and this can be read and written to by all Microsoft Windows® versions.

Operating system interfaces

Microsoft Windows® Explorer

Explorer is the main file manager for all Microsoft Windows® versions. In order to 'explore' any object in the file system, right-click on its icon and choose Explorer from the context menu. The default view of Explorer is shown in Figure 8.7.

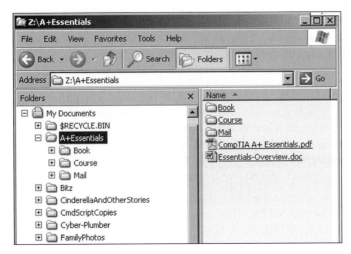

Figure 8.7

This shows a list of folders at the present location in the left pane and files in the right pane. These are file hierarchies that can be expanded to view their contents and files can be copied, moved or deleted from the Explorer interface. This style of presenting information is now so commonplace throughout computing that applications employing it are often described as having an 'Explorer style' interface.

My Computer

This is fundamentally the same interface as Microsoft Windows® Explorer, but it opens with a different default view. Rather than a view of files and folders on the system, My Computer opens with a list of disk drives and without the file list on the left of the display. However, if you click on the **Folders** button, the file system will be displayed 'Explorer style'. You can think of Explorer and My Computer as being different views of the same thing – offering the same choices through buttons for Folders, Search and the navigation controls, and the button (to the right of the Folders button) to change the default view of the folders. Both of these interfaces are all but identical in Microsoft Windows® 2000 and XP.

Control Panel

The Control Panel is a feature of both Microsoft Windows® 2000 and XP. In XP it can be accessed from an entry in the Start menu, in 2000 you navigate to **Start | Settings**. Figure 8.8 shows the default view in Windows 2000.

The contents of the Control Panel are mainly applets that deliver some system functionality such as keyboard adjustments, changing the time and date and so on. Others, like Fonts are folders. In addition to entries placed in the Control Panel by Microsoft Windows® when it is installed, some applications also put their own applets there. Many of the features of the Control panel can be started from a run box or a command prompt. For example, DEVMGMT.MSC at a command prompt (or in a 'Run' box) will start Device Manager. Searching on *.msc will produce a list of applets that can be started like this.

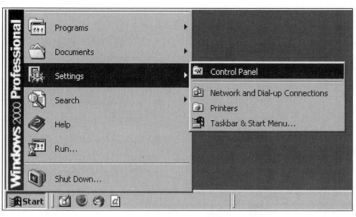

Figure 8.8

The exact contents of the Control Panel will vary from system to system so, for exam purposes, you should know how to access it and be familiar with the standard entries such as Add / Remove Programs, Folder Options, the System applet, and so on. For the most part, Control Panel collects various functions such as these and presents them all in one place as a matter of convenience. The Folder Options and System applets can both be accessed from elsewhere, for example, so you should familiarise yourself with the alternatives. One of the features of Microsoft Windows® operating systems is that they provide alternative ways of doing things. To access the System applet, for example, right-click on the **My Computer** icon on the desktop and choose **Properties** from the context menu. Alternatively, navigate to **Control Panel** and click on the System icon. Most of us have our preferred way of doing things in Microsoft Windows®, but as a working tech or as someone wanting to pass the exam, you need to be familiar with the alternatives.

Command prompt

Both Microsoft Windows® 2000 and XP allow you to use a DOS-style command prompt. The ability to work at a prompt is still an important skill for a working technician, although it does not have quite the same importance for exam purposes as it once had. In Microsoft Windows® XP, the command prompt can be found by navigating to **Start | All Programs | Accessories | Command Prompt**. The route to the prompt is all but identical in Microsoft Windows® 2000. Alternatively, you can type CMD in a 'Run' box on either operating system to launch the default command processor CMD.EXE. You can also launch the older legacy command processor COMMAND.COM by typing COMMAND (no need for the file extension) at a CMD prompt or in a 'Run' box. In general, to use a command, type its name with any switches or options at a system prompt and press the Enter / Carriage Return key. For example, to show a listing of files in the current directory (folder) and to display the output one page at the time, you would issue the command:DIR /P (followed by a carriage return) to make this happen. Command line work is outlined further in 'Working at a Command Prompt' which is available at www.aplusforstudents.co.uk.

My Network Places

This is an Explorer-style interface that allows you to list network computers and drives on the local network. You can also Add a Network Place – using the Microsoft Windows® Wizard to connect to a data store to which you have access rights – on the local network or the Internet, using the http or ftp protocols. Figure 8.9 shows My Network Places in an Explorer-style view in Microsoft Windows® 2000.

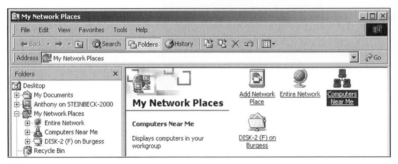

Figure 8.9

Task bar / systray

On a default Microsoft Windows® installation, the taskbar runs along the bottom of the display. The Start button is at the left side and the system tray (or Notification Area) is at the opposite end of the taskbar. The system tray holds icons for programs that are running in the background such as virus scanners, or quick launch icons for applications such as OpenOffice . The centre part of the taskbar displays buttons for each of the open windows and allows you to click on them to bring a running application to the front, or to maximise it if it is minimised. The taskbar can be moved by dragging and dropping elsewhere on screen. Right-clicking on an empty part of the taskbar brings up a context menu and selecting **Properties** from this menu allows you to change the properties of both the taskbar and the Start menu. There is also an option to manage toolbars. Microsoft Windows® 2000 and XP are similar in their implementation of the taskbar and system tray, although XP offers a few extra features.

Start menu

The Start menu is a feature common to all modern Microsoft Windows® releases. It contains some predetermined entries and has room for some optional ones. Figure 8.10 shows the Start menu on a Microsoft Windows® 2000 system. It is accessed by left-clicking on the **Start** button.

The items in the bottom part of the figure are defaults, which have been placed there by the Microsoft Windows® installer. The items at the top of the figure are shortcuts put

Figure 8.10

there by the user. In order to do this, create a desktop shortcut, then drag and drop it on to the Start button and position it where required. XP has the facility simply to 'pin' a shortcut to the Start menu as one of the right-click options when you select a desktop icon to launch an application.

The Start menu is such a highly configurable option in all versions of Microsoft Windows® that you cannot be expected to know every possible permutation of possibilities. You should, however, familiarise yourself with its working in both 2000 and XP.

Identify the names, locations, purposes and characteristics of operating system files

Locations

The location of any object on a Microsoft Windows® system can be described by giving a fully qualified path name. Each drive on a Microsoft Windows® system has a drive letter (terminated with a colon, e.g. C:) and files are arranged in a tree structure that begins with the 'root' of the file system – this is indicated by a single backslash character. The root directory of a drive is created when it is formatted. The backslash character is also used as a path separator between directories (folders) on the system. If we wish to refer to a file called MYFILE.DOC which is in the LETTERS folder in the MYPAPERWORK folder on the C: drive, it would be written as:

C:\MYPAPERWORK\LETTERS\MYFILE.DOC

Note that capital letters have been used for clarity – the Windows command line interpreter is not case-sensitive and myfile, MYfile and myFiLe would be regarded as the same thing. Other operating systems, such as MAC OS® or Linux are case-sensitive.

BOOT.INI

This is a text file in the root of the system partition (usually C:) in both Microsoft Windows® 2000 and XP. By default it has System and Read Only attributes set, so it is greyed out (but visible) in Explorer and can be seen from the system prompt by using the ATTRIB command. The information in the file is read by BIOS at boot time to point to the location of the Master Boot Record (MBR) on the boot volume. On dual boot systems, it also displays the boot menu. The BOOT.INI file has to be present in the root of the system partition for the system to boot.

Because the BOOT.INI is a text file, it can be edited with a text editor, though you will have to change its attributes first. Editing by hand is not recommended; it is easier and more reliable to use the Microsoft Windows® GUI. In both Microsoft Windows® 2000 and XP, open the **System** applet, then click on the **Advanced** tab, then the **Settings** button of the **Start up and Recovery panel**.

NTLDR

NTLDR is a binary file that is used to start loading the operating system on an NT-based system. It must be present in the root of the system partition to work.

NTDETECT.COM

NTDETECT.COM is also required to be in the root of the system partition for the system to boot. Its function is to detect the hardware present at boot time in order to update the registry key HKEY_LOCAL_MACHINE\HARDWARE.

Because the system needs to know the current hardware configuration, this key is held in memory (a 'volatile hive') rather than a disk file. (See registry data files, page 124).

The three files that we have just looked at – BOOT.INI, NTLDR and NTDETECT.COM must all be present in the root of the system partition (usually C:) for an NT-based system to boot. Expect at least one exam question that tests this core knowledge.

NTBOOTDD.SYS

In spite of its important-sounding name and its .sys extension, this file is not normally necessary to the Microsoft Windows® 2000 / XP boot process. NTBOOTDD.SYS is used to recognise and support SCSI boot devices that have their BIOS disabled. On most systems, it is neither needed nor installed. Its main use in A+ exams is to provide a plausible sounding wrong answer (what CompTIA call 'a distracter') to questions on the boot process.

Registry data files

As noted earlier in the chapter, the Microsoft Windows® registry is a database of configuration settings for the system. The information is kept in 'hives' and most of these hives are stored in disk files. Table 8.2 lists the hives / files mapping.

Table 8.2 Microsoft Windows® 2000 / XP Registry hives and files.

Hive Registry Path	Hive File Path
HKEY_LOCAL_MACHINE\SYSTEM	\winnt\system32\config\system
HKEY_LOCAL_MACHINE\SAM	\winnt\system32\config\sam
HKEY_LOCAL_MACHINE\SECURITY	\winnt\system32\config\security
HKEY_LOCAL_MACHINE\SOFTWARE	\winnt\system32\config\software
HKEY_LOCAL_MACHINE\HARDWARE	Volatile hive
HKEY_LOCAL_MACHINE\SYSTEM\Clone	Volatile hive
HKEY_USERS\UserProfile	Profile; usually under \winnt\profiles\users
HKEY_USERS\.DEFAULT	\winnt\system32\config\default

The 'volatile hives' contain registry information that is NOT held in a disk file. Some information – such as the current hardware configuration – is built at boot time and held in memory. This information is deleted when the system is powered down, and recreated at the next boot time.

Identify concepts and procedures for creating, viewing, managing disks, directories and files

Disks

Although you can obtain basic information about attached disk drives through the My Computer interface, much more detail is available if you use the Microsoft Windows® Management tools. Navigate to: **Control Panel | Administrative Tools | Computer Management | Disk Management** in either Microsoft Windows® 2000 or XP and you will see something like Figure 8.11.

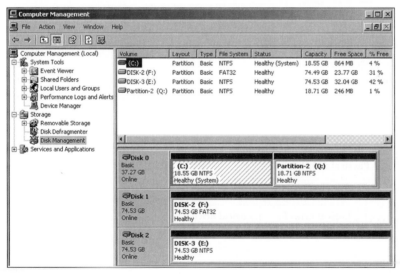

Figure 8.11

Figure 8.11 shows the disks attached to a Microsoft Windows XP® machine. Note that the numbering system starts with 0 for the first disk. The first disk on the system – Disk 0 – has, in this instance, been divided into two partitions. The first of these is C: – the boot volume – and the second has been allocated a Q: drive letter. Each partition on the disk has its own drive letter and appears to the user as a disk drive when viewed through the Explorer or My Computer interface. Figure 8.12 shows this.

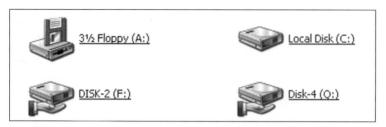

Figure 8.12

Disk 2 is a physical disk and Disk 4 is a partition on a physical disk (in this case the physical disk that also holds C:) but they are indistinguishable when viewed through the My
Computer interface.

Partitions

Hard disk drives may be divided into partitions. Where this is done, the information is
kept in the *partition table* in a reserved area of the disk. There is room in the partition
table to record the locations of four partitions and on modern systems any of these may
be a *primary* partition. Early Microsoft Windows® versions required the boot volume to
be the only primary partition on the system, but this does not apply to Microsoft
Windows® 2000 or XP systems.

The four-partition limitation can be overcome by using an *extended* partition to hold a
number of logical drives. There is only one extended partition and it does *not* have its
own drive letter.

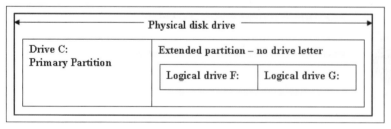

Figure 8.13

Figure 8.13 is a diagrammatic representation of a physical disk drive that has been partitioned with one primary partition, an extended partition and two logical drives within
the extended partition.

Active partition

Where there is more than one partition on a system, one has to be marked as 'Active' so
that the bootstrap loader knows where to look for the operating system. The file
BOOT.INI on a Microsoft Windows® 2000 or XP system points to the active partition.
On a multi-boot system, the user is given a choice of which operation system to start and
this is achieved by setting the 'Active Flag' on the required partition – thus marking it as
'Active' and pointing the bootstrap loader at it.

File systems

We have already looked at file systems earlier in the chapter (see page 119), so all that is needed here is to note that each partition – primary or logical, but NOT extended – may be formatted with a file system. Indeed, one of the reasons for using multiple partitions on a single disk is to accommodate different file systems, which may be the basis of dual or multi-boot machines.

Directory structures

As noted earlier, each drive on a Microsoft Windows® system has a drive letter (terminated with a colon, e.g. C:) and files are arranged in a tree structure beginning with the 'root' of the file system, indicated by a single backslash character. When viewed in Microsoft Windows®, a directory is known as a folder and appears in the display using

the familiar folder icon and its location appears in the Explorer address bar with its contents listed below.

Figure 8.14 shows the folder on the C: drive called 'Example' with a subfolder called 'subfolder'. To create a new subfolder at the present location, right-click and choose **New**, then **Folder**, from the context menu. After the new folder has been created,

Figure 8.14

it can be renamed. To navigate to a folder, simply click on it. To remove a folder, highlight it and choose **Delete** from the context menu, or press the delete key.

The equivalent at a system prompt is to use the CD (or CHDIR) command to navigate between folders, use MD (or MKDIR) to create a new folder or RD (or RMDIR) to remove an empty folder.

To create the directory structure shown in Figure 8.14 from a prompt you could use these commands:

Table 8.3 Commands for creating the directory structure.

Command	Meaning
CD \	Change directory to the root
MD Example	Make a directory called 'Example'
CD Example	Change directory to 'Example'
MD subfolder	Make a new directory called 'subfolder'

Working with files

File creation

Most files are created by the operating system for its own use, or by applications under user control. When you open a new word-processor document, for example, the word-processing software creates a new file. When you save this file to disk, it is written to a physical disk location and the Master File Table is updated accordingly.

In the early days of the PC, the MS-DOS operating system imposed a file-name length limit of eight characters with a three-character file extension – the 8.3 convention. There are some limits on the use of non-alphanumeric characters, and the file name and extension must be unique within its containing directory. Later Microsoft Windows® versions introduced *long file names* and both Microsoft Windows® 2000 and XP allow file names of up to 215 characters and allow embedded spaces. To maintain backward compatibility, all of the later Microsoft Windows® versions generate DOS-style 8.3 aliases for long file names. These consist of the first five or six characters of the long file name followed by a tilde and a system-generated number. So, for example, MyVeryLongFilename.doc may be truncated to MYVERY~1.DOC.

File extensions

Most applications use a particular file extension to indicate the file type. For example, the .DOC extension usually indicates a Microsoft Word® file, the .XLS extension indicates a Microsoft Excel® spreadsheet file. These file associations are recorded in the system registry and can be changed. Thus if you are using, for example, the (free) Open Office suite, you may associate the .DOC and .XLS extensions with that program. In this case, when you click on, say, a .DOC file, it will be opened with Open Office Writer rather than MS Word®.

File attributes

Every file has a set of attributes associated with it. These can be viewed or changed from the command prompt using the ATTRIB command or through the Graphical User Interface (GUI). Every file has the attributes:

- Read Only
- Hidden
- System
- Archive

Each of these attributes can be 'set' or 'clear'. When an attribute is set, it applies to the file in question. Thus, if MYFILE.EXT has the read-only attribute set, then it can be read but not edited.

Hidden files do not show up on a DIR directory listing and system files are protected operating system files such as C:\BOOT.INI on a Microsoft Windows® XP system. These files frequently have the hidden attribute set as well.

The Archive bit indicates a file's back-up status. When a new file is created, the archive bit is set to indicate that it has not yet been backed up. When the file has been backed up – with a back-up program or XCOPY – the archive bit is cleared (unless you deliberately program this not to happen) so that the file will not be backed up again until it has been modified and the changes written to disk. Control of the archive bit is the basis for *full*, *differential* and *incremental* back-up types.

File permissions

Part of the additional security provided in Microsoft Windows® 2000 / XP when installed on the preferred NTFS 5 File System is secure user accounts for each person using the machine, even as a stand-alone system. Each user 'owns' the files and folders that they create and they can set or change various file permissions for themselves and other users or user groups. In order to see or modify the permissions for a file or folder, right-click on the file name, select *Properties*, then the **Security** tab. You will see something like this:

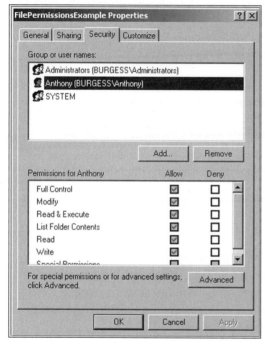

Figure 8.15

Figure 8.15 shows the file permissions for the user Anthony who is the owner of the file. Additional permissions can be added by checking the relevant boxes, or denied by checking the boxes in the **Deny** column. Both users and user groups can be added to the list and each of the permissions can be set for each user or group.

If you are unable to see the **Security** tab in Microsoft Windows® XP, it may be that you have **Simple File Sharing** enabled. To change this, and enable this level of security, navigate to **Folder Options | Tools** and uncheck the box next to the Simple **File Sharing** option. This option is not available in Microsoft Windows® 2000, where full security is implemented by default.

SUMMARY

In this chapter we have looked briefly at some non-Microsoft Windows® operating systems – MAC OS® and Linux. Apart from being able to distinguish them from Microsoft Windows®, you need no detailed knowledge of them. For those who are interested, the Linux operating system has its own CompTIA exam called Linux+.

We have considered the main operating system interfaces – both graphical and command line – and noted some common features and differences.

The key files listed in the exam specification are the same for both Microsoft Windows® 2000 and XP as are the means of working with disks, partitions, file systems, and so on.

For the most part, Microsoft Windows® XP has a more developed set of features than 2000 simply because it is a later release. The best way to approach these operating systems is to use them. No list of features or differences can be an effective substitute for hands-on work.

QUESTIONS

1   You have been asked to fit a second hard drive in a Microsoft Windows® 2000 PC using a disk that has been recovered from an old Microsoft Windows® Millennium machine. The file system on the recovered disk is intact and it is FAT 32. What access will the Microsoft Windows® 2000 host machine have to the new disk?

  a) None

  b) Read only

  c) Depends on file permissions

  d) Full read / write access to all files and folders

2   You have been asked to change the default boot options on a dual boot PC that has the two Windows versions on separate partitions. Which of these files do you need to edit?

  a) NTLDR

  b) BOOT.INI

  c) NTDETECT.COM

  d) All of the above

▶

3   Which of the following Registry keys is NOT held in a disk file?

  a) HKEY_LOCAL_MACHINE\SYSTEM

  b) HKEY_LOCAL_MACHINE\SECURITY

  c) HKEY_LOCAL_MACHINE\SOFTWARE

  d) HKEY_LOCAL_MACHINE\HARDWARE

4   Which of these files are necessary to boot a Microsoft Windows® 2000 system?

  a) NTLDR

  b) BOOT.INI

  c) NTDETECT.COM

  d) NTBOOTDD.SYS

5   Which of these file attributes can be viewed / changed from a command prompt?

  a) Read Only

  b) Hidden

  c) System

  d) Archive

ANSWERS / EXPLANATIONS

1   You have been asked to fit a second hard drive in a Microsoft Windows® 2000 PC using a disk that has been recovered from an old Microsoft Windows® Millennium machine. The file system on the recovered disk is intact and it is FAT 32. What access will the Microsoft Windows® 2000 host machine have to the new disk.

  d) Full read / write access to all files and folders.

2   You have been asked to change the default boot options on a dual boot PC that has the two Microsoft Windows® versions on separate partitions. Which of these files do you need to edit?

  b) BOOT.INI

3   Which of the following registry keys is NOT held in a disk file?

  d) HKEY_LOCAL_MACHINE\HARDWARE

▶

4 Which of these files are necessary to boot a Microsoft Windows® 2000 system?

a) NTLDR

b) BOOT.INI

c) NTDETECT.COM

Note: This applies to Microsoft Windows®XP systems as well. Look out for questions that invite you to see differences between 2000 and XP that are not actually there!

5 Which of these file attributes can be viewed / changed from a command prompt?

a) Read Only

b) Hidden

c) System

d) Archive

All of them can be viewed / changed from both command line and GUI.

CHAPTER 9
Install, configure, optimise and upgrade operating systems

For exam purposes and in order to do the job in the field you need to have a good knowledge of how to install, configure and optimise both Microsoft Windows® 2000 and XP systems. Earlier versions, such as 9.x and NT 4 are relevant only in terms of upgrade paths to the modern Microsoft Windows® releases.

Exam objective 3.2
3.2 Install, configure, optimise and upgrade operating systems

Identify procedures for installing operating systems, including:

> Verification of hardware compatibility and minimum requirements
> Installation methods (e.g. boot media such as CD, floppy or USB, network installation, drive imaging)
> Operating system installation options (e.g. attended / unattended, file system type, network configuration)
> Disk preparation order (e.g. start installation, partition and format drive)
> Device driver configuration (e.g. install and upload device drivers)
> Verification of installation

Identify procedures for upgrading operating systems, including:

> Upgrade considerations (e.g. hardware, application and / or network compatibility)
> Implementation (e.g. back up data, install additional Microsoft Windows® components)

Install / add a device including loading, adding device drivers and required software, including:

> Determine whether permissions are adequate for performing the task
> Device driver installation (e.g. automated and / or manual search and installation of device drivers)
> Using unsigned drivers (e.g. driver signing)
> Verify installation of the driver (e.g. device manager and functionality)

Identify procedures and utilities used to optimise operating systems, for example: virtual memory, hard drives, temporary files, service, start up and applications.

Installing operating systems

The procedures for installing Microsoft Windows® 2000 and XP are all but identical. In this chapter we will use examples from XP Professional with notes on 2000 where necessary.

Hardware compatibility and minimum requirements

Before starting to install an operating system, you need to be sure that it will run on the target hardware. This requires an assessment of both the capacity of the hardware – disk space, installed RAM, etc. – and whether or not a particular hardware device is supported by the operating system. The primary source of information is, of course, Microsoft.

Minimum requirements

Microsoft Windows® 2000 Professional

This version requires the following:

- Processor – 133 MHz or higher Pentium-compatible CPU

- Memory –At least 32 megabytes (MB) of RAM; more memory generally improves responsiveness. (Note: all 2000 systems require a minimum of 64 MB of RAM except 2000 Professional which will, in fact, install on a system with 32 MB, though Microsoft's own documentation is inconsistent on this point.)

- Hard disk – 2 GB with 650 MB free space

- CPU support – supports single and dual CPU systems

- Drive – CD-ROM or DVD drive

- Display – VGA or higher-resolution monitor

- Keyboard.

Microsoft Windows® XP Professional

This version requires the following:

- Processor – PC with 300 MHz or higher processor clock speed recommended; 233 MHz minimum required (single or dual processor system *); Intel Pentium®/Celeron® family, or AMD K6/Athlon™/Duron™ family, or compatible processor recommended

- Memory –128 MB of RAM or higher recommended (64 MB minimum supported; may limit performance and some features)

- Hard disk –1.5 GB of available hard disk space*

- Display – Super VGA (800 × 600) or higher-resolution video adapter and monitor

- Drive – CD-ROM or DVD drive

- Keyboard and mouse or compatible pointing device.

* In terms of basic hardware requirements, Microsoft Windows® XP Professional and Home editions vary only in the number of processors supported: Professional supports dual processors; Home does not.

These minimum requirements are published by Microsoft and it would clearly not be in their interests to overstate the minimum requirements. For any operating system, more is generally better and XP, in particular, benefits greatly from having plenty of RAM.

Hardware compatibility

Microsoft Windows® 2000 and XP both have a SUPPORT folder on the installation CD and this contains a Hardware Compatibility List (HCL) current at the time of the software release. A more up-to-date version can be found on the Microsoft Windows website.

   Microsoft Windows® 2000 and XP also have an option in the installer program – WINNT.EXE – which will check the hardware configuration for possible problems. The installer is on the CD in the \i386\winnt32 folder. Running this with the /CHECKUP-GRADEONLY switch will produce a report in a text file called upgrade.txt. If this report indicates possible problems, you can visit relevant manufacturers' websites for details of new or upgraded drivers. Given the size of the market for Microsoft Windows® XP-compatible products, manufacturers are not generally slow to make drivers available.

Installation methods

In order to install Microsoft Windows® on to a PC, it is necessary to boot the machine and then to run the installer from the installation CD. This may be done by:

- Booting to an installed operating system
- Booting to the Windows installation CD
- Booting to removable media – floppy / external drive /USB / proprietary software on CD.

With the target PC up and running, the installation can be from a local disk (typically the installation CD), installation from a network share or installation from a prepared image of the system using proprietary imaging tools such as Norton Ghost® or Acronis True Image® which are usually on their own bootable CD.

Booting to an installed operating system

This is as simple as putting an installation CD in a drive and selecting from the options displayed when it runs, either automatically or by you clicking on the CD-ROM drive icon in Microsoft Windows®. You will then be presented with various options. This method of installation is discussed further in the Upgrade considerations section later in this chapter (see page 144).

Booting to the installation CD

This is the most straightforward method of installation. Put the installation CD in the drive and boot the PC. Provided the BIOS / CMOS settings are set to boot to CD first, you will be presented with the standard operating system installer menu. From here, make your choices and proceed with the installation. Details of the installation process are described in the Attended Installations section (see page 137)

Booting to removable media

Where there is no CD drive or boot to CD is not supported, you may have to stop and make a set of boot disks. This requires that you have access to a PC with a working floppy drive. You will also need Internet access, though not necessarily from the target machine.

Any Microsoft Windows® version on the host machine will do, we merely need to run a floppy creation program. The method described here is for Microsoft Windows® XP and produces a set of six start-up disks. The procedure in Microsoft Windows® 2000 is similar but produces a set of four start-up disks.

Making a set of start-up disks

1 Make sure that you have six blank floppy disks available.

2 Go to the Microsoft website and download the correct file for your operating system version. There are separate versions for Microsoft Windows® 2000 and for Home and Professional versions of XP. There are even separate versions for each service pack level of XP, so it's important to make sure that you are downloading the right file. This is a self-extracting CAB file.

3 Run as the Administrator. Accept the Supplemental Licence Agreement. Follow the on-screen instructions.

You will end up with a set of six disks (XP) or four disks (2000).
    Note: there is also a BOOTDISK folder on the 2000 Installation CD that contains the files necessary to make a set of Microsoft Windows® 2000 boot disks without a download.

Installing from a Microsoft Windows® 9.x start-up disk

Where it is not possible to make a set of boot disks, it is still possible to install Microsoft Windows® XP by using a Microsoft Windows® 98 start-up disk. You will also need a copy of SMARTDRV.EXE, which you can copy to your start-up floppy from any Microsoft Windows® 9.x installation CD or installed version. With these tools in place, proceed as follows:

Install from a 98 floppy

1 Make sure that you have a formatted FAT 32 partition on the C: drive.

2 Boot to the start-up floppy with CD-ROM support.

3 Run the SMARTDRV.EXE disk cache program.

4 Navigate to the i386 folder on the CD-ROM.

5 Run the WINNT.EXE installer from the command prompt.

Attended installations

Regardless of how you boot the target machine – directly to CD or from other media – the actual installation consists of running the NT installer program WINNT.EXE (the command line version) or WINNT32.EXE – the version that runs in the Microsoft Windows® GUI. Once the installer is running, the process is the same regardless of how it was started. Your main task is to provide information – settings, product key, etc. – when prompted by the installer. Later in the chapter we will look at unattended installation methods, but before that we need to step through the standard attended installation process.

Practical – standard Microsoft Windows® XP installation from bootable CD

1 Boot to the CD-ROM – the installer will load several files and will take a few minutes (or more) depending on the speed of the target machine.

2 At the welcome screen, press **Enter** – ignore the other options for now.

3 Press **F8** to accept the licence terms.

4 Press **Enter** to install to unpartitioned space.

5 If you are confident that the target disk is okay, choose a quick format, otherwise format the target partition with (the default) NTFS. At this stage, there are other options for adjusting partition sizes, etc. Explore these if you wish but return to the default, which is to use the whole of drive C.

6 The installer will now copy a lot of files from the CD to the target machine.

7 When this process is complete, the machine will reboot and the installer will change to graphics mode. The installer will run for a while – several minutes at least.

8 You will be presented with a **Regional and Language Options** screen. Click the **Customise** button and change both language and location from the default US to your region, then click on **Apply**. Click on the **Details** button and add the keyboard for your region. Select the US keyboard for removal – you will see a warning message, which you can ignore. Click on **OK**, and then **Next**.

9 The next dialogue prompts you for a name and organisation. These can be entered as 'USER' and 'COLLEGE' respectively. Click on **Next**.

10 Enter the Product Key. This is a 25-digit code in the form

XXXXX-XXXXX-XXXXX-XXXX-XXXXX

This should be on the packaging of the Installation CD.

11 On acceptance of a valid Product Key, you will be prompted for the computer name. This can be anything you choose, but if you are connecting to a network be sure that it is unique within your LAN. Set the administrator password to, for example, 'Fr1day' – Note that this password conforms to fairly common 'complexity' requirements by containing a mixture of upper-case and lower-case letters and a numeric digit. Some systems may require it to be longer – say eight or ten characters.

12 Set the time zone to your time zone – such as GMT – and select **Next**.

13 The installer will now set up the network components – accept the default **Typical Settings** and select **Next**.

14 Either accept the default workgroup name – WORKGROUP – or change it to something else. Select **Next** – the installer will run for a few minutes copying more files. This is the final stage of the installation and at the end of it the machine will reboot into the newly installed XP.

15 Change the screen resolution if prompted to do so.

16 Select **Next** on the welcome screen. Select **Skip** on the next screen.

17 Select **Not at this time** and **Next** on the registration screen.

18 Enter the user name 'USER' in the top box and select **Next**.

19 Select **Finish**.

The practical exercise in installing Microsoft Windows® XP outlined above is similar in all but a few details to installing Microsoft Windows® 2000. With either operating system you would, in practice, probably need to customise the installation to meet the needs of the end user.

Network installation

This is essentially similar to a local installation from CD. Put the installation CD in a shared drive or copy its contents to a shared network folder, then boot the target PC with network support and run the installer over the network. On large networks based on 2000 server (or later), it is possible to use Microsoft's Remote Installation Service (RIS) or Systems Management Server (SMS). Details of these services can be found on the Microsoft website, but are not required knowledge for A+ Essentials.

Drive imaging

With earlier versions of Microsoft Windows® it was possible to 'clone' a drive – that is, to make an image of a Microsoft Windows® installation – and to 'restore' it on to a differ- ent PC with a similar hardware configuration. This rapidly became a means of stealing copies of Microsoft Windows®; all you needed to do was to buy a single licensed copy, make a disk image and clone it across as many compatible systems as you wanted. There were, of course, legitimate uses for cloning, and it is still used by the volume system builders and by corporations rolling out large fleets of identical, or near identical, PCs. However, in order to make theft by copying more difficult, Microsoft added some extra security features to the modern editions of Microsoft Windows®. They also provided some tools to make legitimate disk imaging possible.

Creating an image of a Microsoft Windows® installation

In order to do this you will need:

▨ Compatible – preferably identical – hardware

▨ Third-party imaging software such as Norton Ghost® or Acronis True Image®

▨ The Microsoft Windows® deployment tools.

Microsoft Windows security identifiers

When you install Microsoft Windows® on a PC, it creates a Security Identifier (SID) and this uniquely identifies that installation on that machine. This is an entirely behind-the- scenes operation that you might never notice until you tried to image a drive without taking it into account. If, however, you were to make an image of a Microsoft Windows® installation on one machine and restore it on another, you would encounter problems when you attempted to network them because you would have two machines with the same SID. The Deployment Tools – specifically SYSPREP.EXE – offer a solution to this. In outline, the cloning process works like this:

- Create a master copy of the installation on the source PC by installing and configuring Micrsoft Windows® and the applications – office suite, browser, etc. – that you want to include in your standard build image.

- Use SYSPREP.EXE to remove SIDs on the source machine.

- Create as many images as you need of the stripped-down installation.

- Restore the cloned image to another (hardware-compatible) PC and allow Microsoft Windows® to create a new SID, unique to that installation, when it first starts up.

Creating the master copy

1   Start with a clean install of Microsoft Windows® – 2000 or XP. DO NOT join a domain during this initial installation even if you intend to join one later.

2   Log on using the ADMINISTRATOR account and install and configure any applications that you want to be part of your software build.

Installing the deployment tools

1   Create a folder on the system partition of the source PC and give it the name \Sysprep. Usually, the system partition will be the C: drive so the location of the folder will be C:\Sysprep. (Note: capitalisation of the name is not important, but its name and location are. When a Sysprepped Microsoft Windows® installation boots for the first time, it automatically removes the \Sysprep folder and its contents to prevent accidental damage by a user idly, or accidentally, clicking on it.)

2   Put the Microsoft Windows® installation CD in the drive and navigate to SUPPORT\TOOLS.

3   Click on the DEPLOY.CAB file to show its contents.

4   Highlight the files SYSPREP.EXE and SETUPCL.EXE and copy them to the \Sysprep folder that you created on the PC's hard disk.

5   Navigate to your \Sysprep folder (if you are not already there) and click on the SYSPREP.EXE icon to run the program. You will be presented with a summary of what the Sysprep tool does.

6   Read the text and, if the licence terms apply to you, click on the **OK** button to continue. You will now be presented with some choices about how to run Sysprep.

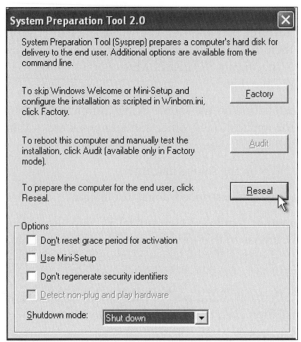

Figure 9.1

7 Choose the options to **Shut down and Reseal** as indicated in the figure.

8 After clicking on the **Reseal** button, you will see a notice which summarises your choices.

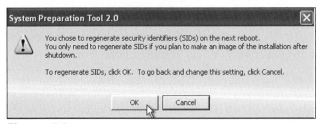

Figure 9.2

9 Removing Security Identifiers (SIDs) to be regenerated on the next boot is exactly what you want to do.

Click on the **OK** button. Sysprep will work in the background for half a minute or so, and then the system will shut down. DO NOT restart the master system until you have made your drive image.

Creating the disk image

The details of how you create the disk image will depend on what disk cloning software you use for the job. In outline, the process is:

1   Run the system preparation utility to remove SIDs on the 'Master' or source PC.

2   Close down the system.

3   Save the contents of the prepared drive to a single file on a separate drive.

Deploying the disk image

Having saved an image file to a disk, you can now copy it as many times as you like, or simply use it as a master copy from which you can 'restore' any number of times. Because you used the Sysprep utility to prepare your disk before imaging, every time it is restored, Microsoft Windows® will run its mini set-up routine on first boot and create new (and unique) security identifiers for the newly installed system.

Operating system installation options

As noted earlier in the chapter, a standard installation of Microsoft Windows® and its variants, such as creating a set of boot disks or using removable media, require you to enter information – Product Keys, time zone data, etc. – in the course of the installation process. Because you are required to be present for most of the process in order to enter the required information, the generic term for these methods is *attended installation*. Obviously, where you have multiple PCs to deal with, typing in the same information each time is tedious and time wasting. The alternative to this is an unattended install.

Unattended installation

In order to save the time involved in an attended installation, it is possible to put all the information – Product Keys, time zone, etc. – in an answer file that the Microsoft Windows® installer will use without user intervention. *Unattended installation* is a feature of Microsoft Windows® 2000 and XP and is not found in earlier releases.

Creating an answer file

To create an answer file:

1   Put the Microsoft Windows® installation CD into the CD drive and navigate to \SUPPORT\TOOLS\DEPLOY.CAB.

2   Click on DEPLOY.CAB and run the file SETUPMGR.EXE.

3   Follow the on-screen prompts and supply the required information just as you would in a standard attended installation. If you are going to install from a network share, you can specify a distribution folder where the Microsoft Windows® installer files can be found. You can also place other files, for example drivers that are not supplied with the Microsoft Windows® disk, in the distribution folder. If you are going to do an unattended install from a local CD-ROM drive, leave this field empty.

4   When you have finished entering all the information, save the resulting text file under the default name of unattend.txt on removable storage such as a floppy disk.

5   Note: you will be given the opportunity to specify network components in the course of creating your answer file. You should accept default values – **Client for Microsoft Networks / File and Print Sharing enabled** and **TCP / IP** – unless told otherwise by your network administrator. Choice of file system type FAT or NTFS cannot be selected as part of the answer file and must be specified as part of the disk preparation – see disk preparation later in this chapter.

Using the answer file

In order to use the answer file that you have created, run the Microsoft Windows® installer from a command line and point it at the unattend.txt file that you created. Depending on the hardware configuration of your system, you will enter a command line that looks something like:

D:\i386\WINNT32 /UNATTEND: A:\UNATTEND.TXT

As the installer runs, it will take its information from the text file without further user intervention. If you need to change the contents of the unattend file, you can use the SETUPMGR.EXE with the **Modify** option. Alternatively, you can use a standard text editor such as NOTEPAD.EXE.

Practical – unattended installation from a local CD

This is a variant on an unattended installation that uses a local CD and a floppy. It can be a useful way of exploring the unattended installation method on a single PC.

1 Create an answer file as in a standard unattended installation.
2 Save it to a floppy, then change the name to WINNT.SIF. Note the floppy that you use for this must NOT be a bootable or start-up disk.
3 With the floppy in the drive, boot to the installation CD.
4 Follow onscreen instructions and select your partitioning and file system preferences.
5 Allow the unattended installer to run to completion.
6 Remove all installation media, reboot and step through the mini set-up program to configure the new installation.

Disk preparation

Earlier versions of Microsoft Windows® required you to create and format a partition before starting the installation. However, Microsoft Windows® 2000 and XP installers all have this capacity built in to the installer program. You can still partition and format manually if you wish, but for the most part it is easier to create a partition as part of the installation process, install Microsoft Windows®, then use the management tools to make any required changes after the initial installation has been completed. To prepare a disk:

1   Boot to an installation CD.

2   Wait while setup copies files – device drivers etc. – to the target machine.

3   Accept the End User Licence Agreement (EULA) by pressing **F8** when prompted. You will then be shown a map of the existing disk space. In this instance, it is a new unpartitioned and unformatted space. If you wish, you can accept the default, which is to use the whole of the space for your installation by pressing **Enter**.

4

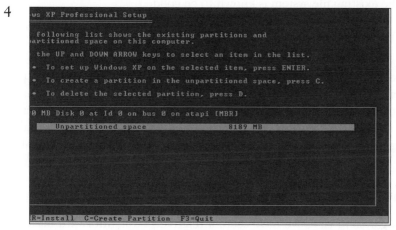

Figure 9.3

5   Alternatively, you can choose C to create a new partition. If, as in this example, you do this, you will be given the option to specify the size of the new partition.

6   Choose your partition size and press **Enter** to continue. You will then be shown the size of the new partition that you have created and the remaining unallocated space.

7

```
8190 MB Disk 0 at Id 0 on bus 0 on atapi [MBR]
     C:   Partition1 [New (Raw)]             4997 MB (   4996 MB free)
          Unpartitioned space                3193 MB
```

Figure 9.4

8   Press **Enter** to install to your new partition.

9   You will now be presented with the choice of file system and the type of format.

```
If you want to select a different partition for Windows XP,
press ESC.

   Format the partition using the NTFS file system (Quick)
   Format the partition using the FAT file system (Quick)
   Format the partition using the NTFS file system
   Format the partition using the FAT file system
```

Figure 9.5

The figure shows the default value which is a full format with the NTFS file system. Unless there are compelling reasons otherwise, accept this by pressing **Enter.** The installer will now format the partition, and then proceed as a standard installation.

The quick format options are only available if the partition has been previously formatted with a file system that you want to use. If you choose a quick format, the installer will blank the File Allocation Table / Master File Table so that the contents of the disk may be overwritten, but will not carry out a full format. This can save time, but should only be used where the existing file system is known to be good.

Post-installation tasks

Once the operating system has been installed, the installation media stored and the PC rebooted, you will need to install device drivers for anything that did not plug and play during the installation. You will also need to test run the installation to make sure that it works as required. As a minimum, you should check for any problems that may be reported in Device Manager and System Information. Even where device drivers are reported as present and working, it may be useful to check whether newer versions are available. There is more on device drivers later in the chapter.

Upgrading operating systems

Installing an operating system is, as we have seen, a relatively straightforward business. Provided the hardware meets the minimum specification and there are no compatibility problems, all you need to do is carry out the installation procedures and post-installation tasks. You then need to reinstall applications and possibly reinstate data. Upgrading an operating system – replacing one operating system with another while attempting to keep the same applications and data – has the same requirements as a clean install in terms so hardware specification and compatibility, as well as presenting some problems of its own. Before starting, you need to consider the hardware specification, whether applications will run under the new system and the availability of device drivers. You also need to consider network compatibility – some of the earlier operating systems used older network protocols such as NetBEUI which may be problematic with newer systems such as Microsoft Windows® XP. There are also connectivity problems between XP and the older MAC OS networking protocol Apple Talk.

Another major consideration – and a favourite for exam questions – is the upgrade path from one Microsoft Windows® version to another.

Microsoft Windows® 2000 can be upgraded from:

- Microsoft Windows® 95

- Microsoft Windows® 98 and 98 (SE)

- NT Workstation 3.51

- NT Workstation 4.0

There is no upgrade path from Microsoft Windows® Millennium to Microsoft Windows® 2000.

Microsoft Windows® XP can be upgraded from:

- Microsoft Windows® 98 and 98 (SE)
- Microsoft Windows® Millennium
- NT Workstation 3.51
- NT Workstation 4.0
- Microsoft Windows® 2000 Professional

It is also possible to upgrade from Microsoft Windows® XP Home to XP Professional or Media Center Edition.

In addition to the full versions of Microsoft Windows® intended for a clean install, there are also upgrade versions which require that a supported version of Windows is present in order to run the upgrade installer.

Implementation

Once you have established that an upgrade is feasible, it is advisable to take a few common-sense steps before starting work.

- Back up all data – and check that your back-up works by restoring at least a couple of the backed up files.
- Remove any unnecessary or infrequently used applications and / or Microsoft Windows® components through **Control Panel**.
- Clean up any temporary files and empty the **Recycle** bin.
- Defragment the disk.
- Disable antivirus protection.

Installing devices and device drivers

Most devices that you install will plug and play and Microsoft Windows® – particularly XP – is usually very well supplied with device drivers, which it will install automatically. Alternatively, most devices come with drivers for various Microsoft Windows® versions on a CD packaged with the device or which can be downloaded from the manufacturer's website.

Permissions

If you are logged on to the system as Administrator, you will have sufficient permissions to install hardware, applications, drivers, etc. Where permissions are insufficient for any operation, you will receive a warning to this effect.

Although it is good practice to use the Administrator account for all administrative tasks such as installing drivers, both Microsoft Windows® 2000 and XP have a 'Run as' option, which allows you temporary administrative privileges.

Where the 'Run as' option is not offered by default, right-click on the program icon (Microsoft Windows® XP) or hold down the Shift key then right-click on the program

(Microsoft Windows® 2000). This option is available on a default install, but can be removed by an administrator for security purposes.

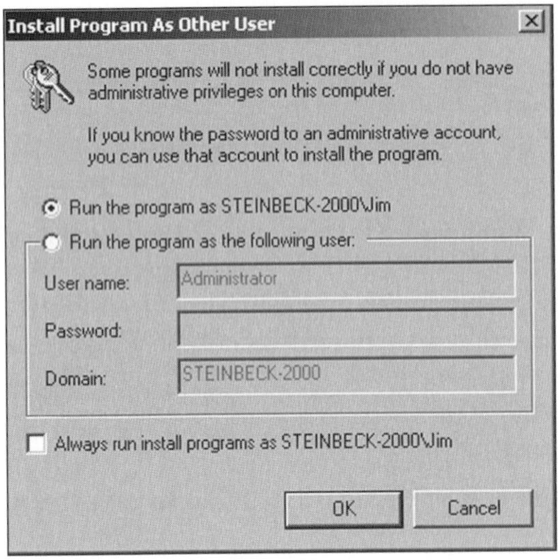

Figure 9.6

Installing drivers

Usually, a new hardware device is attached to the PC and when it is rebooted Microsoft Windows® detects it and looks for drivers. For commonly used devices such as the more popular network cards or printers, Microsoft Windows® XP in particular frequently has suitable drivers bundled with it and will install them by default. Even where this is the case, however, it may be a good idea to find and install the latest drivers from the vendor's website. This can be done by downloading the correct drivers, unzipping them if necessary – then running the executable file that installs them. It may be useful to burn them to disk for future use.

The process of installing a driver is much the same as installing any other piece of software – click on the icon and follow the instructions on the screen. If you do not have the driver, you can search for one by running the Add Hardware wizard in Control Panel.

Driver signing

Driver signing was introduced by Microsoft in the interests of quality control. When a manufacturer releases new drivers for one of their products, they can submit it to Microsoft who test it against their operating systems and, if it meets the necessary criteria, it will be 'signed' as Microsoft approved. However, the signing process has not found favour with many manufacturers so unsigned drivers are commonplace.

The default setting for Microsoft Windows® XP is to issue a warning when you attempt to install unsigned drivers, but this can be changed through the System applet by clicking on the **Hardware** tab, then the **Driver Signing** button.

If you want to check the status of all drivers on the system, then the command SIGVERIF in a Run box or at a prompt will give you a complete list.

Figure 9.7 shows the graphical output of the SIGVERIF command. This information is also written to a text file sigverif.txt.

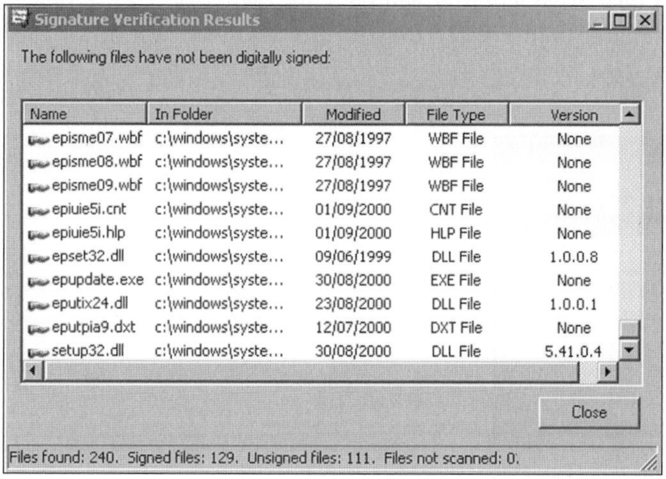

Figure 9.7

Verifying the installed drivers

The obvious first test is that the device is working properly. If, for example, you have installed new graphics drivers, you should be able to change screen resolutions, etc. More formally, you can look at the drivers through Device Manager. Both Microsoft Windows® 2000 and XP give you the means to examine the current drivers for a device, to disable it, uninstall it or to look for an update.

Optimising the operating system

Whether an operating system is newly installed or has been running for some time, it is generally possible to improve performance by changing some of the default settings.

Virtual memory management

(See also Chapter 8, page 117 on this topic.)

All Microsoft Windows® systems use hard disk storage as Virtual Memory. In order to extend the amount of memory that the system 'sees', unused contents of RAM are swapped to and from a disk file. The size and location of this swap file can affect the performance of the system. Generally, the swap file – called PAGEFILE.SYS on both Microsoft Windows® 2000 and XP systems – is set to be 1.5 times the amount of installed physical RAM.

Where there is only one disk drive on a system, the swap file obviously has to be on the same disk as the rest of the operating system, applications, etc. This means that virtual memory is sharing the same read / write heads as the rest of the system. When the read / write heads are busy paging swap information between disk and RAM, they are not available for the rest of the operating system or applications.

Even where there are several disk drives on a system, the swap file is setup on the first drive by default. In Windows® XP, it is usually in the root of C: – C:\PAGEFILE.SYS. You can obtain performance increases by changing the size of the swap file and / or moving it to a different physical disk drive where it will have its 'own' read / write heads. Figure 9.8 shows the default virtual memory settings for an Micrsoft Windows® XP system which has more than one disk drive.

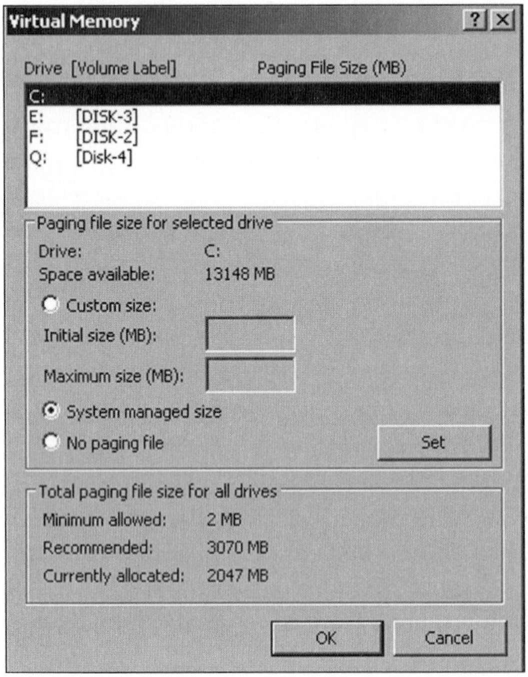

Figure 9.8

Provided you are logged on with Administrator privileges, you can change both the size and location of the swap file. Changing the initial size so that it is the same as the maximum size reduces the management overhead on both the CPU and the disk drive system. Moving the swap file to a faster or underused drive will make better use of resources by giving the swap file its 'own' read / write head. This has to be a separate physical drive of course, as a logical drive or partition shares its read / write heads with other drives or partitions on the disk.

Hard drives

Two factors that cause a hard drive to slow down through time are fragmentation and the accumulation of junk files. Once a disk reaches around two thirds of its capacity, it begins to slow down because it takes longer for the read / write head to find space to write saved information. The cure for this is to remove unneeded files from time to time, either manually or by using the Disk Clean-up Wizard. This can be accessed in either Microsoft Windows® 2000 or XP as one of the System Tools. To see the options available, navigate to **Start | All Programs | Accessories | System Tools** and click on the icon for **Disk Clean-up**.

Defragmentation is best done after junk files have been removed (so that you can consolidate the space you have gained). The defrag utility can be started from the System Tools menu or from the context menu of the drive that you want to Defragment. DEFRAG – along with other disk management tools – is considered further in Chapter 10.

Start-up – services and applications

When a PC boots, it starts various services and applications, which then run in the background. Many, possibly most, of these are useful services, but some are not. For example, you may not want a process running continuously that does nothing more than check for updates of an application, though you would probably want your virus scanner to run as a matter of course. Start-up options can be selected by using the MSCONFIG utility, which is considered in detail in Chapter 10. For the time being, though, note that MSCONFIG is not part of Microsoft Windows® 2000. Many 2000 installations that you work with may well have a copy of MSCONFIG installed as an add-on. If you are working on a system where it is not installed, you can either download a copy from the Internet, or simply copy the file MSCONFIG.EXE from a Microsoft Windows® XP machine. It may be prudent to check the licensing implications before doing this.

SUMMARY

In this chapter, we have considered how to install, configure, upgrade and optimise an operating system. You are strongly advised to try the practical exercises if possible. The fundamental process, as described in the Standard Microsoft Windows® XP installation practical, is core knowledge, so make sure that you are thoroughly familiar with it.

For exam purposes, you should know the variants on the basic install method and memorise the minimum hardware requirements and upgrade paths from earlier Microsoft Windows® versions – these are favourite topics for questions. Knowing the methods used to optimise operating systems – virtual memory management, etc. – is useful in its own right as well as being useful for questions on preventive maintenance topics.

QUESTIONS

1   You have been asked to install Microsoft Windows® XP Professional on a PC. It meets the minimum requirements for hardware specification but you also need to check the compatibility of specific components. Which of the following are valid approaches to this?

    a) Run WINNT.EXE with the /CHECKUPGRADEONLY switch

    b) Visit the Microsoft site

    c) Run WINNT.EXE with the /HARDWARE switch

    d) Run SETUP.EXE with the /CHECKUPGRADEONLY switch

2   You have to install Microsoft Windows® 2000 on a PC that does not support boot to CD. Which of the following are possible approaches?

    a) Download the floppy creation utility from Microsoft and make a set of installation boot floppies

    b) Navigate to the BOOTDISK folder on the installation CD and make a set of floppies from there

    c) Boot to a Microsoft Windows® 98 start-up disk, create a FAT 32 partition on the hard disk and run WINNT from a prompt

    d) Boot to a Microsoft Windows® 98 start-up disk, create a FAT 32 partition on the hard disk and run SETUP.EXE from a prompt

3   You have been asked to prepare an installation for cloning with a third-party utility. You install Microsoft Windows® XP and some applications, then defrag the disk. You create a folder C:\Sysprep on the hard drive. Which two files do you need to copy to that folder?

    a) SYSPREP.EXE

    b) CLONEDRV.EXE

    c) SETUPCL.EXE

    d) DRVPREP.BIN

4   You have been asked to upgrade a PC from Microsoft Windows® Millennium to Microsoft Windows® 2000 Professional. The hardware is known to be compatible with both Windows versions. Do you?

    a) Run the Microsoft Windows® 2000 installer from the installed Millennium version

    b) Boot to the Microsoft Windows® 2000 CD and install from there

    c) Make a set of start-up disks

    d) Tell the customer that it can't be done

▶

5   You install a new network card in a PC. You reboot Microsoft Windows® and the card isn't recognised. You have a CD with drivers from the vendor but when you start to install them you receive a warning about 'unsigned drivers'. Do you?

a)   Go ahead anyway

b)   Use a different network card

c)   Go to the vendor's website for new drivers

d)   Run the Windows update service

ANSWERS / EXPLANATIONS

1   You have been asked to install Microsoft Windows® XP Professional on a PC. It meets the minimum requirements for hardware specification but you also need to check the compatibility of specific components. Which of the following are valid approaches to this?

   a) Run WINNT.EXE with the /CHECKUPGRADEONLY switch

   b) Visit the Microsoft site

2   You have to install Microsoft Windows® 2000 on a PC that does not support boot to CD. Which of the following are possible approaches?

   a) Download the floppy creation utility from Microsoft and make a set of installation boot floppies

   b) Navigate to the BOOTDISK folder on the installation CD and make a set of floppies from there

   Option c would work, but you need to create the partition and format it before running the installer.

3   You have been asked to prepare an installation for cloning with a third-party utility. You install Microsoft Windows® XP and some applications, then defrag the disk. You create a folder C:\Sysprep on the hard drive. Which two files do you need to copy to that folder?

   a) SYSPREP.EXE

   c) SETUPCL.EXE

▶

4   You have been asked to upgrade a PC from Microsoft Windows®
        Millennium to Microsoft Windows® 2000 Professional. The hardware
        is known to be compatible with both Microsoft Windows® versions.
        Do you?

   d) Tell the customer that it can't be done

   Options b and c would be possible for a clean install but there is no
   upgrade path from Microsoft Windows® Millenium to 2000.

5   You install a new network card in a PC. You reboot Windows and the
        card isn't recognised. You have a CD with drivers from the vendor but
        when you start to install them you receive a warning about 'unsigned
        drivers'. Do you?

   a) Go ahead anyway

   Unsigned drivers are not uncommon so a is an acceptable option,
   though it would be prudent to set a Restore Point just in case. Option
   c – obtain new drivers – is good practice, but not relevant in this
   scenario.

CHAPTER 10
Operating systems – tools / diagnostics / preventive maintenance

Modern operating systems provide a range of tools and diagnostics to help the working technician troubleshoot problem systems, and you need to know them for both practical and exam purposes. Additionally, although it is rather unexciting stuff, preventive maintenance is part of the job. It is also a small but important part of the Essentials exam.

Exam objectives 3.3 and 3.4
3.3 Identify tools, diagnostic procedures and troubleshooting techniques for operating systems

Identify basic boot sequences, methods and utilities for recovering operating systems:

> Boot methods (e.g. Safe Mode, Recovery Console, boot to restore point)
> Automated System Recovery (ASR) (e.g. Emergency Repair Disk (ERD))

Identify and apply diagnostic procedures and troubleshooting techniques, for example:

> Identify the problem by questioning the user and identifying user changes to the computer
> Analyse problem including potential causes and initial determination of software and / or hardware problem
> Test related components including connections, hardware / software configurations, Device Manager and consulting vendor documentation
> Evaluate results and take additional steps if needed such as consultation, alternate resources and manuals
> Document activities and outcomes
> Recognise and resolve common operational issues such as 'bluescreen', system lock-up, input / output device, application install, start or load and Microsoft Windows®-specific printing problems (e.g. print spool stalled, incorrect / incompatible driver for print)

▶

Explain common error messages and codes, for example:

Boot (e.g. invalid boot disk, inaccessible boot drive, missing NTLDR)
Startup (e.g. device / service failed to start, device / program in Registry not found)
Event Viewer
Registry
Microsoft Windows® reporting

Identify the names, locations, purposes and characteristics of operating system utilities:

Disk management tools (e.g. DEFRAG, NTBACKUP, CHKDSK, Format)
System management tools (e.g. Device and Task Manager, MSCONFIG.EXE)
File management tools (e.g. Microsoft Windows® Explorer, ATTRIB.EXE)

3.4 Perform preventative maintenance on operating systems

Describe common utilities for performing preventative maintenance on operating systems, for example, software and Microsoft Windows® updates (e.g. service packs), scheduled back-ups / restore, restore points.

Boot sequences

Where a PC is not functioning properly, one of the first things to try is to reboot the machine. This frequently fixes minor problems and is one of the things that you should do early in the diagnostic process. However, rebooting is not just a passive exercise in which you hope that things will put themselves right (though they often do) but a diagnostic procedure in its own right. In order to get the most out of the reboot process, you need to understand the basic boot process, how it works and what the error messages mean. While you are unlikely to be examined on the boot sequence as such, you should be aware of it in outline at least.

Irrespective of the installed operating system, the boot sequence starts with the firmware Power On Self Test (POST), which initialises various devices before loading the operating system itself. When control is passed from the firmware to the operating system, the first file to be processed by Microsoft Windows® 2000 and XP is NTLDR – the bootstrap loader for the operating system. In outline (and skipping a few details) the Microsoft Windows® 2000 / XP boot process follows this sequence:

▓ The Power On Self Test (POST) runs.

▓ Load and process NTLDR (the NT Loader program).

▓ NTLDR reads the BOOT.INI file. Where more than one selection is possible, a menu is displayed. If no selection is made, this times out and loads the default operating system (in this example an NT-based one).

- NTLDR executes a detection file called NTDETECT.COM. This collects information about currently installed hardware, which it passes back to NTLDR for later use.

- NTLDR reads and loads NTOSKRNL.EXE and HAL.DLL (the Hardware Abstraction Layer).

- NTLDR uses the information gathered earlier from NTDETECT.COM to update the registry with details of current hardware. At this point in the process the NT logo and progress bar are displayed while drivers are loaded.

- NTLDR passes control to the NTOSKRNL file to complete the boot process.

- NTOSKRNL initialises the Hardware Abstraction Layer file (HAL.DLL) along with BOOTVID.DLL and the sequence shifts from text mode to graphics mode.

- NTLDR uses the information from NTDETECT to create a temporary volatile registry hive in memory.

- NTOSKRNL runs a session manager file SMSS.EXE for final pre-use functions such as a disk check and setting up virtual memory in the paging file PAGEFILE.SYS.

Boot methods

In addition to the standard turn-it-on-and-watch method of booting, there are some special methods that can be used for diagnostic and repair work. These are:

- Safe Mode

- Recovery console

- Boot to restore point

Safe mode and other advanced options

Safe Mode is one of the *advanced start-up options* in Microsoft Windows® 2000 and XP. To access the advanced options, hold down the F8 key when the system makes the option available. This is fairly early in the boot process – just as NTLDR is processing the BOOT.INI file. The options that you will be offered on a Microsoft Windows® XP system are shown in Figure 10.1. The options in Microsoft Windows® 2000 are roughly similar.

```
Windows Advanced Options Menu
Please select an option:

    Safe Mode
    Safe Mode with Networking
    Safe Mode with Command Prompt

    Enable Boot Logging
    Enable VGA Mode
    Last Known Good Configuration (your most recent settings that worked)
    Directory Services Restore Mode (Windows domain controllers only)
    Debugging Mode
    Disable automatic restart on system failure

    Start Windows Normally
    Reboot
    Return to OS Choices Menu

Use the up and down arrow keys to move the highlight to your choice.
```

Figure 10.1

Safe Mode – this starts Microsoft Windows® 2000 / XP with a minimal set of drivers, basic video and no network connections. XP presents you with a choice to boot to Safe Mode or to roll back the system to a System Restore point of an earlier date.

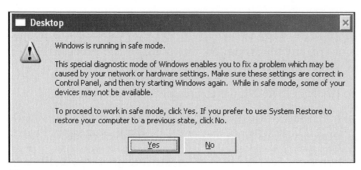

Figure 10.2

This roll-back option is not available in Microsoft Windows® 2000.

Once you are in safe mode – under either operating system – you can restore or edit files or fix a configuration error:

- **Safe Mode with networking**. As the name suggests, this is the standard Safe Mode with networking components in addition to the basic drivers.

- **Safe Mode with command prompt**. This gives you a command prompt instead of the Microsoft Windows® GUI.

- **Enable boot logging**. This boots into the normal Microsoft Windows® GUI and writes a log file to NTBTLOG.TXT to \WINDOWS in Microsoft Windows® XP and to \WINNT in 2000. Information from the log file may be useful in tracking down boot-time errors.

- **Enable VGA mode**. This starts Microsoft Windows® 2000 / XP normally but with only VGA graphics support. Although the display is crude, this is a useful mode for fixing a wrong or corrupted video driver.

- **Last known good configuration**. This is a roll-back feature carried over from early NT systems. It can still be useful if you have Registry problems by rolling back to a previous 'known good' Registry though it cannot do anything about file errors.

- **Directory services restore mode**. This is used exclusively on domain controllers and is beyond the terms of reference for an A+ technician.

- **Debugging mode**. This is an advanced boot-logging option and requires the PC to be connected to another machine over a serial cable. The boot log is then written to the other machine. This is not an option which is frequently used in practice.

- **Disable automatic restart on system failure**. This is a Microsoft Windows® XP-only feature. XP is set up to reboot when it encounters a fatal error. This can be a nuisance and the setting can be changed by editing a registry key. Choosing this option changes they key to prevent repeated reboots. This is a complex undertaking and detailed information can be found on the Microsoft support site – you certainly do not need to know this in detail for the exams.

- **Boot normally**. This is self explanatory.
- **Reboot**. This is an Microsoft Windows® XP-only function.
- **Return to OS choices menu**. This is another Microsoft Windows® XP-only function. Where a machine is set up to give a choice of operating systems, these are displayed by BOOT.INI and this function takes you back to that screen.

Boot to restore point

As we have seen above, the ability to boot to a System Restore Point is an option when booting to Safe Mode in Microsoft Windows® XP. However, if you have a working GUI, you can boot normally and access the Restore points through the **System Restore** option in the **System Tools** menu. Restore points are considered again in the preventive maintenance section later in the chapter (see page 176).

The recovery console

The recovery console is a feature of both Microsoft Windows® 2000 and XP. It is a command line utility that allows you to create and remove partitions, format drives, read and write data, stop and start services, and so on. You can run the recovery console by booting to an installation CD, or you can install it on a working system so that it becomes available as a boot-time option. The following practical was done in Microsoft Windows® XP, but can also be done in Microsoft Windows® 2000.

Installing a recovery console

1 Put the Installation CD into the drive and boot to it.
2 Run the WINNT32 command with the CMDCONS switch, that is,

   D:\i386\WINNT32 /CMDCONS (where D: is the drive letter for your CD drive).

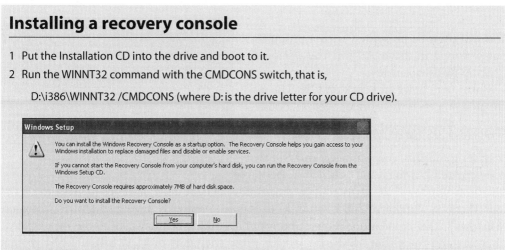

3 Click on **Yes**.

Note: you will need the same service pack level as the installed system. If, for example, you have a system that was installed with Service Pack 1 and then had Service Pack 2 applied, you will need an installation disk that has Service Pack 2 integrated into it.

Figure 10.3

Whether it has been installed or you are working from a bootable CD, you will need the Administrator password for the target system in order to use the Recovery Console on it.

Note: Although the command line interface is similar to the standard system prompt, the command set is different and the facilities offered are more limited. For example, while files can be copied to the system partition on the hard disk, you cannot use a Recovery Console to back up files from the hard disk.

HELP at a prompt will list all documented commands with a one-line entry for each. For detailed help on a *particular* command – usage, options, switches – use HELP <COMMAND NAME> at a prompt.

Boot disks and emergency repair disks – Microsoft Windows® 2000

This is an emergency recovery technique. Like many recovery and repair techniques, it requires some forward planning. In this instance, you need an Emergency Repair Disk (ERD), which is a back-up of key settings so that you can repair the start-up environment, verify and replace system files and repair the boot sector. Obviously, the ERD has to be made prior to any problems arising and should be updated from time to time, especially when there have been significant changes to the system. To make a Microsoft Windows® 2000 ERD, navigate to the **Backup** option in **System Tools** and select the **Welcome** tab. Click on the button to create an ERD.

Emergency Repair Disk
This option helps you create an Emergency Repair Disk that you can use to repair and restart Windows if it is damaged. This option does not back up your files or programs, and it is not a replacement for regularly backing up your system.

Figure 10.4

You will then be presented with a prompt to put a floppy in drive A: and the option to back-up Registry entries.

Make your choice and click on **OK**. The disk creation process is the work of a few seconds.

REPAIRING A SYSTEM FROM AN ERD

In order to do this, you will need an ERD that   Figure 10.5
you created earlier and either a bootable
Microsoft Windows® 2000 installation disk or a set of boot disks. In order to make the set of four Microsoft Windows® 2000 boot disks (if you do not already have them), put a Microsoft Windows® 2000 installation CD in the drive of a working PC, navigate to the BOOTDISK directory and run either MAKEBT32.EXE (from the GUI) or MAKEBOOT.EXE from a command line prompt and follow the instructions on screen. Note that the PC that you use for this task need not necessarily be running Microsoft Windows® 2000 to carry out this task.

The repair process is the same whether you use a bootable CD or a set of boot disks to carry out the repair. Boot the PC to either a set of floppies or a bootable installation CD. The system will load various files and drivers. You will then be given a choice of restoring from your ERD or of running a Recovery Console. In this case, you would choose the ERD option.

A FURTHER NOTE ON BOOT DISKS

The boot disks used in Microsoft Windows® 2000 are specific to that operating system and can be made by the method described above or by downloading the appropriate utility from the Microsoft site. The older Microsoft Windows® NT system had a utility called RDISK.EXE for this purpose – this is NOT part of Microsoft Windows® 2000 and may be given as a plausible (but wrong) answer in an exam question. Another possible cause of confusion can come from standard boot disks made with earlier versions of Microsoft Windows® such as 98 or Millennium. You can boot a modern PC to one of these disks – they are boot disks after all – but if the target system has been formatted with the default NTFS file system, you won't even be able to read the hard disk, let alone carry out any useful work on it.

Automated System Recovery – Microsoft Windows® XP

This is part of the Backup system in Microsoft Windows® XP – so if you are working with a default installation of the Home edition, you will have to install it from the installation CD first. Other XP versions have Backup installed by default. In order to use Automated System Recovery (ASR):

- Navigate to **System Tools | Backup** and start the backup utility.

- If Backup starts in Wizard mode, uncheck the box marked **Always start in wizard mode**, click **Cancel**, then start again. This will take you to the Welcome tab in **Advanced** mode.

- Click the **Automated System Recovery** button, then click **Next**. You will then be prompted for the destination where you want the back-up to be stored.

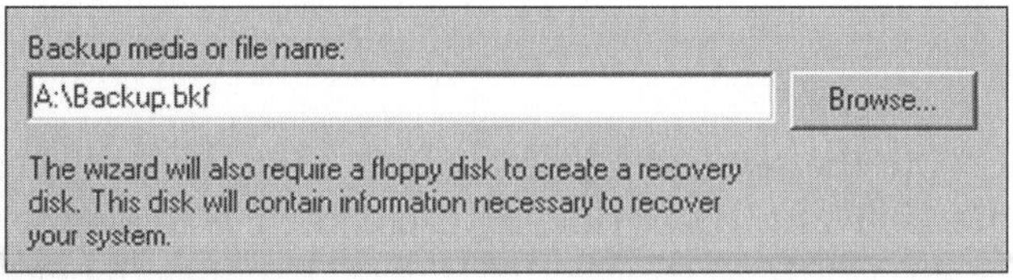

Backup media or file name:

A:\Backup.bkf   Browse...

The wizard will also require a floppy disk to create a recovery disk. This disk will contain information necessary to recover your system.

Figure 10.6

As you can see from the figure, the default is to write to a floppy disk on drive A. You will need to change this to another drive letter where there will be space for the back-up file. You cannot use the C: drive for this, nor can you use another partition on the same physical drive, because the whole of the first physical disk is reformatted as part of the restore operation. Another limitation is that ASR works only with locally attached disks – it cannot be used to back-up or restore to a network drive.

Having chosen your destination drive, click **Next** to start the back-up process.

After the back-up process has finished, you will be prompted to insert a floppy disk in Drive A. Do this and click on **Next**. Information about the ASR backup will be written to the floppy.

Store the ASR back-up disk and the floppy somewhere safe until they are needed.

Running ASR requires that you have administrative rights on the system that you are backing up or restoring.

Restoring from ASR back-up

To restore from an ASR back-up, you will need to boot the PC to an installation CD – or, if you can not do this, boot from CD using a set of six boot disks – and wait until you see a screen message prompting you for the ASR disk.

Diagnostic procedures and troubleshooting techniques

Troubleshooting – hardware or software – requires an approach rather than a set of pre-defined answers. Whatever the problem, the approach is:

1   Gather the facts. Observe, use diagnostic utilities, ask the user.

2   Make a list of the possibilities.

3   Work through the list carefully and methodically, testing and noting results until a solution is found.

Obviously there are times when the 'list' is just couple of items in your head and the process of 'working though it' is brief and informal. At other times, you may have to adopt a more formal approach, making written notes and recording test results.

Systematic diagnostic and troubleshooting techniques are amongst the key skills which distinguish the professional technician from the talented (or even not so talented) amateur. The basic methodology is the one outlined in Chapter 7 in relation to hardware, but it applies with equal validity to operating systems and is worth revisiting here.

Whatever the problem – hardware, operating system, network connection or a sulky printer the same fundamental approach is required to achieve a solution.

Ask the user

Most technical support call-outs are the result of a user making a support call because they are experiencing some sort of difficulty. An obvious first step, then, is to ask the customer what the problem is. It is also worth asking whether anyone else uses the PC that you are examining. This may be particularly important where you are working on a family PC where children may have access to it.

This first step in the troubleshooting process is definitely more art than science. It is easy to forget that most users are not familiar with the terminology of computing and may, for example, confuse memory with disk storage or not even know what version of Microsoft Windows® they are running. They certainly cannot be expected to know, down to the last mouse click, what other users have been doing.

This initial investigation of a problem will require you to exercise all of the communication and professionalism skills that are discussed in Chapter 19.

The initial problem is, as often as not, described along the lines of, 'When I click on so-and-so nothing happens'. The next step, then, is to ask the user to reproduce the problem.

Reproduce the problem

Having listened to the user's description of the problem, simply ask them to show you the steps that lead to the error they reported. Note exactly what they do and the error messages (if any) that the system puts out. At this stage, the problem and its solution may become apparent. Frequently, it is something simple like a missing desktop shortcut or a wrongly mapped drive and such problems can be fixed there and then.

Before proceeding further, you should always reboot the machine. There are often one-off failures caused by memory allocation failures and the like which can be 'fixed' by rebooting. A fault isn't really a fault unless it happens more than once.

Identifying changes

Systems that have had hardware or software changes are more likely to exhibit faults. Ask for, and note, information about recent changes: hardware upgrades, new software installation, operating system updates or service packs from disk or over the Internet. It may be possible to track down and fix the problem from this information or even to restore the system to its earlier state and start again.

Microsoft Windows® can also be useful in tracking down changes. System Information – one of the System Tools – summarises the current configuration and the Microsoft Windows® XP version has the facility to look at changes made after a specified date. The Add / Remove programs applet in Microsoft Windows® 2000 and XP can also be a useful source of information, particularly about automatic updates that may have been installed without the user's knowledge.

Beware, though, of giving too much credibility to recent changes. The fault may have arisen through other causes. For example, if a machine boots fine after a memory upgrade but crashes after a few minutes' operation, this is probably not a memory fault. The crash-after-five-minutes symptom is typical of an overheating CPU – possibly the CPU fan became disconnected in the course of the memory upgrade.

Analysing the problem

Isolating the symptom

Given the complexity of a modern multimedia PC, it is necessary to try at least to narrow the search for the cause of the problem. When diagnosing hardware, this usually means removing suspect parts systematically, one at a time until the problem rights itself. Using this approach, the last piece of hardware removed is a strong candidate for the defective part.

With software, this means removing any background programs (typically TSRs such as quick launchers for applications) until only the suspect program is running.

Separating hardware from software

It is often difficult to know whether a problem is caused by a software or hardware fault. The following are all worth trying:

- **Known good hardware**. The best way to separate hardware from software in diagnosing a problem is to replace the hardware with a known good component. For example, a reported memory fault may be caused by a software fault or a defective stick of RAM. If replacing the RAM cures the problem, then it was a hardware fault. If not, it is probably a software problem, though it would be as well to consider the possibility that it could be both.

- **Uninstall / Reinstall.** Uninstalling and reinstalling suspect software often provides a quick fix.

- **Patching / Upgrading.** A frequent cause of problems is incompatibility between hardware and the associated software drivers. Download patches or upgrades where these are available, especially if the hardware and the drivers are more than two years different in age.

- **Virus check.** At some point in the investigation a virus check with an up-to-date scanner is a necessity. Where a system has sufficient functionality, it may be a good idea to check for viruses at the start.

- **Common sense.** No set of rules or guidelines or procedures can provide a substitute for common sense. Think carefully about what the user reports, note symptoms and make written notes if necessary. Assume nothing and always look for the obvious: if the fuse in the plug on the wall has blown there is not much point in testing the power supply in the computer.

Testing related components and connections

Sometimes the easiest way of tracking down a problem is to strip the PC down to its constituent parts and rebuild it, testing from time to time. There are many connections in the PC and one poorly seated component can be sufficient to cause a failure. The key to this process – like all troubleshooting – is being systematic. Rebuild and test with the minimum hardware necessary to boot (motherboard, RAM, CPU and power) – then add components and test from time to time. Once you have a working GUI, you can also check in Device Manager. For example, a poorly seated expansion card – sound card, modem, or whatever – may not even show up in Device Manager, whereas a card that appears but reports a fault may simply have a driver problem. Also worth checking is the vendor's website for a particular suspect component. There are occasionally 'known issues' with components and these are often documented either in product documentation or on the website. There may also be user forums where you can find any workarounds that other users may have found for your problem.

Evaluate results

Troubleshooting is an iterative process. Go through the steps, making notes where necessary; evaluate your results in the light of your experiences, information gained from product manuals and websites. Then step through the process again until you find a solution.

Document activities and outcomes

Once you have found your solution, write it down. Describe the problem, the symptoms, the methods of investigation and the outcome. This need not be long or complex documentation – indeed the shorter the better. All that is required is that when you, or anyone else, encounters a similar problem in the future, there are some clear notes on the problem, the methods of investigation and the solution.

Common operational issues

The exam specification lists some common operational problems and, although these are less prevalent in modern Microsoft Windows® versions and less of a nuisance when you are working in the field, you still need to know about them.

Blue screens

Also known as Blue Screen of Death (BSOD) errors, these stop errors occur when 2000 / XP systems experience an irrecoverable fault. In these situations, the system stops responding and a screen of information – usually white text on a blue or black background – appears.

The most common cause of the errors is newly installed hardware or drivers. The errors can also occur when disk space is getting tight, or even 'just happen' for no apparent reason. If the error occurs after installing new hardware, uninstall it, reboot and check the Event Viewer to see the error messages logged before the crash. If the system will not boot normally, boot to Safe Mode or attempt to start using last known good configuration.

Once you have re-established some level of working system, check in the **Add | Remove Programs | Windows Components** applet in **Control Panel** to see the status of Windows Updates and Service Packs. Use third-party diagnostics to check for memory errors. Conduct a full virus scan with an up-to-date scanner.

System lock-ups

These are not much different to blue screens. Instead of the white-on-blue message, the system just stops working. The problem and possible solutions are likely to be similar to those of a blue screen error, that is probably caused by incompatible hardware or a virus. Remove suspect hardware and reboot. Scan for viruses.

Input / output devices

The most common causes of failure are poor physical connections and / or driver problems. Reseat or reconnect the suspect device – keyboard, mouse, screen, etc. – and if that does not fix the problem, check in Device Manager and try reinstalling or updating drivers.

Application failures

A one-off failure or lock-up of an application may be 'just one of those things'. The first action in such a situation is to access the Task List – press Ctrl+Alt+Del and select **Task Manager** in Microsoft Windows® 2000 / XP – kill the application and restart it. If this does not work, try rebooting the system. It is also worth checking any log files that the application may have made and looking in Event Viewer.

If the problem persists – in an application that will not start or load after it has been working satisfactorily for some time – this may indicate corrupt files or virus activity. Check for viruses and if necessary uninstall and reinstall the application.

Failure to install in the first place or to load or run immediately after installation is probably a compatibility problem. It may be as simple as a failure of the installation CD to autorun when placed in the drive. Check the CD – using Explorer – for the presence of an AUTORUN.INF file. Although most installers are intended to autorun, this may not be the case with a particular application. If this is the case, there is probably a SETUP.EXE that you can run from the CD or through the **Add / Remove Programs** applet in the **Control Panel**.

It may, of course, be that the application is not compatible with your Microsoft Windows® version. Just as there is a Hardware Compatibility List (HCL) for Microsoft Windows® versions, there is a software / applications equivalent for Microsoft Windows® 2000 and XP. The Application Compatibility Toolkit (ACT) can be downloaded from the Microsoft website and used to check the compatibility of an application.

Printing problems

The most common cause of failure to print is a poor physical connection and the most common cause of poor quality output from a printer is the wrong paper or other print media. The exam specification cites print spool stalled and incorrect / incompatible driver for print as problems that may be examined. These, and other printer and printing problems, are discussed at some length in Chapter 12.

Common error messages and codes

Invalid boot disk / Inaccessible boot device / Missing NTLDR

If an NT system such as Microsoft Windows® XP fails to boot to hard disk and returns an error message such as 'Invalid boot disk' or 'Inaccessible boot device', or reports a missing file with a message such as 'Missing NTLDR' then – if the hardware is okay – there is a problem with the Master Boot Record (MBR) and / or the key files:

- NTLDR
- NTDETECT.COM
- BOOT.INI

The role of these three files in the boot process is discussed in Chapter 8. If they are missing or corrupt, the answer is to replace them, which is a good reason for backing them up in the first place. BOOT.INI in particular is specific to the system on which it was made.

To fix a problem in this category, you need to boot the machine to a Recovery Console. If the target machine does not have a Recovery Console installed as an option or it is otherwise inaccessible, you will need to boot to an XP installation CD and work from there.

From a Recovery Console, you can fix the Master Boot Record by issuing the command: FIXMBR from a prompt. This puts a new Master Boot Record on the C: drive.

The next step is to replace – by copying from back-up – the three key files necessary to boot a Microsoft Windows® 2000 or XP system.

On Microsoft Windows® 2000 systems, you can restore all of the key files by booting to an installation CD (or a set of start-up floppies). When the text mode part of the installer runs, follow the on-screen instructions until you are prompted to **Repair an Installation**. Choose the **Fast Repair** option and follow the instructions for using the Emergency Repair Disk (ERD).

On Microsoft Windows® XP systems, the ERD has been replaced by Automated System Recovery (ASR).To access the ASR feature, you will need to have administrator rights. ASR has been described earlier in the chapter and all that needs to be noted here is that it is a last resort option, only to be used after trying Last Known Good Configuration, Safe Mode, etc. If the measures outlined here fail, then you will probably need to reinstall the operating system.

Start-up problems

Device / service has failed to start

This message indicates a failure in the network logon phase of Microsoft Windows® 2000 / XP start-up. Usually, at this stage of the start-up, the desktop is already on screen, while other system services are being loaded behind the scenes. If the machine is working 'normally' in stand-alone mode you can access the Event Viewer from the desktop. If this isn't possible, boot to Safe Mode. Either way, provided you have administrator privileges, you can access the Event Viewer through the GUI or by typing EVENTWR.MSC at a system prompt. From here, and by using the log files for information, you should be able to trace and fix the fault.

Event Viewer

The Event Viewer maintains logs of system events. Provided that you have administrator rights, you can launch Event Viewer by clicking on the **Administrative Tools** applet in **Control Panel** and clicking on the icon for the **Event Viewer**, or type EVENTVWR at a prompt. Either way, you will see something like Figure 10.7.

Event Viewer groups its entries under three headings:

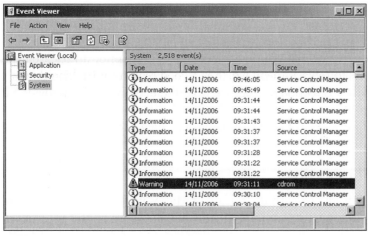

Figure 10.7

░ The Application log – shows messages that relate to applications

░ The Security log – shows security events such as logins and login failures

░ The System log – shows messages that relate to the operation of Microsoft Windows®

Where there appears to be a problem, click on the entry in the list to see further details of the reported event. Figure 10.8 shows details of the warning event highlighted in Figure 10.7.

One of the problems with the event logs is the amount of detail they record. Usually you are interested in recent events, and the size of the log can be overwhelming. Where you are trying to track a particular problem, you can clear the log (there is an option to save it to a file first), then examine the log for fresh events that relate to the problem that you are investigating. You may also need to clear the log if you see an 'Event log is full' message. The log can be cleared by selecting **Clear all events** from the **Action** menu. This clears the events for the selected log – Application, Security, or System.

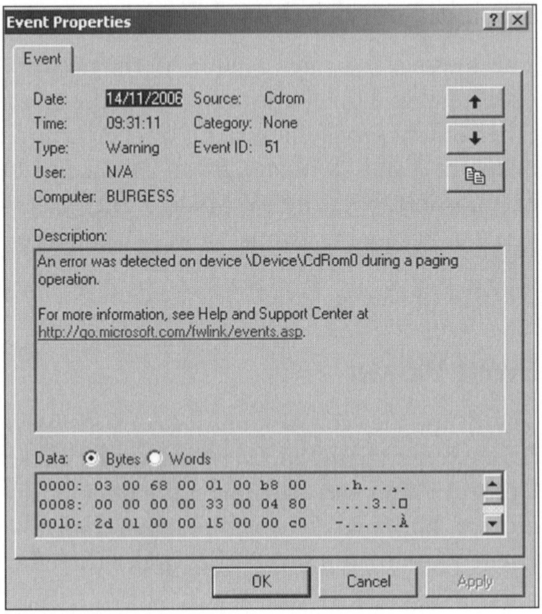

The Registry

If you encounter a message that indicates that there are problems with the Registry such as a 'not found' message for an application, you can, of course, edit the Registry with one of the available

Figure 10.8

Registry editing tools. However, this can be a hazardous undertaking unless you are pretty sure of what you are doing, so it may be better to restore an old Registry.

As we have already seen, Microsoft Windows® 2000 gives the option to back up the Registry when making an Emergency Repair Disk (ERD). Navigate to **Start | Programs | Accessories | System Tools | Backup** and back up from there. Microsoft Windows® XP, of course, uses the System Restore utility. This is described elsewhere in the chapter and can be used after trying Last Known Good Configuration, Safe Mode, etc. to restore a previous Registry.

Microsoft Windows® reporting

This is a feature that was introduced with the release of Microsoft Windows® XP. If there is a problem with an application and you are currently connected to the Internet, a window pops up and asks if you want to report the problem to Microsoft. If you choose to do this, technical information about the problem is sent to Microsoft. If there have been other reports of the same problem, you will be able to access this to help you to find a solution. The reporting feature can be configured through the **System** applet in **Control Panel** or through the **Properties** sheet of **My Computer**.

Operating system utilities

Disk management tools

Like many of the utilities in Microsoft Windows®, the disk management tools can be accessed by more than one method. For example, the defragmenter can be accessed by:

- Typing DEFRAG [Drive letter] at a prompt (DEFRAG /? for details of usage) – Microsoft Windows® XP only – to start a command line version.

- Typing DFRG.MSC at a prompt – to start the GUI version – Microsoft Windows® XP and 2000.

- Right-clicking on the drive icon for a disk drive and selecting **Properties | Tools | Defragment now** – Microsoft Windows® XP and 2000.

- Navigate to **Control Panel | Administrative Tools | Computer Management | Disk Defragmenter** – Microsoft Windows® XP and 2000.

Similarly, other disk management tools can be accessed through a command line or the GUI. For exam purposes at least, you should familiarise yourself with the various paths to the different tools in both XP and 2000.

Defrag

Imagine a library where returned books are placed on the first available shelf space and the catalogue is updated to record their new position. After a while, books would be shelved all over the place, and something like a multi-volume encyclopaedia would take a long time to find because the individual volumes would be on different shelves or even different floors of the building.

Microsoft Windows® stores files rather like the books in this library example. When a file is written to the hard disk, it is written to the first available storage unit (cluster). A large file may be written across several clusters and these may be widely separated. When files are deleted, this makes more clusters available, possibly in the middle of other files. This is known as fragmentation and the answer to the problem is defragmentation: that is rearranging the storage clusters so that all parts of the file are on the same part of the hard disk, making them easier to find and quicker to load. As a practical exercise, you could try starting the defragmenter by one or more of the means outlined earlier and observing the results.

NTBACKUP

This is the standard back-up utility in both Microsoft Windows® 2000 and XP. It can be accessed by navigating to the Backup entry in the **Accessories | System tools** menu or by typing NTBACKUP at a system prompt. Once launched – by either method – it presents you with a wizard interface that guides you through the back-up / restore process. NTBACKUP is installed by default on Microsoft Windows® 2000 and XP Professional systems, but not in XP Home Edition. If you are working with XP Home, you will need to install the back-up utility from the installation CD. It is in:

[CD-ROM drive letter:] \VALUEADD\MSFT \NTBACKUP. Once installed, it works in exactly the same way as the XP Professional edition.

CHKDSK

The CHKDSK utility is used to create and display reports on the state of the target disk drive. It also gives you options to automatically fix any problems that it encounters. Like many Microsoft Windows® utilities, it can be started through the GUI or from a command line prompt. Whichever option you choose, you will be running the same utility. In order to check a disk in either Microsoft Windows® 2000 or XP:

1   Click on **My Computer** to show attached disk drives.

2   Right-click on the drive you want to check.

3   Select **Properties** from the context menu.

4   Click on the **Tools** tab.

Figure 10.9

5   Click on the **Check Now** button. By default, this will offer the option to check and report only. Checking either of the boxes (as in Figure 10.10) gives you the options to fix errors as they are encountered and / or attempt to recover any bad sectors on the disk.

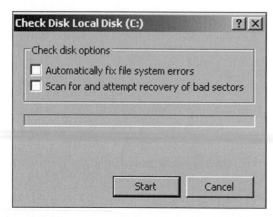

Figure 10.10

If you check the box to Automatically fix file system errors, Microsoft Windows® will warn you that this will require a reboot of the PC and give you an option to cancel if you do not want to do this.

An alternative route to the GUI implementation of CHKDSK is through **Control Panel | Administrative Tools | Computer Management | Disk Management**. If you use this route, highlight the drive that you want to check and proceed as in steps 2–5 above.

To start CHKDSK from a prompt, type CHKDSK. By default, this will run the CHKDSK utility on the C: drive and generate a report. To check other drives, you need to specify a drive letter, and other options can be invoked by the use of appropriate command line switches. As with nearly all commands, the /? option will give you a summary of the options. To see this for yourself, type CHKDSK /? at a system prompt in either Microsoft Windows® 2000 or XP.

Format

On a modern installed Microsoft Windows® version, you can format any disk – except the system or boot partitions – through the GUI and, as we saw in Chapter 9, disks can be partitioned and formatted as part of the standard installation process. The underlying command line tools for these operations are DISKPART.EXE and FORMAT.COM. DISKPART is not a part of the standard Microsoft Windows® 2000 installation but can be downloaded from the Microsoft site. It is available by default in Microsoft Windows® XP. DISKPART is not specifically listed in the Essentials exam specification (so in theory you do not even need to know of its existence) – however, it can be very useful occasionally in the field. FORMAT.COM is required knowledge.

The FORMAT command creates the basic structures that allow data to be written to a partition on a disk. Where this is a new disk, the system will perform a full format. Where there is an existing formatted partition, you can specify a Quick Format with the /Q switch. This option blanks the File Allocation Table / Master File Table and allows a disk to be reused, allowing the old data to be overwritten.

Because modern Microsoft Windows® versions support both FAT and NTFS file systems, you have to specify the file system type on the command line. For example, to format drive Q with the NTFS file system, you would use the command:

FORMAT Q: /FS:NTFS

There are other switches and options for the format command, and typing FORMAT /? at a prompt will list them for you.

System management tools

Device Manager

Device Manager displays installed hardware on the system and reports any problems. The most straightforward route to Device Manager is:

1   Right click on **My Computer**.

2   Select **Properties** from the context menu.

3   Click on the **Hardware** tab.

4   Click the button for **Device Manager**.

Figure 10.11 shows Device Manager in Microsoft Windows® XP. Where there are no problems with a device, the list is closed up. Where there are problems – as with the multimedia audio controller in the figure – the list is open and the problem device is marked with a yellow blob and a question mark and exclamation mark.

Device Manager gives many options such as the ability to disable a device, to uninstall it, to roll back device drivers or to look for new ones. Device Manager is a useful tool when troubleshooting a PC in the field, as well as being core knowledge for exams, so you are strongly recommended to explore its features for yourself.

Device Manager can also be accessed through the **System** applet in **Control Panel** in both Microsoft Windows® 2000 and XP.

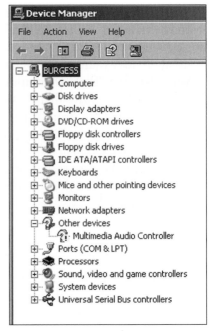

Figure 10.11

Task Manager

To access the **Task Manager** in Microsoft Windows® 2000 or XP, hold down the Ctrl+Alt+Del keys simultaneously. This will take you to a security screen as shown in Figure 10.12.

Figure 10.12

To access the Task Manager, click on the **Task Manager** button.

A quicker route to Task Manager is to hold down Ctrl+Shift+Esc keys.

As you might expect, the Microsoft Windows® XP version of Task Manager has more features than its counterpart in Microsoft Windows® 2000. This is reflected in the number of tabs displayed by the system – three in Microsoft Windows® 2000 and four or five in XP.

TASK MANAGER OPTIONS

The Task Manager options are as follows:

- **Applications tab**. This shows applications that are currently running and reports them as 'not responding' when they hang. You can kill off a non-responding application from here. You can also switch to a running application or launch a new application from here.

- **Processes tab**. This shows currently running processes, their usage of CPU and RAM and the name of the user who owns the process. For these purposes, there are non-human 'users' such as 'System' and 'Network Service' as well as users in the more conventional sense of the term.

- **Performance tab**. This shows CPU usage and swap file (aka Page file / Virtual memory) usage and the number of running processes.

- **Networking tab** (Microsoft Windows® XP only). This tab appears in XP only if you are connected to a network. It shows a graphical representation of the performance of each installed network adapter.

- **Users tab** (Microsoft Windows® XP only). This tab only shows where there is more than one local user account on the PC and user switching is enabled. You can see the user name and status of the other user(s) and have the option to disconnect them, log them out, or send them a message.

MSCONFIG.EXE

This is a Microsoft Windows® XP utility that can be launched by typing MSCONFIG in a Run box – it does not run from a command prompt unless you tweak the system to make this happen. Microsoft Windows® 2000 does not include MSCONFIG.EXE but the XP version will run on a 2000 machine. The XP version – running on XP – looks like this:

Like many utilities, MSCON-FIG groups its functions under tabs. These are:

- **General**. The General tab gives many options to control the system at start-up: normal, diagnostic or selective. There is a button to launch the System Restore utility and an Expand File option that allows you to extract a single file from an installation disk.

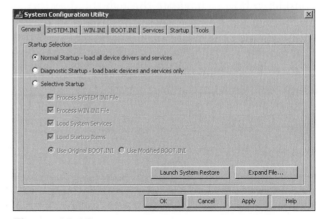

Figure 10.13

▓ **SYSTEM.INI**. This shows the contents of the SYSTEM.INI configuration file. Lines in the file can be disabled or enabled. They can be re-ordered, that is moved up or down within the file, or a new line added. There is also a 'find' function that means you can search for a text string within the file.

▓ **WIN.INI**. This tab shows the contents of the WIN.INI configuration file and has the same editing capabilities.

▓ **BOOT.INI**. This tab shows the contents of the BOOT.INI configuration file. It provides a number of options such as the ability to boot to Safe Mode, a logged boot and so on. On systems where there is a choice of operating systems at boot time, the default time to wait is 30 seconds. This value can be edited from this tab.

▓ **Services**. Most systems start a variety of services at boot time. Many of these services are essential for the working of the system. Others, such as routines that check for the availability of software updates may be useful but inessential. Services can be enabled / disabled by checking / unchecking the boxes next to them.

▓ **Startup**. Many applications are started at boot time and run as background processes. Typically, these are things like a virus scanner or a quick launcher for a frequently used application. These can be selectively enabled / disabled by checking / unchecking the boxes next to them.

▓ **Tools**. This lists various system tools such as the Registry editor, a command prompt, Add / Remove programs, etc. In order to launch a particular tool, highlight it in the list and click on the **Launch** button. The tools listed here are all available elsewhere on the system – the tools tab just puts them together in one convenient place.

▓ **MSCONFIG**. This is a useful utility when working in the field as well as being required knowledge for exam purposes. Like many aspects of operating systems, the best way to really get to grips with it is to use it.

File management tools

We looked at Microsoft Windows® Explorer / My Computer in Chapter 8, where we considered how to navigate through the directory hierarchy and to create, copy, delete etc. files and directories. A further aspect of file management is viewing and changing file attributes.

File attributes

Every file has a set of attributes associated with it. These can be viewed or changed from the command prompt using the ATTRIB command or through the Microsoft Windows® GUI. Every file has the attributes:

- Read Only
- Hidden
- System
- Archive

Each of these attributes can be 'set' or 'clear'. When an attribute is set, it applies to the file in question. Thus, if MYFILE.EXT has the Read Only attribute set, then it can be read but not edited.

Hidden files do not show up on a DIR directory listing and System files are protected operating system files such as \BOOT.INI on a Microsoft Windows® 2000 / XP system. These files frequently have the hidden attribute set as well.

The Archive bit indicates a file's back-up status. When a new file is created, the archive bit is set to indicate that it has not yet been backed up. When the file has been backed up – with a back-up program or XCOPY – the archive bit is cleared (unless you deliberately program this not to happen) so the file will not be backed up again until it has been modified and the changes written to disk. Control of the archive bit is the basis for Full, Differential and Incremental back-up types.

Note: File attributes are a characteristic of all files on Microsoft Windows® systems and have been in use since the early DOS systems. Modern Microsoft Windows® versions implement other controls such as file permissions based on ownership and administered though Access Control Lists in addition to these basic properties.

Viewing / changing file attributes through Microsoft Windows® Explorer

To view the attributes of a file through Explorer, right-click on the file name and select the **Properties** entry from the context menu.

Microsoft Windows® shows the file attributes of the selected file. Where it is a normal file, you will see the attributes shown in the figure and you may change them by checking / unchecking the appropriate boxes. Where a file is marked as a System file – files such as NTLDR or BOOT.INI – you will be able to view the attributes, but will not be able to change the System setting. If you cannot see the system files in Microsoft Windows® 2000 or XP, you may need to change the default view of the file system. To do this, click on the **Tools** menu item at the top of any Explorer window, choose **Folder options** from the context menu, then

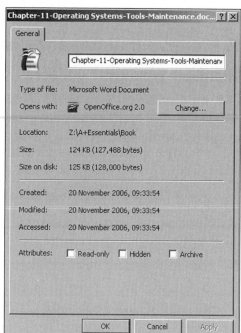

Figure 10.14

select the **View tab**. From here, you can check the radio button to **Show hidden files and folders**. You may also want to uncheck the boxes to **Hide extensions for known file types** and **Hide protected operating system files**.

Viewing / changing file attributes with ATTRIB.EXE

Using the command ATTRIB at a system prompt lists files in the current directory and shows which attributes are set and a blank where an attribute is clear.

Figure 10.15 shows the output of the ATTRIB command on the root of the C: drive of a Microsoft Windows® XP system. Note that only attributes which are set are shown. For example, the file PAGEFILE.SYS (the Microsoft Windows® XP swap file) has a blank in the read-only attribute field because it is not a read-only file.

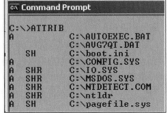

Figure 10.15

In order to set an attribute with the ATTRIB command, use the symbol + and the letter for the attribute, and to clear it use the symbol – and the appropriate letter. Thus to set the file MYFILE.EXT to be read only issue the command:

ATTRIB +R MYFILE.EXT

To make it read/write, use the command:

ATTRIB – R MYFILE.EXT

Other attributes may be reset using the same syntax.

Preventive maintenance on operating systems

Microsoft Windows® updates

Like any operating system, Microsoft Windows® is a work in progress. Both Microsoft Windows® 2000 and XP have an update service which you can use to download and install various updates and security patches. After installing Microsoft Windows® on a PC, it is good practice to visit the Microsoft site to download and install the latest updates. Any of these will work:

▧ Type WUPDMGR at a system prompt or in a 'Run' box.

▧ If you use the Microsoft Windows® Internet Explorer browser, choose the **Windows Update** option from the **Tools** menu.

▧ Point your browser (Internet Explorer or other) to http://windowsupdate.microsoft.com.

▧ Navigate to **Start | All programs | windows update** (top part of column) – Microsoft Windows® XP only.

In order to stay up to date, both Microsoft Windows® 2000 and XP offer an automatic update service. The settings for this can be seen and changed by navigating to the **Control Panel** and clicking on the **Automatic Updates** icon. You will be presented with the choices shown in figure 10.16.

Automatic updates can be a useful way of keeping a system current.

Service packs

A service pack is a collection of updates packaged as an entity and made available for download. For individual PCs, this can be downloaded and installed or, particularly where you have a fleet of PCs to maintain, you can download a stand-alone executable file which can be burned to CD or

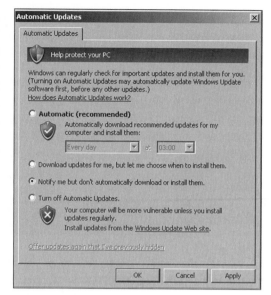

Figure 10.16

placed on a network share to be used on multiple machines. The last service pack to be released for Microsoft Windows® 2000 was SP4 and for XP it was SP2. There is a widely available unofficial 'service pack 3' for XP that has been assembled from various Microsoft updates, but this has not been released by Microsoft at the time of writing (March 2007).

Other software updates

Other software on the system may need updating from time to time. Particularly important in this respect are definition files and updates for virus and malware protection – this topic is considered more fully in Chapter 17 (see pages 272–275).

Another important set of updates to bear in mind is device drivers for installed hardware.

Scheduled tasks

There are a number of maintenance tasks such as back-ups, Microsoft Windows® updates, definition file updates, etc. which can be set up either through Microsoft Windows® or the application concerned. There is also a service – Scheduled tasks – which can be used to automate any process. To add a Scheduled task, navigate to **Control Panel** and click on the **Add Scheduled Task** applet. This starts a wizard that will guide you through scheduling a task to run at a particular time of day at specified time intervals.

Figure 10.17 shows the choices for a custom-written back-up script in Microsoft Windows® XP using the Task Scheduler. To see the standard scheduling interface in the Backup utility, navigate to **System Tools** and start **Backup** in Wizard mode.

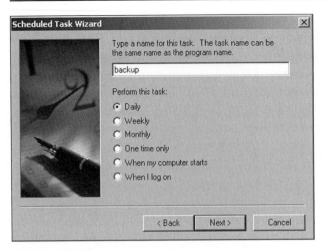

Figure 10.17

Restore / restore points

The system Restore utility was introduced with the release of Microsoft Windows® XP. It is one of the System Tools and can be accessed by clicking on the **System Restore** entry in the **System Tools** menu.

A restore point is a copy of your system configuration at a given time and date and there are three types:

- Restore points created by the system – Scheduled restore points

- Restore points which you create – Manual restore points

- Restore points when some programs are installed – Automatic restore points

By default, Microsoft Windows® monitors all attached disk drives and allocates12 per cent of the available space for restore points. The size of this allocation can be changed and, where a drive is used exclusively for data storage, for example, it can be turned off to save both the processing overhead and the storage space. Current settings can be viewed and changed through the **System Restore** tab in the **Systems** applet.

It is useful to set a manual system restore point before making significant changes to a system so that you can roll back to a previous state if you experience problems. Rolling back to a previous restore point has been described earlier in the chapter. It is worth noting, perhaps, that if you upgrade from Microsoft Windows® XP Home edition to XP Professional edition, you will lose all restore points made before the upgrade.

SUMMARY

This chapter has considered the tools and diagnostic procedures available in Microsoft Windows® 2000 and XP as well as the 'soft skills' needed to elicit information from the user / customer. We have looked at an outline of the boot sequence and considered various boot methods such as custom-made boot disks, the use of Safe Mode and a Recovery Console. We have also considered preventive maintenance as it applies to operating systems.

The content of this chapter, taken with that of chapters 8 and 9, accounts for 21 per cent of the available marks for the A+ Essentials exam. In preparing for the exam, you need to memorise facts about the two Microsoft Windows® versions, their similarities and their differences. You also need to know the different ways to access system facilities both through the GUI and the command line. The best way to do this is to sit at a PC, do any suggested practicals, explore, experiment and even devise your own practicals.

QUESTIONS

1   You want to boot a Microsoft Windows® 2000 PC into Safe Mode. You restart the machine. Which key combination will take you to Safe Mode?

   a) Ctrl+Alt+Del

   b) Shift+F8

   c) F8

   d) Shift+F10

2   A user calls you to say that they are having difficulties in accessing files on the network. Before booking a desktop visit, you try to address the problem over the phone. Having established that the PC in question is running Microsoft Windows® XP and was working properly earlier in the day, what do you suggest that the user does next?

   a) Attempt to log in at a different workstation

   b) Reboot the PC

   c) Try a different password

   d) Defragment the hard disk

▶

3   How do you make an Emergency Repair Disk (ERD) in Microsoft Windows® XP?

   a) Navigate to **System Tools | Backup** and run the ERD Wizard

   b) Run RDISK.EXE from a command prompt

   c) Download one from the Microsoft site

   d) None of the above

4   You want to defragment a disk on a Microsoft Windows® 2000 system. Which of the following actions will launch this utility?

   a) Click on the drive icon, then choose **Properties | Tools | Defragment now**.

   b) Type DFRG.MSC at a command prompt

   c) Type DEFRAG at a system prompt

   d) Any of the above

5   You are working on a dual-boot Microsoft Windows® 2000 / XP PC and you want to change the default wait time of 30 seconds at the boot screen. Which of the following would achieve this?

   a) Change the timeout from the BOOT.INI tab in MSCONFIG

   b) Edit the BOOT.INI file with Notepad

   c) EDIT the NTLDR file with Notepad.

   d) Any of the above

ANSWERS / EXPLANATIONS

1   You want to boot a Microsoft Windows® 2000 PC into Safe Mode. You restart the machine. Which key combination will take you to Safe Mode?

c) F8

Note: This is the same in XP as well.

2   A user calls you to say that they are having difficulties in accessing files on the network. Before booking a desktop visit, you try to address the problem over the phone. Having established that the PC in question is running Microsoft Windows® XP and was working properly earlier in the day, what do you suggest that the user does next?

b) Reboot the PC

Always reboot first!

3   How do you make an Emergency Repair Disk (ERD) in Microsoft Windows® XP?

d) None of the above

XP doesn't use Emergency Repair Disks.

4   You want to defragment a disk on a Microsoft Windows®2000 system. Which of the following actions will launch this utility?

a) Click on the drive icon, then choose **Properties | Tools | Defragment now**.

b) Type DFRG.MSC at a command prompt.

Option c is not available in 2000, but would work in XP.

5   You are working on a dual-boot Microsoft Windows® 2000 / XP PC and you want to change the default wait time of 30 seconds at the boot screen. Which of the following would achieve this?

a) Change the timeout from the BOOT.INI tab in MSCONFIG

b) Edit the BOOT.INI file with Notepad

Option a would be the easier; b would be feasible.

CHAPTER 11
Laptops and portable systems

Laptop computers and other portable devices such as Personal Digital Assistants (PDAs) and 'Palmtops' have increased in popularity and power as hardware prices and reliability have improved over the years. There are many similarities between portable and desktop PCs, as well as some important differences. As a working technician, you need to be aware of these, and in terms of exams, 11 per cent of the marks for the Essentials exam are awarded for the topics covered in this chapter.

Exam objectives 2.1, 2.2, 2.3 and 2.4
2.1 Identify the fundamental principles of using laptops and portable devices
Identify names, purposes and characteristics of laptop-specific:

    Form factors such as memory and hard drives
    Peripherals (e.g. docking station, port replicator and media / accessory bay)
    Expansion slots (e.g. PCMCIA I, II and III, card and express bus)
    Ports (e.g. mini PCI slot)
    Communication connections (e.g. Bluetooth, infrared, cellular WAN, Ethernet)
    Power and electrical input devices (e.g. auto-switching and fixed-input power supplies, batteries)
    LCD technologies (e.g. active and passive matrix, resolution such as XGA, SXGA+, UXGA, WUXGA, contrast radio, native resolution)
    Input devices (e.g. stylus / digitiser, function (Fn) keys and pointing devices such as touch pad, point stick / track point)

Identify and distinguish between mobile and desktop motherboards and processors including throttling, power management and WiFi.

2.2 Install, configure, optimise and upgrade laptops and portable devices
Configure power management.
Identify the features of BIOS-ACPI.
Identify the difference between suspend, hibernate and standby.
Demonstrate safe removal of laptop-specific hardware such as peripherals, hot-swappable devices and non-hot-swappable devices.

▶

2.3 Identify tools, basic diagnostic procedures and troubleshooting techniques for laptops and portable devices
Use procedures and techniques to diagnose power conditions, video, keyboard, pointer and wireless card issues, for example:

Verify AC power (e.g. LEDs, swap AC adapter)
Verify DC power
Remove unneeded peripherals
Plug in external monitor
Toggle Fn keys
Check LCD cut-off switch
Verify backlight functionality and pixilation
Stylus issues (e.g. digitiser problems)
Unique laptop keypad issues
Antenna wires

2.4 Perform preventative maintenance on laptops and portable devices
Identify and apply common preventative maintenance techniques for laptops and portable devices, for example: cooling devices, hardware and video cleaning materials, operating environments including temperature and air quality, storage, transportation and shipping.

Laptop specifics

Laptop systems deliver the same functionality as their desktop counterparts and therefore use similar components. However, whereas desktop machines can usually be opened up easily and use industry-standard components that are frequently interchangeable across a variety of makes and models (an ATX motherboard, for example will fit in any ATX case, regardless of maker or vendor), laptops tend to use manufacturer-specific components. Frequently, components from a particular manufacturer are not just incompatible with machines from other makers, but may also be specific to a particular model (or group of models) within their product range. This means that the usual advice about reading the manual and other manufacturer's documentation is particularly applicable when working with laptop or other portable systems.

Form factors

Most, if not quite all, components on a desktop system comply with published standards from bodies such as the American National Standards Institute (ANSI) or the Institute of Electrical and Electronics Engineers (IEEE), which define performance characteristics and physical connections with other devices. This means that desktop PCs use components that are readily available and widely interchangeable. With a couple of notable exceptions – RAM and hard drives – this is not generally the case with laptop machines.

RAM form factors

Main system memory (RAM) uses laptop-specific form factors, which are for the most part as interchangeable as RAM sticks in desktop PCs, that is providing the pin count and RAM type are correct, RAM can be fitted in any laptop machine with the necessary spare RAM slots irrespective of the system manufacturer. As with desktop PCs, the basic RAM packaging is almost always some type of Dual Inline Memory Module (DIMM). Obviously, where you are upgrading memory on a laptop, the same considerations of packaging and compatibility with existing installed RAM will apply as they do to a desktop PC.

The Small Outline DIMM (SODIMM) is the most widely used form factor for laptop RAM modules. There are several variants on the pin count and capacity (just as there are with desktop modules) and these include 72-pin and 144-pin Extended Data Out (EDO) RAM and SDRAM types as well as the more modern 200-pin Double Data Rate (DDR) RAM and 200-pin DDR2 RAM. The standards that apply to desktop modules, PC2700, DDR2 etc. apply to SODIMMs. Capacities of modern SODIMM types are currently up to 2 GB per module. Figure 11.1 shows a 256 MB PC2700 DDR SODIMM RAM module.

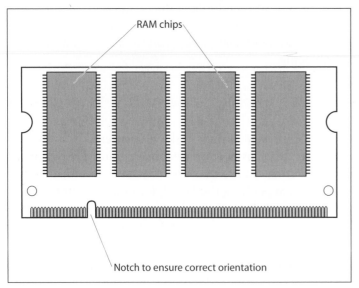

RAM chips

Notch to ensure correct orientation

Figure 11.1

144-pin SODIMMs have a notch in their underside, close to (but not exactly at) the centre to ensure correct orientation; 200-pin modules have a single notch as shown in Figure 11.1 that is closer to the edge of the module: this indicates that the module is Double Data Rate (DDR) RAM. DDR 2 RAM has its notch nearer to the centre of the module than DDR but not as near centre as the older (144-pin) SDRAM type. Although the different notch positions mean that you cannot accidentally fit DDR into a DDR 2 slot, it is not always easy to distinguish them by visual inspection, so exercise care when specifying RAM for an upgrade using memory of these types.

The MicroDIMM is a smaller and newer form factor for RAM packages. It provides the same range of RAM types – DDR, DDR 2, etc. but in a DIMM package that has either 144 or 172 pins. The module is not symmetric about centre, so there is no need for an orientation notch on its underside.

Installing laptop RAM

Most modern laptop systems have a removable cover – usually on the underside of the machine – which can be removed to expose the RAM slots.

▓ Read the manufacturer's documentation for the system.

▓ Locate the memory cover and remove it.

▓ Check the type of installed RAM and that there is a spare slot.

▓ Establish the type of RAM required either by visual inspection, manufacturer's documentation or by visiting the website of one of the major RAM vendors.

▓ With the machine powered down and observing standard antistatic precautions, fit the new module into an empty slot.

▓ Replace the cover, power up and test for correct operation.

Hard drives

Internal hard drives on laptop machines almost invariably use an EIDE / PATA type hard disk, though serial ATA (SATA) drives are available. Both PATA and SATA drives for laptops are smaller than their desktop counterparts. A typical laptop hard disk is 2.5 inches instead of the standard 3.5 inch for a desktop unit and are usually less than 0.5 inches high compared with a little under an inch for a desktop drive. There are also 1.8 inches-wide drives made by Toshiba, but these are less commonly encountered in the field. Capacities of laptop drives are (in 2007) between 20 and 100 GB, although this will probably increase with time and technological progress.

Installing a laptop hard drive

Compared with installing a drive on a desktop PC, this is slightly more complicated because of the way that laptop machines are constructed. In addition, because notebook machines are not designed to take a second hard disk, you will need to back-up all data and install the operating system afresh on the new disk before replacing the applications and data. Alternatively, you may want to clone the contents of the old drive to the new one. Either way, you are in for some extra work.

▓ Check the manufacturer's documentation for the type of hard disk required for that make and model, where it is located in the system, how it is mounted and cabling requirements.

▓ Back-up all data or make an image (clone) of the whole drive.

▓ Obtain a drive of the correct type and – observing standard antistatic precautions – physically install it.

▓ Either flash the cloned image of the old drive onto the new one or reinstall the operating system, the applications and the data.

▓ Test thoroughly for proper operation.

Note: If you want to clone the old drive, you will have to use the system preparation tools described in Chapter 9 (see page 138). You can connect the 2.5 inch drive to a standard PATA cable with an adapter for cloning and data transfers, if you wish to do this prior to physical installation.

Form factors for other components

Apart from RAM modules and disks, most other components are specific to a make or model of laptop machine. You need to know the specifications of laptop components for exam purposes and as criteria for choosing a laptop system or advising a customer on making such a choice. However most laptop components – other than RAM and disks – are specific to a make and model and while it may by technically feasible to replace them, it is not often a cost-effective choice. In reality, most upgrades to laptop systems will consist of adding extra features by attaching additional devices through Cardbus / PCMCIA slots – more on these later in the chapter.

Cases

Laptop cases are as manufacturer-specific as the motherboard that they use. They are a 'clamshell' design – that is, the lid that incorporates the display is designed to close over a specially modified keyboard layout when the case is closed. Considerations such as cost and availability of a laptop case out of warranty are the same as those noted for motherboards above.

Docking stations and port replicators

Some laptop systems are intended to be used as replacements for desktop systems and the capabilities of the laptop system may be extended by connecting it to a *docking station* through a docking port built into the laptop – these are manufacturer-specific – or through one of the standard interfaces such as USB. The docking station is a permanent fixture in (say) the office and provides a connection through a single port for the laptop system. The docking station acts, in effect, as an extension of the motherboard and may contain full-size drive bays and expansion slots that the laptop can access while it is connected.

A *port replicator* is similar in so far as it allows access to additional peripherals through a single port on the laptop machine. Rather than connecting, say, a full-size keyboard, mouse and monitor directly to the ports on the laptop each time it is used, the additional peripherals are connected permanently to the individual ports on the port replicator and the laptop is dropped into place and connected through a single port when needed.

Accessory bays are the external bays on a laptop that allow for the connection of external devices such as disk drives. They are also referred to as laptop drive bays.

The essential difference between these laptop extensions is the level of extra functionality they provide: a docking station is like connecting to a full-featured PC, motherboard and all; a port replicator allows connection to a group of externally connected peripherals through a single port on the laptop; accessory or drive bays are built-in features of a laptop that allow for connection of additional components.

Expansion slots

PCMCIA types I, II and III

The Personal Computer Memory Card International Association (PCMCIA) is a trade association with a web site at www.pcmcia.org. It defines the standards for expansion cards used to extend the capabilities of laptop systems. The PCMCIA name tag was dropped from the description of the expansion bus and the card that it supports and is now known as PC Card or, in later versions, Cardbus.

The expansion cards are roughly the size of a credit card and come in three types – I, II, and III – which are of different thicknesses. They are mainly used on laptop machines, but can also be deployed on desktop PCs.

Table 11.1 Sizes and typical uses of PCMCIA cards.

Type	Thickness	Connectors	Typical use
I	3.3 mm	1 row of connectors	Memory cards
II	5.0 mm	2 rows of connectors	LAN adapters, modems, sound cards
III	10.5 mm	4 rows of connectors	PC Card hard disks

All cards in all versions are 85.6 mm long and 54.0 mm wide. The original specification was for a bus that supported only memory expansion, but the second release (PCMCIA 2) extended support to other devices. The third release of the specification – known, confusingly, as PCMCIA 5 – increased the bus width from the earlier 16 bits to the current 32 bits. 16-bit cards are designed to fit in a 32-bit slot, but 32-bit cards are keyed to prevent insertion into a 16-bit slot.

Like any device attached to a PC, PCMCIA cards require BIOS and operating system support:

- Socket services: a layer of BIOS-level software that detects insertion and removal of cards

- Card services: a higher level of software that manages IRQ assignments and I/O addresses after the card has been detected.

Note: PC card architecture is not tied to the Intel platform, it is fully supported by Apple thus allowing Modem and LAN cards to be used interchangeably across hardware platforms.

Mini PCI

As the name suggests, this is an adaptation of the standard PCI bus that is a standard part of desktop systems. Mini PCI cards are fitted internally in the laptop with the connector ports lining up with the edge of the case. Functionally, mini PCI provides the same services as its full-sized counterpart. You usually have to unscrew a back panel, as in memory installation, to access the slot. Form factors and pin counts are shown in Table 11.2.

Table 11.2 Mini PCI form factors.

Type	Connector	Size (millimetres)
I A	100 pin, stacking	7.5 × 70 × 45
I B	100 pin, stacking	5.5 × 70 × 45
II A	100 pin, stacking	7.5 × 70 × 45
II B	100 pin, stacking	17.44 × 78 × 45
III A	124 pin, card edge	2.4 × 59.6 × 50.95
III B	124 pin, card edge	2.4 × 59.6 × 44.6

The extra pins on the Type III cards allow information to be sent back to the system for audio, phone or network devices. Anything available as a full-sized PCI card is feasible as a mini PCI and vice versa and there are adapters to convert between the two physical formats.

Express bus

This is a type of USB hub that allows for the connection of multiple USB devices to a single USB port on the PC. Hubs can be daisy-chained and there is a theoretical limit of 127 devices – with the hubs themselves being part of the device count.

Other ports

In addition to their own characteristic ports for docking stations and port replicators, laptop systems usually have all of the standard ports that you would expect of a desktop PC for video output and the attachment of an external keyboard and / or mouse, as well as USB and FireWire (IEEE 1394) general purpose ports. Ports and connectors are considered in detail in Chapter 5 (see pages 67–72).

Communications connections

Bluetooth

Bluetooth is a wireless communication standard for Wireless Personal Area Networks. It is not intended for use with structured networks, but for short distance communication between devices such as phones, cameras, microphones and, of course, PCs. Many modern laptop PCs in particular are Bluetooth-enabled. Bluetooth devices use a radio frequency that does not require a licence, and devices 'discover' one another when they come in range. A typical use is for ad hoc connections for tasks such as the transfer of files from phones or PDAs to a PC. The current version of Bluetooth is 2.1, which is backward-compatible with earlier versions.

The range of a Bluetooth device depends on its class and its power rating, of which there are three.

- Class 1 devices have a maximum power rating of 100 milliwatts and a range of 100 metres.

- Class 2 devices have a maximum power rating of 2.5 milliwatts and a range of 10 metres.

- Class 3 devices have a maximum power rating of 1 milliwatt and a range of 1 metre.

Line of sight is not necessary for communication, but it can help at the extremes of range. Where a PC does not have Bluetooth capability built in, it can be added by using an adapter that fits in a USB port and looks quite similar to a 'pen drive', and is particularly suitable for the sort of ad hoc communications that use Bluetooth. Figure 11.2 shows a typical USB Bluetooth adapter.

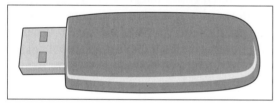

Figure 11.2

Bluetooth technology is also described in Chapter 14 Network connectivity (see pages 240–241).

Infrared

Infrared is an older technology than Bluetooth. The port is usually on the front of a desktop PC or on the side of it. It is usually dark maroon in colour and rectangular in shape. Communications are line of sight only and restricted to four metres between devices. A typical use is point-to-point short range communications such as remote controls. Infrared, as a computing technology, is controlled by a trade association – the Infrared Data Association – and their website (www.irda.org) is a source of up-to-date information.

Infrared is also described in Chapter 14 Network connectivity (see page 240).

Cellular WAN

This is essentially an extension of mobile phone technology to computing. A cellular network is provided (usually by a phone company) and appropriately enabled devices can access the network as a subscription service. Devices that use cellular WAN technology are, typically, mobile phones and hand-held devices such as Personal Digital Assistants

(PDAs). The best known of these is probably the BlackBerry, which is typically used for mobile email access to corporate email systems which use a BlackBerry Enterprise Server. Some laptop manufacturers fit their machines with antennae, which make it possible to connect to a service to which you subscribe.

Cellular WAN communications are also described in Chapter 14 Network Connectivity (see page 241).

Ethernet

Ethernet is the most widely used networking technology in personal computing. Nearly all systems are equipped with wireless or wired (or both) Ethernet adapters. Where an adapter is not built into the system, you can add one through PCMCIA / Cardbus or a USB adapter.

Ethernet is described in some detail in Chapter 14 Network connectivity (see page 240) and underlies the bulk of the material in Chapters 13 and 15.

Power and electrical input devices

Like all PCs, laptop machines require a steady supply of *direct current* in order to function. In a desktop PC, the conversion of the *alternating current* to direct current (AC / DC conversion) is usually performed by the internally mounted Power Supply Unit (PSU). Laptop machines use either an external unit, which performs the necessary conversions or battery power. When a PC is attached to the mains supply, its battery is being recharged. When it is switched to battery power, the system will sense this and will implement power-saving measures. Power management is considered later in this chapter (see page 194).

Power sources

Like most components of portable systems, there are no generally accepted standards for power sources. Both external sources – adapters that convert mains power – and various battery types vary greatly between manufacturers and even between models from the same manufacturer.

AC adapter

An AC adapter for a portable computer does the same job as its counterpart in a desktop machine. It takes alternating current AC mains power, reduces the voltage to that which is appropriate to a PC and converts the AC power to direct current DC.

These units are external to the portable machine and although they use a standard plug at the mains power end, there are many different connector types at the computer end. Even where these may be plug-compatible, the voltage and current delivery capacity may be different on different systems and you can damage a system by using the wrong AC adapter. In general, use only the proprietary adapter intended for that particular make and model of portable machine.

DC adapter

These are also external units. They convert and condition external direct current sources – such as the cigarette lighter socket in a car – to meet the voltage and current requirements of the portable system. As with AC adapters, these are proprietary units and even where they are plug-compatible, the voltage and current delivery capacity may be different on different systems and you can damage a system by using the wrong adapter. In general, use only the proprietary adapter intended for that particular make and model of portable machine.

Battery

Extending battery life has always been one of the major aims of the manufacturers of portable systems. Hardware is designed for minimal power consumption and modern machines – portable or desktop – have power-saving features. Power management is discussed later in the chapter, but for all the sophistication of modern hardware and operating systems in this respect, the main determinant of battery life is the type of battery in use. The main types are:

- **Alkaline**. These are the familiar type used in calculators, tape recorders, etc. They are disposable after a single use and relatively cheap. You are more likely to encounter these in very small hand-held devices than in PCs.

- **Nickel cadmium**. These are cheap rechargeables. They contain many toxic substances and require special disposal requirements at the end of their life – typically 700 or so charge / discharge cycles.

- **Nickel-metal hydride**. These are more expensive and less toxic but have a shorter life – typically 400 charge / discharge cycles.

- **Lithium Ion**. These are the most expensive and probably the battery of choice – where you have a choice – as they are very lightweight, hold twice the power of nickel cadmium and will run for around twice as long on each charging. These are the most commonly used battery types in PCs.

Laptop displays – LCD technologies

Given the sheer bulk of a CRT monitor, a successful portable design only became possible with the development of flat-panel monitors that could be built into the lid of a notebook system.

There are different types of flat-panel display technologies, but the most commonly encountered types are:

- **Active Matrix / TFT**. This is the higher quality of the two display types. It employs Thin Film Transistor (TFT) technology, which has a transistor for each pixel in the display. It has relatively high power consumption and can drain a notebook battery in a couple of hours.

▪ **Passive Matrix.** This is an older (and cruder) technology in which there is a row of transistors for the vertical axis and another row for the horizontal axis. The display itself consists of a matrix of wires, and a pixel is darkened by sending a current to its x, y coordinates from the controlling rows of transistors. This uses less power, but is slower and produces a lower-quality image.

Resolutions

Screen resolutions are measured by the number of pixels used to display the screen image: the greater the number of pixels, the greater the level of detail. Displays are described in terms of the grid of pixels they use, thus a screen display of 1024 rows of pixels with 768 pixels will be written as 1024 × 768 and, if you do the arithmetic, you can see that this amounts to a total of 786,432 pixels. Obviously the greater the number of pixels used, the better the image will be, though at a cost of higher video memory requirements.

The *aspect ratio* of a display is expressed as the width of its image divided by its height, thus our 1024 × 768 display has an aspect ratio of 4:3, which is the standard aspect ratio for standard (CRT) desktop monitors and television sets. However, modern high-definition television displays and newer monitors may use an aspect ratio of 16:9 or 16:10. Table 11.3 shows some of the common LCD standards listed in the exam specification and their aspect ratios.

Table 11.3

Display	Resolution	Ratio
Extended Graphics Array (XGA)	800 × 600	4:3
	1024 × 768	4:3
Super Extended Graphics Array plus (SXGA+)	1400 × 1050	4:3
Ultra Extended Graphics Array (UXGA)	1600 × 1200	4:3
Widescreen Extended Graphics Array (WUXGA)	1920 × 1200	16:10

There are other video standards – over 20 of them – and, like many areas of computing, there are constant new developments. For the Essentials exam, you should know the more common ones and what they mean.

Native resolution

Unlike CRT monitors that may support a number of resolutions equally well, LCD displays have a single native resolution compatible with the graphics adapter. This does not normally produce problems because the display on a laptop is proprietary and specific to that make and model and built into the lid of the clamshell case. Providing that you replace like with like (and you probably will not have much choice in the matter) when replacing a defective panel, you will not experience any problems. If you attach an external LCD monitor to a port, you will need to check that you are using the appropriate settings to avoid the distortion that will occur if you set the wrong resolution or aspect ratio.

Contrast ratio

The contrast ratio of a display is a measure of the ratio of the darkest colour to the lightest colour that the screen can show. A higher ratio is better than a lower one because the difference in intensity between dark and light colours is the main determinant of the clarity of the display. Ratios for LCD monitors at the bottom end of the price / performance scale generally start with a ratio of 500:1, though ratios of 600:1 and 800:1 are not uncommon. Higher-end monitors may have a contrast ratio of 1200:1 or more. However, the choice of a monitor is highly subjective and the real test (for you or your customer) is to try it and see.

Input devices

Keyboards

The keyboard of a laptop PC has to fit into the lower half of the clamshell case so the keys tend to be smaller and closer together than on a standard keyboard. The layout of the letter keys follows the standard QWERTY layout, but 'special' keys such as Home, Insert, etc. may not be present on older machines, or may be in non-standard locations.. To access the functions normally provided by these keys, there is an additional function key – usually labelled Fn – which modifies the actions of one of the regular keys. Just as holding down the Shift key and a letter key causes the system to display the upper case version of the character, holding down the Fn key allows you to access the additional function allocated to that key. There is usually no separate numeric keypad, but some standard keys may be labelled for use as numeric keys by using the Fn key to activate them as an alternative to the 'top row' of the standard QWERTY layout. In addition to the built-in keyboard, you can also attach a standard a desktop-style keyboard through a PS/2 or USB port.

Stylus / digitiser

A stylus is essentially a pointing stick which has neither ink (as in a pen) nor any electrical connection. Styli (or styluses, if you prefer) are commonly used with touch screens or, more frequently, with the smaller displays of Personal Digital Assistants (PDAs) or Tablet PC machines. Its advantages over pointing with a finger are lack of grease from the skin – which can be a problem with full-sized touch screens – and its accuracy. The business end of a stylus is comparable in diameter with that of a sharpened pencil and it can be used to draw or hand-write characters on the input surface of a PDA, which then digitises the (analogue) input for processing and storage by the hand-held device.

Pointing devices

The standard pointing device for most systems is the mouse, and other pointing devices have the same basic functions: the user can point to an object on screen and select it by 'clicking' on it. Most laptop systems allow you to connect a standard mouse though either a PS/2 or USB port.

Alternatives / complements to mice include:

- **Trackball.** The trackball is much like a mouse that has been turned upside down. The ball is moved by thumb or fingers and there are buttons for selecting by clicking. These were cheap to produce, but finger grease and dust from the atmosphere meant that – like ball mice – they deteriorate quickly with use and need frequent cleaning. They are no longer widely used.

- **Touchpad.** This is actually a tradename of a product but it has been so widely used to describe similar devices that it is generally regarded as a generic term. A touchpad is a rectangle of touch-sensitive material usually sited just below the laptop keyboard. The user draws on the touch-sensitive rectangle and the cursor moves across the display. There are also two buttons, which correspond to the buttons of a mouse. In addition, you can usually left-click by tapping the surface of the touch-sensitive rectangle.

- **Touchpoint.** The touchpoint was introduced by IBM with their Thinkpad series of laptops. It is also known as a finger mouse. It consists of a small rubber-tipped stick – usually in the centre of the keyboard – that allows you to move the on-screen pointer much as you would with a mouse. The main problem with these is a tendency to 'drift' off centre as they deteriorate with age.

- **Touchscreen.** This is more usually found on full-sized displays in which a user points and 'clicks' with a finger-end on the screen. It has been adapted for use in Tablet PC laptops where the device is held like a pad of paper. This type of device may also support input with a stylus (see above).

Motherboards

The probability of your ever having to replace a motherboard in a portable system is small. Motherboards are usually designed to fit in a particular case which is, in turn, part of the design of a particular model or a narrow range of models. Replacement motherboards are therefore expensive. Nearly every new system sold will have at least a year's warranty from the manufacturer who will replace a defective motherboard – or even the whole unit – during the warranty period. By the time the warranty period is over, technology has moved on, prices have fallen and hardware specifications have increased to the point where replacing a major proprietary component is probably not cost-effective.

The standard form factors for motherboards – ATX, Micro-ATX, BTX, etc. – simply do not apply to the manufacturer-specific designs used in portable systems. The chief characteristic of laptop motherboards is the fact that they have nearly all the standard ports and connectors integrated into the board and there are no on-board expansion slots. The most commonly used functional equivalent of the PCI slot on a desktop motherboard is the Cardbus / PCMCIA slot, which is a feature of most laptop PCs.

Processors

Like all laptop components, CPU chips are designed to economise on space and with a view to reducing the operating temperature of the system as far as possible. Frequently, they are not attached to the motherboard by pins in a ZIF socket – like most of the desktop processors that you will encounter – but use some variant of the Flip Chip Ball Grid Array (FCBGA) or are soldered directly to the board. Recently, however, many of the major manufacturers have started to use ZIF sockets on newer machines and this may be a consideration when buying a new portable system. With a ZIF socket, it may be technically feasible to replace or upgrade a laptop processor, though whether or not it will be cost-effective is open to doubt.

From the point of view of a working technician, the important aspects of laptop CPUs are their speed and performance ratings – so that you can select or advise on purchase decisions – and knowledge of how to configure them especially in terms of the power management features which are discussed later in the chapter.

Popular laptop processors

The processor market is dominated by the two big names, Intel and AMD, and of these, Intel is the larger manufacturer of mobile CPUs.

Intel introduced the Pentium® M series of chips in 2003 – the 'M' indicating 'Mobile' – as a replacement for its earlier Pentium® 4 Mobile (P4 M).

Intel's Centrino® platform is a marketing initiative introduced in March 2003 and upgraded a couple of times since. It is not, however, a chip. The Centrino® label may only be applied to a system by a manufacturer if it uses an approved Intel chip in conjunction with a qualifying motherboard chipset and wireless network interface. Systems that do not meet the Centrino® requirements – that use only the CPU chip and chipset – carry the Intel Core™ label instead.

Intel Core™ chips are sold in solo and duo formats – that is there is a single-core and dual-core version available. In fact, the chips are identical internally, but have either one or two cores enabled depending on how they are badged. Neither of these chips support 64-bit operations however, so a newer range of chips were introduced in 2006 under the name of Intel Core 2. Like their predecessors, they are available as single-core or dual-core processors and there is an Extreme model which is quad-core. All of the Core 2 processors are 64-bit.

Advanced Micro Devices (AMD) also produce a range of laptop processors, which they simply tag as Mobile. The current range of AMD Mobile processors is:

- Mobile AMD Sempron™ – a budget chip that supports only 32-bit operations.

- Mobile AMD Athlon™ 64 – supports 32-bit and 64-bit operation.

- Mobile AMD Turion™ 64 Mobile Technology – supports 32-bit and 64-bit operation. Generally deployed in 'thin' and 'light' notebook systems.

- AMD Turion™ 64 X2 Dual-Core Mobile Technology– supports 32-bit and 64-bit operation.

Throttling

Both heat and power consumption are particularly important considerations on laptop systems. One of the means of reducing power consumption and heat production is 'throttling' back a processor when it is not necessary to use it at full power. Two commonly encountered proprietary technologies used to achieve this are Intel's Speedstep® which can reduce CPU clock speed and voltage, and AMD's Power Now!™, which provides similar functionality for their chips. Throttling is discussed in Chapter 2 (see page 32) in the context of CPUs for both desktop and laptop machines.

Power management

Power management is a feature of all modern PCs, but is especially significant in portable systems because of the significance of heat and, crucially, battery life. A laptop PC that is running flat out while not actually doing any work is not just wasting power and generating unnecessary heat, it is reducing the lifespan of the battery.

Power management is a feature of the Basic Input Output System (BIOS) and uses the Advanced Configuration and Power Interface (ACPI). BIOS-ACPI was first released as an open standard in 1996 and will be found on just about any modern PC – desktop or laptop. Figure 11.3 shows the power saving settings in a Phoenix BIOS.

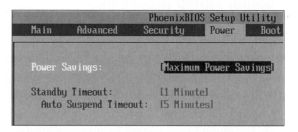

Figure 11.3

Providing that the hardware is ACPI compliant – and on modern systems it almost invariably is – both Microsoft Windows® 2000 and XP allow the user to control the power settings. Like many settings in Microsoft Windows®, the controls can be accessed through the Control Panel. Clicking on the **Power Options** applet allows you to select one of the pre-configured power schemes or to modify one of them and save it under its own name.

The Power Options applet is available on all Microsoft Windows® PCs, but on a laptop there are a couple of additional tabs: one for a Power Meter and another for Alarms. Figure 11.4 shows these on a laptop which is running XP Professional.

Figure 11.4

The Power Meter monitors battery life and you can access it by clicking on the battery icon which is in the System Tray / Notification Area on the right of the Microsoft Windows® task bar. The Alarms tab allows you to configure how the system will respond when battery power gets low. The Alarms tab allows you to activate an alarm when battery power level reaches low battery or critical battery thresholds and set the action that the system should take when one of these thresholds is reached. Figure 11.5 shows some typical settings for a laptop system.

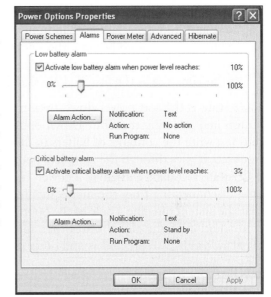

Figure 11.5

Features of BIOS-ACPI

The power management features you can set through Microsoft Windows® or the BIOS set-up utility depend on the implementation of ACPI in BIOS. This defines four power level states that apply to the whole system and they are numbered from G0 to G3. These are known as *global* states.

Global states

G0 state is the normal operational state and all devices are assumed to be working at full power, although some devices can be put into lower power modes – 'C' and 'D' states. These are examined below.

G1 state is known as 'sleeping' and has four modes labelled as S1 to S4. The higher the number of the sleep mode, the greater will be the power savings. The system will take slightly longer to wake from the higher-numbered modes.

- S1 mode uses the most power. The CPU stops processing and its cache is flushed, but both CPU and RAM are still fully powered up. Other devices that are in use are powered down.

- S2 mode uses less power because the processor is powered down. This is not often implemented.

- S3 mode is the Microsoft Windows® Standby mode. In this state, power is maintained to system memory (RAM). Because information about running applications is stored in RAM, they can be restarted by the user at the press of a key. This mode is also known as 'suspend to RAM'.

- S4 mode is what Microsoft Windows® calls 'hibernation'. In this mode, the contents of RAM are written to a disk file and when the system is brought out of hibernation, the contents of the disk file are read into RAM and the system can resume from where it left off. Hibernation mode is also known as 'suspend to disk'. It takes longer to restart from hibernation than from standby, but suspend to disk mode can survive even a power failure because the information is held in a disk file. Where hibernation is enabled on a system, the information is held in a file called hiberfil.sys, which is the same size as the installed physical RAM on the system.

G2 state is the soft power-down option that most of us use by clicking on the **Start** button and selecting the **Shut Down** option. This causes Microsoft Windows® to save settings, write the contents of buffers to disk and shut down cleanly. When the system is restarted, it goes through the complete boot sequence.

G3 state is usually caused by a power failure or – where a system is completely locked up – disconnecting from the mains supply. Obviously, recovery from this state requires that the system runs the whole of the boot process.

In addition to the global states that apply to the whole system, there are states that apply individually to processors and other devices.

Processor states

C0 state is the normal fully working state of the CPU. No power saving is implemented in this state.

C1 state is also known as the 'halt' state. The CPU does not process instructions in this state, but can resume all but instantaneously.

C2 state is also known as 'stop clock' state. The processor remains visible to applications but takes longer to wake up.

C3 state is Sleep mode, in which the processor cache is flushed. Restoration from this mode takes longer than from the C1 or C2 states.

Device states

There are four *device* states that apply to peripheral devices and details of each are device dependent. In outline they are:

- D0 state – fully operational
- D1 state – power saving, but implementation details are device specific
- D2 state – power saving, but implementation details are device specific
- D3 state – turned off

Performance states

While a device of a processor is working (C0 or D0 state) it may implement some form of power saving through a series of *performance states*. These are implementation dependent and have proprietary names, but in outline, P0 is the highest performance state and successive numbers up to 16 indicate higher levels of power saving and lower levels of performance.

Managing power saving in Microsoft Windows®

The Power schemes tab displayed by the
Power Options applet presents you with a
drop-down list from which you can select one
of the predetermined power schemes for the
system. These include Home/Office Desk,
Portable/Laptop, Always on, etc. You can
modify any of these schemes to suit your preferences and save it under its own name.
Whether you choose one of the predetermined schemes or create your own, the
variables under your control from this tab are
the timings that control when power-saving
measures are implemented. Figure 11.6 shows
the settings for a laptop system, which are different depending on whether the machine is
running on mains or battery power.

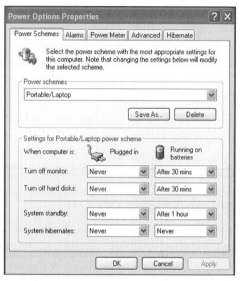

Figure 11.6

Under this power scheme, the laptop has
no power saving in place when it is running on
mains power and power-saving measures when running on batteries. As you can see from
the figure, this system has been configured so that when running on batteries, inactivity
for 30 minutes will result in the system turning off the display in order to conserve power.
Hard disks will be stopped after 30 minutes of inactivity and, after an hour, the system
will go into standby mode. This corresponds to the S3 state outlined previously.

The Advanced tab displayed by the Power Options applet allows you to show an icon
in the task bar that indicates whether the system is running on mains or battery power,
to password-protect the system on resuming from standby, and to determine what the
system will do when the Power Off button is pressed.

Hibernation is controlled through its own tab. When hibernation is enabled and the
system is unused for a selected time period, the system will go into Hibernation mode,
which corresponds to the S4 state outlined earlier.

Power management is also discussed in Chapter 2 (see page 32).

Wi-Fi

Wi-Fi is generally thought to be a contraction of Wireless Fidelity and is the trademark
of the trade association the Wi-Fi Alliance, though they discourage the notion that the
trademark stands for anything. Nearly every laptop system that you encounter will be
Wi-Fi compliant, usually through connectivity that is built into the motherboard or
through an adapter in one of the expansion slots such as mini PCI or PCMCIA /
Cardbus. Any system carrying the Intel Centrino® mark is Wi-Fi compliant, though you
should bear in mind that Centrino® is a marketing term, not a chip type.

Wireless networking is based on the IEEE 802.11x standards and is a form of Ethernet
– see the Ethernet section earlier in the chapter (see page 188) and its references to the
networking chapters of the book.

Safely removing hardware

There is little in the way of removable internal hardware components on laptop systems. The most you should expect to have to do is a RAM upgrade or to add or remove a mini PCI card. These tasks are essentially similar to their counterparts in desktop PCs and the key considerations – antistatic precautions, checking for compatibility, etc. – are the same.

Peripheral devices

The majority of devices that are used to expand the functionality of laptops and portable systems are added as peripheral devices attached to either a manufacturer-specific hardware interface or, increasingly these days, one of the standard ports such as USB, FireWire or PCMCIA / Cardbus.

Hot-swappable devices

USB, FireWire and Cardbus devices are generally hot-swappable; that is they can simply be connected or disconnected without harm to the system. On connection a device that has been installed will simply be recognised and Microsoft Windows® will indicate this. However, you should be careful that the device in question is not in use when you come to disconnect it. If, for example, you were to disconnect a USB printer in the middle of a print job you would, at best, lose the print job, although you are unlikely to have caused any real problems. However, Microsoft Windows® provides a safe way of removing peripherals. When a device is connected, the operating system recognises it, loads drivers and puts an icon in the system tray / notification area, which allows for safe removal. In Microsoft Windows® 2000, this is labelled Unplug or eject hardware, and in Microsoft Windows® XP it is labelled Safely Remove Hardware. In either case, clicking on the icon will give you information about the device and its current status and will confirm when it is safe to disconnect. Figure 11.7 shows a USB printer attached to a Microsoft Windows® XP machine.

Clicking on the Stop button will list the devices and prompt for confirmation and when this has been done and the device has been stopped, XP confirms this in one of its notification bubbles in the system tray as shown in Figure 11.8.

Figure 11.7

Figure 11.8

Microsoft Windows® 2000 provides the same functionality, but the notification is not a bubble but a Microsoft Windows® information box that is displayed on screen.

These features for safely removing peripherals are not, of course, peculiar to laptops but are provided by Microsoft Windows® irrespective of the PC type.

Non-hot-swappable devices

Where a device is not hot-swappable, it is necessary to power down the machine, remove the device and reboot and check that the system is functioning properly. Where the disconnection or removal is permanent, you may want to remove unnecessary software components such as drivers.

Diagnostics and troubleshooting

Diagnosing and troubleshooting a laptop system have many features in common with troubleshooting a desktop system and the basic procedures – backing up data, asking the user to reproduce the problem and generally adopting a calm systematic approach – have been discussed at some length in Chapter 7 (see page 94) (for hardware) and Chapter 10 (see page 160) (for operating systems). There are, however, four areas identified in the Essentials exam specification that are particularly applicable to laptop systems: power conditions, video problems, keyboard and pointer problems, and problems with wireless network cards.

Power problems

One of the basic principles of troubleshooting anything is to check the obvious first. In the case of a laptop PC, the first thing to check is that it has power. Check that the battery is properly connected by removing and reseating it. Then check that the mains power supply is working. If the mains power is okay at the wall socket, check the power adapter. Most power adapters have a light to indicate that they are working. If the power adapter appears not to be working, test its output with a multimeter and if you have a spare of the same type, try using that. You should only do this is if it is an identical specification; using the wrong adapter, even where it is plug-compatible, could damage the system.

Another of the fundamentals of all troubleshooting is to isolate the problem. On a desktop machine, you may have to power down, open the case and start systematically removing components. Because of the way laptops rely heavily on externally connected components, this is one of the (few) areas where working on a laptop is easier than working on a desktop PC. Remove devices in a systematic way to see if any of them is a cause of the problem. If this leads to no conclusion, follow the standard procedures for diagnosing operating system problems as you would for a desktop system; remove suspect software, temporarily disable any Terminate and Stay Resident (TSR) programs, and do not forget Safe Mode!

Video problems

As always, start with the obvious; that the system has power and that brightness and contrast controls on the display have not been turned down or off. Once you have disposed of the obvious, the next step is to attach a known good external monitor. All modern systems support the connection of an external monitor and, as often as not, all you need to do is to attach it and make sure that it has power. If there is a key that turns the LCD display on / off, then check it by pressing it a few times, waiting a few seconds between tries to see if this affects the video output. Some systems may require you to press some combination of keys to direct video output to an external device, so check the system-specific requirements in the manufacturer's documentation.

Where a system will send video output to an external monitor but fails to display on its own built-in LCD, then it is probably the laptop display that has failed. In this case, you may be able to buy and fit a replacement but for a machine that is old enough to be out of manufacturer's warranty, you need to consider carefully if this is likely to be a cost-effective solution. Where a system fails to send output to either its own or a known good external monitor, the problem is almost certainly with the motherboard (although you cannot completely rule out the possibility that it is both motherboard and display) so, whatever the technical considerations, you need to consider whether any repair option will be preferable to replacement.

On small hand-held devices – palm-top-style systems – you should try turning the back light feature on or off; you will probably need to consult the manufacturer's documentation to find out how to do this.

Problems with input devices

Because laptop keyboards are built into the case, they cannot be quickly or easily swapped out. However, you should be able to connect a PS/2 or USB external keyboard to an available port to isolate any keyboard problems.

A keyboard problem that is laptop-specific is the Function key – usually labelled Fn – which is used in the fashion of a Shift key to modify the behaviour of the standard keys. If this becomes stuck, then only the modified behaviour of the standard keys will be available – try toggling it just as you would any other 'special' key such as the Caps Lock or Num Lock keys.

Other problems unique to laptops are with Touchpoint and Touchpad features. On many systems, these can be configured for sensitivity or even disabled altogether. In order to check or modify the working of these components, open the Microsoft Windows® Control Panel and work with the appropriate applets. A 'failed' device may actually have been accidentally disabled though the Control Panel.

Where a system – such as a hand-held or tablet PC – uses a touch screen, this may indicate that the digitiser that converts mechanical analogue input to computer processable digital signals has failed. The answer may be (specialist) repair or replacement if this is judged to be cost-effective.

Networking problems

Many of the networking problems that you may encounter will be similar to those familiar from work with desktop systems: IP address, default gateway address, and so on. These are outlined in the networking chapters: 13 (see page 224), 14 (see page 236) and 15 (see page 244).

Most modern laptops have wireless networking capabilities built into them and often the wireless antenna is built into the LCD panel housing. Alternatively, you may connect through a Cardbus LAN card or a USB LAN card. Whatever the connection type, it will almost certainly have some form of LED to indicate that it is working; this is the first (obvious) thing to check. Another 'obvious' point is that some laptops have a button to enable wireless connectivity and this is quite easy to overlook.

If the button is 'on' and the card is okay, then check settings in Microsoft Windows® to make sure that the device is enabled and that there are no driver problems. Some cards may have their own configuration utility that places its own applet in Control Panel in place of the Microsoft Windows® default utility. With a wireless network, you should also check the signal strength through Microsoft Windows® or proprietary software applicable to that particular card.

With a USB or Cardbus card, try removing and replacing the device, and where you have a conventional RJ45 LAN port to connect to a wired network, you can use this as a means of isolating wireless problems, that is if the system can connect to the network through a cable connection, then the network is okay and you have a problem – hardware, software or configuration – with the wireless LAN adapter.

Preventive maintenance

Many of the preventive maintenance procedures that apply to desktop PCs such as defragmenting disks and keeping device drivers and antivirus files up to date apply in equal measure to laptop systems. However, laptops have some additional requirements caused mainly by their design and patterns of use.

Operating environments

A desktop PC, once it has been set up, is not subjected to the same degree of environmental changes as a laptop, which may be taken from home, to office and back again; which may be used outdoors or on a factory floor, or transported on the back seat of the car after being stuffed in a rucksack or a supermarket carrier bag. In short, laptops can have a rough life and much of the preventive maintenance is the responsibility of the user rather than the technician. Part of your role as a support worker is to advise users on what is best practice in addition to any hands-on maintenance work that may be required from time to time.

A laptop system should be transported in its own carrying case or if that is not available, a proper laptop carrying case, which will give adequate protection from the knocks and shocks that it will be subjected to in transit. The nature of the folding clamshell case means that mechanical pressure can cause the keyboard to come into contact with the screen, leading to cumulative damage to the display. In addition to using a proper carrying case, then, it is a sensible precaution to place a screen-sized piece of foam or a heavy

cloth between the keyboard and the display when transporting it. This is how manufacturers usually pack their laptops for distribution so you may be able to save this part of
their packaging for your own use. Obviously, the arguments that apply to transporting a
laptop apply with equal force when preparing a system which is to be placed in storage.

Operating environments are perhaps a little easier to manage. The conditions that suit
a computer – not too hot, not too cold, moderate humidity and lack of dust – are the
same as those that suit their owners, so a good rule of thumb is that if you are comfortable, the PC will be okay. Obviously you should advise your users to avoid using the
machine for long periods in direct sunlight, extremes of temperature or conditions where
there is atmospheric dust. Where necessary, you may be able to physically clean the fan
on a laptop system to maintain or improve air flow without too much difficulty, though
the non-standard designs of laptop systems means that this may not always be feasible.

The biggest single threat to any microprocessor-based system is heat and the necessarily compact construction of laptop machines makes them especially prone to
overheating. This can be countered, if necessary, by using additional cooling devices such
as a *cooling pad*. This is a sort of box, about an inch high, on which you stand the laptop
PC. Fans in the cooling pad draw air under the system and remove heat from the underside of the system where it would normally be trapped by direct contact with the work
surface. Cooling pads are also available for other associated equipment such as docking
stations and port replicators.

Cleaning a laptop is not very different to cleaning a desktop PC; a natural bristle brush
and canned air can be used to clean the keyboard, and the outer case can be cleaned
with a damp cloth with mild detergent solution or a rub down with alcohol. Like any
LCD screen, the laptop display is especially sensitive to inappropriate cleaning materials
or methods. It is possible to clean an LCD screen with a soft cloth that has been moistened, but it is much better to use a cleaner that has been specifically produced for the
purpose. As with all cleaning and maintenance work on any system, it should be carried
out with the system powered down and where any moisture – alcohol or water – is
involved, the system should not be rebooted until it is fully dry.

SUMMARY

In this chapter, we have considered the particular needs and problems of portable systems, especially laptop PCs. We have noted that the number of serviceable hardware components on such systems is small and that most extensions to their functionality are achieved through devices that are connected through various hardware interfaces; some of them proprietary and others that use industry standard interfaces such as USB, FireWire / IEEE 1394 and PCMCIA / Cardbus cards. In addition to these physical connections, we have also considered other means of connectivity and communication such as Bluetooth and (wireless) Ethernet. We have looked at power supplies – mains and battery – and power management. We have considered troubleshooting of laptop systems and the tools and techniques required to clean and maintain them. Laptop systems are popular with users and they have developed from low-performance heavyweight 'luggables' to powerful modern systems that can come close to desktop performance, albeit at a higher cost. In terms of your work as a technician there is always a demand for people who will 'do laptops' because so many technicians dislike working on them. Laptop systems also account for 11 per cent of the Essentials exam.

QUESTIONS

1 You have been asked to fit additional RAM in a laptop system. You determine by physical examination that there is an empty RAM slot available. You remove the existing RAM stick to determine its type. It is a 172-pin DIMM type and there is no location notch on its underside. What form factor is this?

   a) Rambus RDIMM

   b) SODIMM

   c) MicroDIMM

   d) EDO RAM

2 You have been asked to increase the disk storage on a laptop PC running Microsoft Windows® XP Professional. The current hard disk has a capacity of 40 GB. Which of the following would be feasible methods of increasing storage capacity?

   a) Replace the hard disk with a larger one

   b) Use the compression facilities of Microsoft Windows® XP to store more data on the existing disk

   c) Fit a second internal hard disk

   d) Use a type III PCMCIA / Cardbus disk

▶

3   You have a laptop system that simply refuses to boot. You check that the mains power from the wall socket is working and the power adapter is displaying a light, which appears to indicate that it is working. What do you check next?

   a) The battery

   b) The DC output of the power adapter

   c) The fuse in the mains plug

   d) The connection between the adapter and the laptop

4   You are working on a laptop that won't display anything on its LCD display, though it boots and emits a single beep at the end of the boot sequence. You check the brightness and contrast controls and they appear to be okay. You then attach a known good monitor and this, too, fails to display anything from the system no matter what you try. Which of the following components in the laptop system is most likely to be at fault?

   a) The display

   b) The motherboard

   c) The power supply

   d) RAM

5   A user has asked your advice on cleaning a laptop display. Which of the following would you recommend?

   a) Water with a splash of lemon juice applied with a soft cloth

   b) Denatured alcohol applied with a soft cloth

   c) Pre-wrapped 'screen wipes' for LCD displays from a PC shop

   d) Window cleaning fluid

ANSWERS / EXPLANATIONS

1   You have been asked to fit additional RAM in a laptop system. You determine by physical examination that there is an empty RAM slot available. You remove the existing RAM stick to determine its type. It is a 172-pin DIMM type and there is no location notch on its underside. What form factor is this?

c) MicroDIMM

MicroDIMMs are asymmetric so they do not need a notch to ensure proper orientation.

2   You have been asked to increase the disk storage on a laptop PC running Microsoft Windows® XP Professional. The current hard disk has a capacity of 40 GB. Which of the following would be feasible methods of increasing storage capacity?

a) Replace the hard disk with a larger one

b) Use the compression facilities of Microsoft Windows® XP to store more data on the existing disk

d) Use a type III PCMCIA / Cardbus disk

Option c is not feasible because there is no room for a second disk in a laptop. Option d is possible but would use all of the PCMCIA slot capacity. Answers a and b are commonplace solutions.

3   You have a laptop system that simply refuses to boot. You check that the mains power from the wall socket is working and the power adapter is displaying a light which appears to indicate that it is working. What do you check next?

d) The connection between the adapter and the laptop

This is quick and easy to check; poor-quality connections are also the most common causes of hardware failures on any system. Answer b would be the next logical step after a basic connectivity check. The status of the battery is irrelevant in this context and the fuse in the wall plug must be okay or the light on the power adapter would not be lit.

▶

4   You are working on a laptop that won't display anything on its LCD display, though it boots and emits a single beep at the end of the boot sequence. You check the brightness and contrast controls and they appear to be okay. You then attach a known good monitor and this, too, fails to display anything from the system no matter what you try. Which of the following components in the laptop system is most likely to be at fault?

b) The motherboard

The motherboard is the most likely cause of this failure, though the possibility that answer a – the display – is also faulty should be considered.

5   A user has asked your advice on cleaning a laptop display. Which of the following would you recommend?

c) Pre-wrapped 'screen wipes' for LCD displays from a PC shop

CHAPTER 12
Printers and scanners

Working with printers and scanners is part of the technician's everyday work. Each generation of printers and scanners offers a greater number of features than the previous generation so there is much more to know about the machines themselves and various connectivity technologies than there used to be. The material in this chapter covers all of the objectives of the printers and scanners domain and accounts for 9 per cent of the marks in the Essentials exam.

Exam objectives 4.1, 4.2 & 4.3
4.1 Identify the fundamental principles of using printers and scanners

Identify differences between types of printer and scanner technologies (e.g. laser, inkjet, thermal, solid ink, impact).

Identify names, purposes and characteristics of printer and scanner components (e.g. memory, driver, firmware) and consumables (e.g. toner, ink cartridge, paper).

Identify the names, purposes and characteristics of interfaces used by printers and scanners including port and cable types, for example:

    Parallel
    Network (e.g. NIC, print servers)
    USB
    Serial
    IEEE 1394 / FireWire
    Wireless (e.g. Bluetooth, 802.11, infrared)
    SCSI

4.2 Identify basic concepts of installing, configuring, optimising and upgrading printers and scanners
Install and configure printers / scanners.
Power and connect the device using local or network port.
Install and update device driver and calibrate the device.
Configure options and default settings.

▶

Print a test page.

Optimise printer performance, for example: printer settings such as tray switching, print spool settings, device calibration, media types and paper orientation.

4.3 Identify tools, basic diagnostic procedures and troubleshooting techniques for printers and scanners

Gather information about printer / scanner problems.

Identify symptom.

Review device error codes, computer error messages and history (e.g. event log, user reports).

Print or scan test page.

Use appropriate generic or vendor-specific diagnostic tools including web-based utilities.

Review and analyse collected data.

Establish probable causes.

Review service documentation.

Review knowledge base and define and isolate the problem (e.g. software vs. hardware, driver, connectivity, printer).

Identify solutions to identified printer / scanner problems.

Define specific cause and apply fix.

Replace consumables as needed.

Verify functionality and get user acceptance of problem fix.

Printer and scanner technologies

Printers and scanners are both used to transfer images – text, pictures or both – between electronic files and paper or other 'stock' such as overhead projector pages. The basic technologies for doing this are the same and many scanners these days are built into printer / scanner combination devices. The fundamental technologies for printers use a number of well-established technologies, as well as some newer ones.

Laser printers

In the commercial world, the laser printer is the most common printer type that you will encounter and, with the downward trend in all hardware prices, they are becoming increasingly popular with home and micro-business users.

The laser-printing process was developed by Xerox and is known as *electrophotographic reproduction*. There are some variants on the laser-printing process, but these are mainly a matter of patent law. In order to work with laser printers and to troubleshoot them, you need to understand the generic process.

1   **Cleaning**. The photosensitive drum is electrically erased, that is the previous image is removed.

2   **Charging**. The drum is given a uniform negative charge by the primary corona.

3   **Writing**. The laser sweeps the length of the drum, writing the image, much as the 'gun' in a CRT monitor sweeps the display, illuminating particular pixels. The laser reduces the negative charge to −100v on the drum. This lower-charged area is the image to be printed, although at this stage it is simply an electric charge invisible to the human eye.

4   **Developing**. As the developing roller moves past the drum, toner is pulled to the lower-charged areas on the drum that have been exposed to laser light.

5   **Transferring**. Once the image is on the drum, as a coating of toner held in place by static electricity, the paper is fed through the printer and the transfer corona wire attracts the image from the drum to the paper. This is achieved by giving the paper positive charge, which attracts the negatively charged toner on to the paper.

6   **Fusing**. The image is now fused on to the paper by passing it through a heated roller, which uses a non-stick roller surface to prevent the toner fusing with the roller rather than the paper. This final fusing process accounts for the slightly 'cooked' feel of a fresh laser print.

One of the key elements in laser printing is the make-up of the toner. It is an extremely fine (almost liquid) powder, consisting of plastic particles bonded to iron particles. The presence of iron means that the toner is susceptible to electromagnetic fields, so it can be attracted to the drum, etc., and the plastic means that it can be fused to the paper to give a stable human-readable image.

Inkjet printers

Ink dispersion printer is the generic name for printers more commonly referred to as inkjet and bubble-jet printers. This printer type squirts a stream of ink drops on to the paper (or other print medium). There are two fairly similar technologies used to achieve this: *thermal shock* and *mechanical vibration*. Thermal shock 'boils' the ink in a capillary tube behind the nozzle in the print head and then it is squirted on to the paper. Mechanical vibration achieves the same effect by using a *piezoelectric crystal*. This crystal type has the property of expanding when an electric charge is applied to it and this is used to force ink through the nozzles in the print head.

Inkjets form an image by squirting very small dots of ink on to the paper. The print quality is measured by the number of these dots per inch and may range from 150 Dots Per Inch (DPI) to 1400.

There are various arrangements for supplying ink to the printer. Usually there is a cartridge of black ink and a combined magenta / cyan / yellow (red / blue / yellow) cartridge. Separate cartridges for each of the colours are increasingly popular.

Some printers have the print head built into the reservoir so that the electronics are replaced every time the ink is renewed. Other printers have the print head as part of the printer itself, so that only the ink and its container are replaced. Clearly there are price / reliability trade-offs here and this is a decision to be made when considering a new printer.

Impact printers

Although laser and inkjet printers are the dominant printer types for business and home use, there is still a place for the older impact printers. Like the typewriter, an *impact* printer forms an image on the paper by striking through an inked (or similarly coated) typewriter-style ribbon. A number of typewriter technologies were carried forward to the computer era such as the 'Golf Ball' and the 'Daisy Wheel' but these are to all intents and purposes antiques. The only commonly encountered impact printer in modern use is the *dot matrix* printer, which is chiefly used where verifiable copies of documents such as sales invoices in point-of-sale applications are required; multipart forms – such as invoices – can be seen to be authentic copies if they are printed by impact methods on pre-printed and sequentially numbered forms.

Dot matrix printers use an array of pins – or printwires – in the print head to strike an inked ribbon to produce images on paper. The usual number of pins is 9, 18 or 24. Printers with 24 pins are capable of producing Near Letter Quality (NLQ) output; those with fewer pins produce 'draft' quality output.

The printer 'sees' the print image in much the same way as a monitor: a series of dots which may be 'on' or 'off'.

In order to print, paper is pulled through a set of rollers and around a drum (platen). The print head moves across the length of the line, and the printwires strike the paper through a typewriter-style ribbon. Higher-quality (NLQ) printing may require more than one pass. Printing is usually bidirectional.

Thermal

Thermal printing techniques are no longer widely used except in some specialist applications like bar-code printing or hand-held devices. It was used extensively on early fax machines but has generally been replace by inkjet on modern faxes.

Rather than a print head that moves across the page, a thermal printer has a fixed strip of print wires that are heated to produce an image (dot matrix style) on special thermal paper. This has the advantage of being quiet in operation, but the need for special paper is a limitation. Moreover, the paper does not store well after use. It tends to darken with age and the print becomes difficult to read.

A variation on thermal printing is thermal wax transfer, in which a thermal print head melts wax-based dots on to the paper. This does not require special paper and may be available as a colour printer – see solid ink printers, below.

Solid ink

The solid ink printer was first introduced by Xerox in 1991. It uses solid ink sticks – trade-marked as Colorstix™ – and Xerox claim that a set of sticks will produce 'up to 7000 pages with typical ink coverage'.

These are sometimes known as wax-jet printers because they use a similar method of applying colour to paper. These printers apply heat to the 'colorstix' and squirt it on to the paper. The result is brightly coloured prints on almost any kind of paper. The process is relatively slow and expensive compared with other methods so it tends to be used mainly in professional reprographics operations such as advertising agencies.

Printer and scanner components

Memory

Both printers and scanners need to hold pages of information prior to printing and the more memory that they have, the bigger the print job they can handle. Many printers – like many PCs – are sold with enough RAM to provide basic functionality, and a common and easy upgrade, particularly for laser printers, is to increase the amount of installed RAM. Printers almost invariably use proprietary RAM formats so you will need to check the manufacturer's documentation and / or website. Installing the RAM is a matter of powering down the printer, removing any access covers and physically fitting the module. Obviously you will need to observe standard antistatic precautions and test for proper operation after installing.

Drivers

Like any device that is attached to a PC, a printer or scanner needs device drivers to communicate between the PC and the device's proprietary interface. Manufacturers provide drivers on disk with the printer and these may be updated from time to time. It is generally good practice to obtain up-to-date drivers and to install them particularly if there are problems with the printer.

Firmware

Firmware consists of micro-programs that have been 'flashed' onto a chip that uses Electronically Erasable Programmable Read Only Memory (EEPROM). This is similar to the way in which BIOS chips are used in PCs and this type of memory is used in printers and other devices such as CD / DVD drives, etc. Updating firmware, like updating device drivers, is a matter of visiting the manufacturer's website and downloading the appropriate update. It is, of course, important to make sure that you are using the correct version and to follow all of the manufacturer's instructions for carrying out the update.

Consumables

Toner

The laser-printing process is closely related to (was, in fact, developed out of) photo-copier technology and uses the same type of toner. Toner is a fine – near liquid – dust that contains both magnetic particles and plastic, and the laser-printing process fuses it on to the paper. Toner needs to be replaced from time to time, and this is usually a matter of removing a whole sealed unit and dropping a replacement into place. It may be possible to refill a toner cartridge, but this is often more trouble than it is worth. The dust is messy and hazardous to health, particularly if inhaled. It is also sufficiently fine that it will pass through the mesh of a standard vacuum-cleaner bag – even with the cleaners sold for use with PCs –- so unless you use an especially fine vacuum-cleaner bag, the toner dust will pass through it into the mechanism, where the heat of operation will fuse it together and damage the cleaner.

Ink cartridges

Ink cartridges need to be replaced when they run dry. There is normally a printer-specific key, or combination of keys, required to move the print head to an accessible area where the old cartridge can be removed and a new one dropped into place. It is good practice to run the head-cleaning routines immediately after replacing a cartridge to ensure a clean, consistent flow of ink and this can be done either though software (usually utilities bundled with the printer drivers) or by using a key, or key combination, to run built-in routines in the printer itself. This second option has the advantage of being available even if the printer is not connected to a PC.

It is possible to buy refill kits to refill cartridges, but this is a messy and time-consuming business. You can also buy refilled cartridges and 'clones' of cartridges for popular printers and, while these will save you money, they will invalidate any manufacturer's warranty on the printer.

Paper

One of the most common causes of printing problems is using the wrong type of paper or other stock. Each printer is designed to use a particular range of papers in terms of weight and finish, and even where a paper is of the right type, storage in sub-optimal conditions can be sufficient to make it unusable. A good first test where a printer is producing unsatisfactory output is to open a new pack of standard photocopy paper and print a test page or two on that. Another trap for the unwary is with overhead projector transparencies; these must be of the right type for the printer. A laser transparency has too smooth a surface for use with an inkjet printer – the image will 'run' – and an inkjet transparency will melt if it is subjected to the heat of the laser-printer process. The printer can be severely damaged as a result.

Printer and scanner interfaces

In order to print from a PC, the printer / scanner has to be attached to it, either directly through a cable, or across a network, or connected by one of the 'unbounded' connection methods: Bluetooth, WiFi or Infrared. The Chapter 5 section on ports and cables contains a lot of material relevant to this topic, as printers use one of the standard ports and connectors to attach to a PC.

Parallel

Connection to the parallel port on the back of the PC is probably still the most common method of printer connection, especially for the home user or micro-business, though USB is increasingly popular. The parallel port is so commonly used for a printer connection that it is often referred to as the 'printer port'.

The earliest PCs used a unidirectional parallel port and the specification for this was later formalised by the Institute of Electrical and Electronic Engineers (IEEE) as the Standard Printer Port (SPP) in their standard IEEE 1284. This standard also defines the more modern bidirectional connections: the Enhanced Parallel Port (EPP) and the Enhanced Capabilities Port (ECP).

Network (e.g. NIC, print servers)

The rapid growth of networking in recent years means that network printing is the norm rather than the exception in most workplaces and is increasingly popular with home users. Indeed, the possibility of sharing printers was one of the reasons for setting up networks in the early days of small-scale networking.

There are three basic approaches to connecting a network printer:

- Attach the printer to a PC on the network, and then set up a Microsoft Windows® 'Share' on it.

- Use a network-ready printer that has its own Network Interface Card (NIC) built in to it.

- Attach a dedicated print server device to the network and attach the printer to that.

The simplest and most commonly encountered method for connecting a network printer is to attach it to a port – such as the parallel port – of one machine on the LAN and then set up a share on it. In order to do this:

Installing a shared network printer in Microsoft Windows®

(If you are unsure about how to install a printer locally – as summarised in step 1 – look at the Installing and configuring printers and scanners heading later in the chapter, see page 216).

1 Install a printer on one of the local ports of a networked PC.

2 Physically attach the printer.

3 Install drivers.

4 Print a test page locally.

5 Navigate to the **Printers and Faxes** folder in Microsoft Windows® XP or the **Printers** folder in Microsoft Windows® 2000 on the local PC. You will see a list of installed printers. In this example (from XP Professional) we can see two printers, one of which is the default printer.

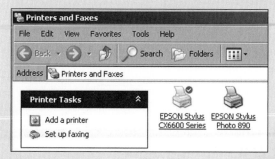

Figure 12.1

6 To make the new printer the default printer locally, right-click on the printer icon and select **Set as default Printer** from the context menu. A 'tick' mark will appear over the newly created default printer.

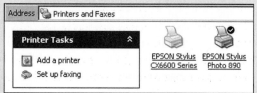

Figure 12.2

7 In order to set up the share – to make it available on the network, right-click on the printer icon and click on **Sharing** from the context menu as in Figure 12.3.

8 Select the Radio button to enable the share as in Figure 12.4.

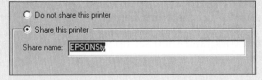

Figure 12.3

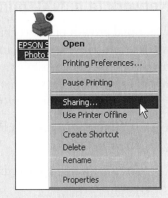

9 A hand will appear under the printer icon to indicate that it is shared on the network.

Figure 12.4

10 The newly installed and shared printer is now available over the network.

In order to use the newly shared printer it must be installed on the networked PC that needs to use it. In order to do this, you will need to log on to another PC that is connected to the network. The following example uses Microsoft Windows® 2000 to do this.

Connecting to a shared network printer in Microsoft Windows®

1 Navigate to the **Printers** folder and click on the **Add Printer** icon to start the **Add Printer Wizard**. You will be asked to select either a local or a network printer.

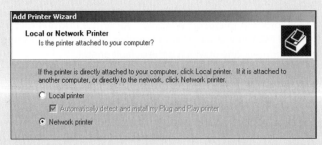

Figure 12.5

2 Choose the **Network Printer** option and click on **Next**.

3 At the next screen, browse for available network printers. You will be presented with a list as in Figure 12.6. (The PC that has the printer attached to it has to be powered up and attached to the network, of course!).

4 Select your shared printer from the previous exercise and click on **Next**.

Figure 12.6

5 You will now be given the option to make this the new default printer for the system; do this if that is what is required, otherwise leave it as non-default but available. Microsoft Windows® will show that the printer is available over the network by displaying its icon with a stylised network cable beneath it and a tick if (as in Figure 12.7) it is also the default printer.

6 Print a test page to make sure that the set-up is working. You will need to be logged in to the PC with a password-protected user account and sufficient permissions to do this.

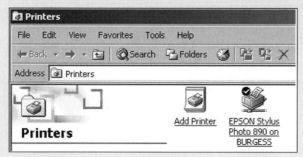

Figure 12.7

The method that we have considered for attaching a network printer is suitable for attaching a printer where print needs are not too demanding. However, where there is a lot of printing to do, the PC that hosts the printer will slow down substantially as the volume of printing increases. In most workplaces, where there is the need for higher volumes of print jobs, it is usual to use a 'true' network printer: that is one that has its own IP (network) address either through having a Network Interface Card (NIC) built into it or by attaching it to a dedicated print server box. In either case, you will need to allocate an IP address to the device and install it through Microsoft Windows®. This may require you to use proprietary software from the manufacturer and the key – as is so often the case – is to read the manufacturer's documentation before starting work.

USB

The Universal Serial Bus (USB) is a popular means of connecting many peripherals including printers and seems set to overtake the popularity of the standard parallel 'printer' port for doing this. A USB printer is connected to a USB port and any necessary drivers installed. Once it is in place, it is the same in operation as a parallel port printer and can be used locally or set up as a network share.

Serial

The standard serial port is slow by today's standards and is no longer widely used for printers. One of the advantages of serial communication is that it supports faster transfer rates on longer cable segments than parallel cables. The limit for a parallel cable is 15 feet; for a serial cable it is 50 feet. Before the widespread adoption of networking in almost every workplace, a serial cable was frequently the only realistic option for connecting a printer that was more than a few feet from the PC to which it was attached. These printer types are no longer widely used.

IEEE 1394 / FireWire

IEEE 1394 / FireWire is in many ways similar to USB; that is it is a high-speed serial interface that can be used to connect a variety of devices including printers. The disadvantage of IEEE 1394 is mainly that of cost when compared to USB or parallel connection and for most users the higher data transfer rates of FireWire are not necessary. Consequently, this type of connection is normally only used in applications such as typesetting or complex graphics, where it is cost-effective.

Wireless (e.g. Bluetooth, 802.11, infrared)

Any of the 'unbounded' communications technologies can be used to connect a printer and many printers have wireless Ethernet (802.11), Bluetooth or infrared interfaces built into them. In terms of operation, once connected, they are indistinguishable from any other printer as far as the user is concerned. Obviously, the limitations of the connection technologies – such as range and data transfer rates – will apply. The unbounded connection technologies are discussed in Chapter 14 (see page 240).

SCSI

The Small Computer Systems Interface (SCSI) is not widely used for printing because, like FireWire, it is a relatively expensive connection that can deliver high speed data transfers seldom necessary for most users. The advantages of SCSI are its speed and the ability to connect several devices on a single SCSI chain, and problems are as likely to be with termination and SCSI IDs as printing or printer problems as such. SCSI technology is discussed in Chapter 5 (see page 67).

Installing and configuring printers and scanners

The details of how to connect a particular scanner or printer may vary in some of their details so it is always sensible to check with any manufacturer's documentation, manual or set-up instructions before starting work. However, there are similarities in the approach required to installation and, in outline, these are:

- Attach the device to a port and connect its power supply.
- Install and / or update device drivers and carry out any calibration tasks.
- Configure any options and set any required default values.
- Print or scan a test page.

Attach the device

Unpack the printer or scanner and check that all parts have been provided; there is usually a checklist from the manufacturer and, if you are lucky, some sort of diagram or assembly instructions for things like paper guides, etc. Physically attach the device to the appropriate local or network port and connect it to the power supply. Note, however, that some USB devices may require the drivers to be installed before physical installation of the device and that some lower-power USB devices may draw their power from the USB interface rather than having their own power supply. Attaching the device to the PC is usually done with the host PC powered down.

Install / update the device drivers

On rebooting the host PC, Microsoft Windows® will probably recognise the device and may even have a driver for it. If this is the case, all you need to do is to follow the instructions on the screen. If Microsoft Windows® doesn't recognise the device, then run the **Add / Remove Hardware Wizard** (2000) or **Add Hardware** (XP); either way, click on the applet in **Control Panel** and follow the instructions on screen. You may be prompted to provide drivers from a manufacturer's disk; again, follow the instructions on screen. When the driver installation is complete, the Microsoft Windows® wizard will confirm this and you should have basic functionality. However, some devices – particularly inkjet printers and scanners – require the further step of calibration. The exact steps required will vary from device to device and between manufacturers, so it is necessary to read any product-specific documentation. However, in outline the process is:

1   As part of the installation process, you will probably be prompted 'Do you want to calibrate now?' Accept this option with an **OK** or a **Yes** at the prompt.

2   In the case of a printer, the printer will print several numbered lines that correspond with different head alignments.

3   Choose the alignment that looks best and enter the line number before pressing / clicking **OK** or **Continue**.

4   At this point, you may be given the opportunity to check the calibration by printing a new test sheet and recalibrating if necessary.

5   When you are satisfied that you have the best alignment, click on **Finish**.

6   As scanners deal with input rather than output, the calibration process is concerned mainly with the accuracy of the colours compared with those shown on screen. Many manufacturers provide a test pattern that can be scanned and the on-screen output corrected until they correspond. Again, it is important to read manufacturer-specific details and to carry out the work in accordance with them.

Configure options and default settings

Once the printer or scanner (or these days a multifunction device that incorporates both) is installed and working, you can configure any other options. This may require you to run manufacturer-provided software to configure sheet feeders, trays, etc. With a printer, it is sensible to ensure that the default paper size is appropriate to the country of use.

Print / scan a test page

Obviously the job isn't done until you have tested it. Microsoft Windows® provides a standard test page for printing. To use it, right-click on the printer icon and select **Properties** from the context menu. Select the **General** tab, and click on the **Print test** page button. This will send a standard test page to the printer. In the case of a scanner, place a suitable page on the scanner and scan it. If it shows on-screen, then the scanner is working. If you are setting up a printer or scanner for someone else – a customer or someone in a workplace – this is a good time at which to ask them to test the installation by printing or scanning a test page.

Optimising printer and scanner performance

For the most part, printers and scanners either work or not and in terms of hardware there is not a lot to optimise, unless you are working with a big multifunction device with multiple trays, staplers, finishers, etc., in which case you will need to follow themanufacturer's instructions. For really high-end equipment, you may need additional manufacturer-specific training before you can work with their products. In software terms, there may be more that you can do. For example, most printers can be set to give different qualities of output or to print in monochrome only in order to economise on consumables.

Troubleshooting printers and scanners

As with all troubleshooting, the keys to success are a calm systematic approach, attention to detail and not overlooking the obvious. The first thing to check is that the device has power and is connected to the host PC. If the power and connections appear to be okay, then the next step is to reboot the host PC and try the device again.

With printers of all types, a common cause of poor quality prints is using the wrong paper or other stock. To test for this, open a new pack of standard photocopy paper and try printing on that. Having ruled out the obvious (and easy), it is now time to look at some specifics.

Identify the symptom

Printer problems can be divided into two groups: failure to print at all and poor quality prints. Failure to print at all is almost invariably a connectivity problem, that is a printing rather than a printer problem. Most printers have a built-in diagnostic mode, which can be accessed by holding down some combination of keys while restarting the printer. Consult the manufacturer's documentation to find the key combination and print a test page. As this is generated by the printer's firmware, it is independent of the PC and will work even if they are not connected. If the printer can print its own test page, but not a test page from the PC, then you have a connectivity or setting problem that is unconnected with the printer hardware. On the other hand, if the printer won't print its own test page, you have a hardware problem and there is no point in looking at the PC end of the connection until you have fixed it or even replaced the printer. Either way, you have made a significant step towards isolating and identifying the problem.

Review device error codes / user reports

Many of the more sophisticated devices, such as the laser printers that are used in most workplaces, have an LED panel that displays error messages and codes. The printers usually come with a detailed manual that you can use to try to track down their meaning.

Another source of information may be an event log; both Microsoft Windows® 2000 and XP maintain event logs for just about everything that happens on the system and your main problem here is not being overwhelmed by the volume of information available. User reports are, of course, potentially a very valuable source of information. In most situations, you will have been called by a user who is experiencing a particular problem, so listen carefully to what they have to say and do not forget the most useful troubleshooting words of them all: 'Show me'.

Print or scan a test page

The inability to print or scan a page is the reason that you have been asked to troubleshoot the printer or scanner in the first place. As your examination of the system proceeds, you should print / scan a test page to see if you have identified and fixed the problem. You need to do this fairly frequently for two reasons; firstly, because it saves time, and secondly, if you have tried three things and the device starts to work as a result you will have no indication of the nature of the fault or the action that fixed it. This may be acceptable when doing a one-off job on your own kit, but it doesn't do much for the shared knowledge base of a formal technical support operation.

Use appropriate tools

This can be anything from using denatured alcohol to clean the platen on an ageing dot matrix printer to using software diagnostic tools such as PINGing a network printer on its IP address. Many tools are, of course, vendor-specific so a search on the Internet, including a search of the vendor's site for product-specific utilities, may be a useful step.

Review and analyse collected data

Troubleshooting is an iterative process and the basic procedures are the same for troubleshooting a printer as for any other device: check the obvious, ask the user, formulate a theory about the possible cause and test it. Keep doing this until a solution is reached. The process, the iteration through probable causes and testing them, will usually lead to a solution. However, once you have disposed of the obvious, considering the service history of the device may provide further insights. High-end devices such as the larger laser printers often have a recommended service regime and there should be a documentary record of this. Even where this is not the case, if you are working as part of the technical support operation in a large organisation, there will be an in-house record of previous service calls, fixes and known problems. Over time, such a system may evolve into an in-house knowledge base focused on the specific products that you support.

At a more general level, there is usually a manufacturer's knowledge base for their products. Most major vendors have a section of their website devoted to troubleshooting information, lists of Frequently Asked Questions (FAQs) and, often, user forums and discussion boards.

Armed with the additional knowledge from these sources, you can now attack the problem again, stepping through the process of isolating symptoms and their causes: printer or printing, hardware or software, connectivity, correct and up-to-date device drivers, etc.

Identify solutions and apply them

Various printer types and scanners tend to have problems and solutions that are typical of that type of device. As a working technician, and for exam purposes, you should be familiar with common problems and their solutions.

Obviously, before you start on the troubleshooting process in detail, you will check the obvious, for example, power to the device and connectivity. You also need to check the consumables – ink cartridges, toner cartridges, etc. – and replace them if necessary. At the other end of the troubleshooting process, the job is not finished until you have a satisfied customer. After you have fixed the problem with the scanner or printer, the best way of verifying the fix is to scan or print a test page, then make sure that the customer is satisfied with the result. One possibility is for the customer to use the device in their usual way – using 'real' rather than 'test' data – to establish that the device is fixed to the customer's satisfaction. In some workplaces, there may even be a form for the customer to sign to confirm their acceptance. When this is done, you can log the job as complete and add details of the problem, its cause and the solution to your records.

Common problems and their solutions

Care and service of laser printers

Laser printers are usually robust and reliable. When toner is exhausted, most laser printers use a complete sealed unit rather then simply replacing the toner dust. This means that many of the critical parts are replaced as a matter of routine. For example, Hewlett-Packard replacement cartridges contain not just toner, but the corona, the drum assembly and the developing roller. In addition, many of the major manufacturers, such as Hewlett-Packard, can supply maintenance kits for many of their range, that is replacement parts for the items most likely to wear in each particular type of printer.

This being the case, the chief cause of problems is the build-up of dirt from toner and paper remnants. This should be removed as part of regular servicing and maintenance.

Toner dust is potentially hazardous to health, so you should exercise great care if you blow it out with canned air. If you use a vacuum cleaner for removing the detritus, it needs to be an antistatic cleaner designed for use with electronic components. You should also check that the bag inside the cleaner has a very fine mesh because toner dust particles are small enough to pass though a standard mesh size and could fuse themselves into the moving parts of the cleaner.

Inkjet printers

Inkjet printers are usually fairly robust and reliable. At the bottom end of the market, they are sufficiently cheap that replacement may be more cost-effective than extensive repairs.

The main maintenance problem is the tendency of the ink to dry in the nozzles and block them. To counter this, all inkjet printers move the print head to a special position known variously as the 'park', 'cleaning', or 'maintenance' area.

Most printers have some sort of head cleaning or diagnostic mode built into them, which is accessed by holding down some combination of keys: it may be necessary to consult the manual for the particular model of printer. Additionally, there is frequently software support for cleaning and aligning print heads as a supplement to the printer drivers on the manufacturer's disk. This may be operating system-specific.

Dot matrix printers

Dot matrix printers are a well-proven technology and require only simple maintenance. Clean the platen and the print head with denatured alcohol. Lubricate gears and pulleys. DO NOT lubricate the print head because this will cause the print to smear.

Scanners

Scanners present few service problems that can be fixed in the field and, at the bottom of the price range, replacement may be a better option than repair. However, the following are some common problems reported by users:

- **Just won't work.** This, of course, is a problem frequently reported for all sorts of equipment and the solution for you, the technician, probably lies with the obvious: power to the scanner or connectivity between the scanner and the PC.

- **Strange noises.** As often as not, this is just the sound of the scanner's start-up process; the stepper motor runs and the light source flashes on and off as the device performs its internal calibration routines. The answer to this is to walk the user through the process and assure them that all is well. Being able to do this without appearing to be critical of the customer or appearing to be superior is one of the important 'soft skills' that are as necessary to the working technician as a screwdriver, a multimeter, or a stock of technical know-how.

- **Scanner won't scan.** The first thing to do is simply try again. If this does not work, restart the scanner and if that does not work, try rebooting the PC. Another possibility in this scenario is that the scanner head has been locked; a physical setting that is provided in order to prevent damage during transit. This lock can sometimes be applied accidentally and cause the scanner to fail.

SUMMARY

This chapter has considered the main printer and scanner technologies and the various means of connecting them to individual PCs or a network. We have considered how the standard troubleshooting methods can be applied to the specifics of printers and scanners and some of the common problems that you may encounter when working with them. We have considered the role of consumables in the printing process and the problems that can be caused by using inappropriate or badly stored paper or other printing stock. We have noted the need to involve the user / customer in the process and the need to verify that the work has been carried out to their satisfaction.

QUESTIONS

1   Which of the following is NOT a part of the laser printing process?

a) Cleaning

b) Charging

c) Writing

d) Fixing

2   A user has reported that a scanner is 'just not working'. You check that the scanner has power and is connected to the host PC. What do you do next?

a) Reboot the PC

b) Restart the scanner

c) Check device drivers

d) Check the transportation lock on the scanner

3   You are setting up a shared printer on a Microsoft Windows® XP peer network. You have installed the printer and necessary drivers on the parallel port of a PC called GIRAFFE. What is the next step?

a) Log on to GIRAFFE across the network, right-click on the printer and select Share

b) Navigate to the new printer through **Start | Printers and Faxes** on GIRAFFE and set up the share from there

c) Type the UNC pathname \\GIRAFFE\Printer Name in the browser bar on any network-connected PC

d) Any of the above

4   An inkjet printer connected to a stand-alone PC on its parallel port is failing to print at all. You have checked that it has fully charged ink cartridges and have successfully printed a test page using its self-test. What do you check next?

a) Printer cable

b) Mains power

c) Drivers

d) Print wires

5   What is the upper limit for the length of a serial printer cable?

a) 10 feet

b) 15 feet

c) 50 feet

d) 75 feet

ANSWERS / EXPLANATIONS

1   Which of the following is NOT a part of the laser printing process:

d) Fixing

2   A user has reported that a scanner is 'just not working'. You check that the scanner has power and is connected to the host PC. What do you do next?

b) Restart the scanner

Any of the listed options is a possible step towards a solution but the general rule for all troubleshooting is to check the simplest option first; in this case, restart the scanner.

3   You are setting up a shared printer on a Microsoft Windows® XP peer network. You have installed the printer and necessary drivers on the parallel port of a PC called GIRAFFE. What is the next step?

b) Navigate to the new printer through **Start | Printers and Faxes** on GIRAFFE and set up the share from there

4   An inkjet printer connected to a stand-alone PC on its parallel port is failing to print at all. You have checked that it has fully charged ink cartridges and have successfully printed a test page using its self-test. What do you check next?

a) Printer cable

The printer has mains power or it would not work at all. Drivers are a possible problem, but less likely and will take longer to check than basic connectivity. There are no print wires on an inkjet.

5   What is the upper limit for the length of a serial printer cable?

c) 50 feet

CHAPTER 13
Network fundamentals

Network topics account for 12 per cent of the Essentials exam. This chapter, and the next two, cover the requirements of the exam. There are other CompTIA qualifications in different aspects of networks, so all that is needed of the A+ technician are the fundamentals at the 'client' end of a connection.

Exam objective 5.1 (part)
Identify the fundamental principles of networks.

Describe basic networking concepts:
  Addressing
  Bandwidth
  Status indicators
  Protocols (e.g. TCP / IP including IP, classful subnet, IPX / SPX including NWLINK, NETBEUI / NETBIOS)
  Full-duplex, half-duplex
  Cabling (e.g. twisted pair, coaxial cable, fibre optic, RS-232)
  Networking models including peer-to-peer and client / server

Identify names, purposes and characteristics of the common network cables:

  Plenum / PVC
  UTP (e.g. CAT3, CAT5 / 5e, CAT6)
  STP
  Fiber/fibre (e.g. single-mode and multi-mode)

Identify names, purposes and characteristics of network connectors
(e.g. RJ45 and RJ11, ST / SC / LC, USB, IEEE 1394 / FireWire).

Fundamental principles of networks

Networks offer a lot of advantages for businesses, colleges, schools, even home users. They make it possible for several users to exchange information (files) and to share devices and services such as printers or an Internet connection. There are various models and types of networks, but a reasonable general definition may be: 'Two or more computers that can connect with one another without direct human intervention.' This is sufficiently generalised that it can include a home network that shares a printer and a modem, through to a college or corporate network of some hundreds of nodes, to the entire Internet.

Whatever the size and shape of the network, it will have many similar characteristics: computers, cables (or wireless links), network cards (or on-board connectors), and a Network Operating System (NOS), which implements the various network protocols needed to make it work. Protocols – the 'rules' governing the working of a particular network are discussed later in the chapter (see page 226).

Note: A+ is only concerned with networking basics. You need to know, for example, how to connect a Microsoft Windows® PC to a network. There are other qualifications, such as Network+, i-Net+ and Server+, which cover more advanced topics.

Basic networking concepts

Addressing

Every PC (or other computer) that is attached to a network has a network address. Just as a telephone has an exchange or area code followed by a telephone number that is unique to that exchange or area, a networked PC has an address that identifies the network to which it is attached (the equivalent of the exchange or area code) and the identifier that is unique to that network (the equivalent of a phone number). The network address of a PC is related to the physical (or MAC) address of the Network Interface Card (NIC); more on this below (see page 227). The form of the address will depend on the network protocol in use: TCP / IP maps logical addresses to MAC addresses, while IPX / SPX (used by Novell Netware®) incorporates the physical address as part of the PC's address on the network. TCP / IP and IPX / SPX are considered further later in the chapter.

Bandwidth

The capacity of network communications – bandwidth – is measured in millions of bits per second – Megabits per second (Mbps). Typical Ethernet LAN speeds are: 10Mbps – 'Standard Ethernet', 100 Mbps – 'Fast Ethernet' and 1000 Mbps – 'Gigabit Ethernet'. Note that although 10 Mbps is still called 'standard', 100 Mbps is the most common Ethernet speed that you are likely to encounter in practice, and most equipment these days is dual-speed and backward-compatible, generally being labelled as '10 / 100' Mbps. Token Ring networks are usually described as 4 Mbps or 16 Mbps, but the speed measurements are not directly comparable because of the different Media Access methods.

Status indicators

In addition to a bandwidth rating, a network card will generally have some LEDs that indicate its status. These will vary from card to card and it may be necessary to consult the manufacturer's documentation for details. However, as a minimum, you should expect a Link Indicator and an Activity Indicator. The Link Indicator will show a steady light to indicate that the NIC is connected to a valid network connection and the

Activity Indicator flashes as network data is sent or received. There may be other indicators to show, for example, the operation speed of a dual-speed card, collision detection and whether it is working in full- or half-duplex mode. In full-duplex mode, a card can send and receive data simultaneously; in half-duplex, it can either transmit or receive, but not both simultaneously.

Protocols

Outside computing and networking, the term 'protocols' indicates a set of generally accepted rules or behaviour appropriate to a particular situation or setting. The procedures of a court of law or the rules governing a visit by an overseas Head of State are all examples of protocols in the everyday sense of the word. In networking, the term indicates agreed standards or rules governing how computers interact.

TCP / IP including IP, classful subnet

TCP / IP is the dominant protocol in networking today. It is the native language of the Internet and because of this it is also widely used in Local Area Networks (LANs) because of the ease of connecting them to the Internet.

The term TCP / IP actually refers to two separate but related things. It is the overall name of a suite of protocols that includes the Transmission Control Protocol (TCP) and the Internet Protocol (IP) and many others, such as the Simple Mail Transfer Protocol (SMTP) and the File Transfer Protocol (FTP). You should be aware of this broader meaning of the term but, for our present purposes, we are only interested in the (narrowly defined) TCP / IP pair.

Network addressing with TCP / IP

The easiest way to understand this is to look at how it works in practice. If you have access to a PC that has a working network card and TCP / IP installed, then the command IPCONFIG /ALL at a system prompt will produce output that looks something like this:

```
Ethernet adapter Local Area Connection 2:

        Connection-specific DNS Suffix  . : elenmar
        Description . . . . . . . . . . . : Intel(R) PRO/100+ PCI Adapter
        Physical Address. . . . . . . . . : 00-A0-C9-E6-23-F9
        Dhcp Enabled. . . . . . . . . . . : Yes
        Autoconfiguration Enabled . . . . : Yes
        IP Address. . . . . . . . . . . . : 192.168.2.104
        Subnet Mask . . . . . . . . . . . : 255.255.255.0
        Default Gateway . . . . . . . . . : 192.168.2.1
        DHCP Server . . . . . . . . . . . : 192.168.2.1
        DNS Servers . . . . . . . . . . . : 192.168.2.1
        Lease Obtained. . . . . . . . . . : 25 September 2006 08:12:36
        Lease Expires . . . . . . . . . . : 02 October 2006 08:12:36
```

Figure 13.1

The entries in the figure which are of interest at present are the physical address and the IP address.

Physical (MAC) addresses

The *physical address* – also known as a MAC (Media Access Control) address or burnt-on address – is a string of hexadecimal numbers unique to that network card. The first three fields make up the Organisationally Unique Identifier (OUI) and the remainder are the Device ID allocated by the card manufacturer. This means that every NIC in the world has a unique identifier, or physical address.

MAC addresses are sufficient to provide a unique identity – address – for the host machine. However, there is no pattern to the addressing scheme and if a network card has to be replaced, then the host changes its address. This can be made to work on a small LAN, but it would be difficult to imagine the Internet working if changing a network card changed the web server's address in cyberspace.

Logical addresses

In order to impose some sort of logical structure on the random collection of MAC addresses, we can impose a logical addressing scheme on them. The most important and most frequently used of these logical addressing schemes is TCP / IP.

In the example shown, we can see a physical address, an IP address and a subnet mask. The subnet mask is necessary to distinguish two pieces of information in the IP address: the network address and the host address.

IP addresses and subnet masks

Rather as a telephone number can be split into an exchange part and a phone number part, an IP address can be split into a network address and a host address. Unfortunately, while we know from experience how to split a phone number into its constituent parts, we need to calculate this in order to divide an IP address into its elements.

An IP address consists of four fields of decimal numbers, each of which can hold a value in the range 0–255. In binary notation, 255 is represented as a row of eight 1s, 11111111, so each of the fields is known as an 'octet'. Figure 13.2 shows the IP Address and subnet mask on a Microsoft Windows® XP PC.

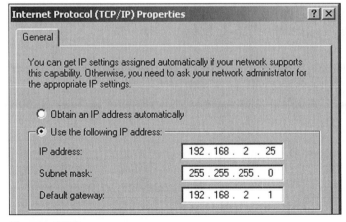

Figure 13.2

Calculating addresses using the subnet mask

In order to split the network address into its elements, we have to convert both the IP address and the subnet mask into binary notation and do some arithmetic with the results.

The IP address and subnet mask in the example above are:

192.168.2.25 and 255.255.255.0

In binary notation this is:

11000000 10101000 00000010 00011001 (IP address)
11111111 11111111 11111111 00000000 (subnet mask)

A binary 'AND' of these values gives the result:

11000000 10101000 00000010 00000000

The non-zero results in the first three fields indicate that these are the network part of the address and they can be converted back to decimal values to give us:

192.168.2.

The zero values in the last field indicate that the original value in the IP address should be interpreted as the host (or node) address, in this case 25. We therefore have a network defined by the network address 192.168.2 and we can have up to 256 (0-255) values in the host address field. Because 0 and 255 in this final field are reserved values, this means that, in effect, we have a network defined by the network address 192.168.2 with room for 254 attached nodes.

Obviously, different subnet mask and IP address combinations will produce different divisions between network and host address ranges.

For exam purposes, you should be aware of how subnet masks work. It is not necessary to be able to perform the type of calculation shown above under exam conditions. It has been included as an aid to understanding rather than something to be learned in detail.

Classful subnets

Although an IP address and subnet combination can be anything permitted by the IP addressing system, there are some standard classes.

For exam purposes, you should be able to identify the class of a network by examining the subnet mask.

Table 13.1 Subnets.

Class	Subnet mask	Start of address range	End of address range
Class A	255.0.0.0	0.0.0.0	127.255.255.255
Class B	255.255.0.0	128.0.0.0	191.255.255.255
Class C	255.255.255.0	192.0.0.0	223.255.255.255
Class D (multicast)		224.0.0.0	239.255.255.255
Class E (reserved)		240.0.0.0	255.255.255.255

IPX / SPX including NWLINK

Internet Packet Exchange (IPX) and Sequenced Packet Exchange (SPX) are proprietary protocols in Novell Netware®. These are routable protocols and correspond in functionality with the TCP / IP pair. From a technical point of view, they are considered to be more efficient than TCP / IP and they are still used, mainly, but not exclusively, in Netware® networks.

Versions of Novell Netware® from 5.0 onwards use TCP / IP, though they may implement IPX / SPX as well. However, TCP / IP is the basis for all Internet communications and it is the dominant protocol in all networking as a result.

NWLINK is the IPX / SPX compatible protocol developed by Microsoft. If you need to connect a Microsoft Windows® client to a Netware® LAN that runs IPX / SPX, it is necessary to install the NWLINK protocol on the Microsoft Windows® client computer.

NetBEUI / NetBIOS

NetBIOS – Network Basic Input Output System – was developed in the 1980s for IBM systems. It was later extended into the NetBIOS Extended User Interface – NetBEUI: a simple non-routable protocol that is still available, but rarely used.

NetBEUI has the lowest non-data overhead of any of the protocols and is fast and efficient on very small networks. However, because it is not routable, it cannot be used on networks that use routers. This means that it is not suitable for large networks or even small networks that are required to access the Internet.

NetBEUI was available in the old Microsoft Windows® 9.x family of operating systems and in Microsoft Windows® 2000, though TCP / IP has always been preferred and installed by default. Microsoft Windows XP does not make NetBEUI available in a standard installation, although it is available if you care to 'dig it out' from the installation CD. If you do this, you will be warned that its use is 'unsupported'. For exam purposes, simply remember these differences of implementation, the NetBEUI acronym and the fact that it is not routable.

Full- and half-duplex communications

These terms are not exclusive to networking. They are derived from telephony. Both of these communication types allow for traffic in both directions. Half duplex allows transmission in either direction, but not at the same time – rather like a single lane road controlled by traffic lights. Full duplex allows for simultaneous transmission in both directions, rather like an ordinary voice telephone call.

Networking models

The main division in networking models is between peer (or peer-to-peer) networks and client / server networks.

Peer-to-peer

The simplest network to implement for a small number of computers is the peer-to-peer network. The word 'peer' means, literally, 'equal', and in a peer network all machines act as both clients and servers in more or less equal measure.

A peer network allows the sharing of resources: printers, Internet connection, even a centralised file store for all users, but there is no central control and only minimal security. Shared resources can be secured to some extent by password protection on each of the 'shares', but as the number of computers involved increases, this rapidly becomes unmanageable.

Client/server

The client / server model of networking is more appropriate to business or other large networks. Whereas in a peer network each computer both provides and uses services through *shares*, the distinction between a server and a client *node* in a client / server set-up is clear.

Clients – also known as *hosts* – rely on a central server to provide services such as print, file storage, etc. The key difference is that the server controls access to the services. On client / server networks, the server keeps a file of user names and passwords and it is necessary to login to the server in order to gain access to any network resource. This level of centralised control results in improved security and, once a network grows beyond a handful of nodes, it is also simpler to administer.

Network cabling and connectors

Coaxial cable types

One of the earlier network cable types was coaxial. This is a familiar cable type because it is similar to that used for terrestrial television. It has a copper core, surrounded by a plastic jacket, with a braided shield over it.

The only coaxial cable in current use – and this is regarded as legacy technology – is thinnet, or 10Base-2. It is usually found on older type 'bus' networks.

Twisted pair cable types

These cable types have individually insulated cables in which pairs are twisted in order to minimise crosstalk between cables. There is then an outer layer of insulation around the whole cable. This is the Unshielded Twisted Pair (UTP) cable type and various categories of UTP are the most commonly encountered cable types in the workplace. UTP cabling is usually associated with 'star' network topologies.

There is also a Shielded Twisted Pair (STP) type, which has an addition layer of insulation around the inner pairs.

Fibre optic cable types

Fibre optic cable uses light rather than electrical signals to transmit data. This means that it is not subject to ElectroMagnetic Interference (EMI). It delivers higher performance than copper-based media but is more expensive and difficult to work with so it is generally reserved for high-speed 'backbones' or locations where there may be problems with EMI.

RS-232 cable types

This is the standard serial port on all PCs. It is not used for 'real' networking, but it can be used for data transfers between machines by connecting them with a *null modem* cable and using appropriate software.

Characteristics of cable types

Plenum / PVC

Standard network cables – coaxial or twisted pair – have an outer cover of PVC for insulation. This is suitable for many uses, but where cabling is pulled through something like a ventilation duct (not an uncommon practice, particularly when cabling older premises) there is a risk that toxic fumes could be released in the event of a fire. Building regulations may require the use of *plenum grade* cable in these circumstances. This is cable that has been given an additional layer of fire-retardant covering – usually Teflon – to reduce the risk to personnel in the event of fire.

UTP (e.g. CAT3, CAT5 / 5e, CAT6)

Unshielded Twisted Pair (UTP) is the most widely used cable type in networking today. It consists of eight individually insulated strands arranged as four pairs, which are twisted in order to minimise 'crosstalk'. Each pair has a different number of twists per inch. There is then an outer layer of insulation around the whole cable.

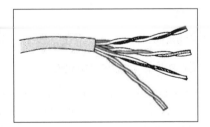

Figure 13.3 shows a Category 5 cable with the outer layer of insulation removed to show the twisted pairs inside. This is the general pattern for all twisted pair cable types.

Figure 13.3

The cable categories pre-date their adoption for networking and reflect their origins in telephony. Their characteristics are summarised in Table 13.2.

Table 13.2 Cable categories.

Category	Frequency	Typical Applications
1	< 1MHz	Telephony; alarm systems, etc.
2	<=1MHz	Telephony; mini computer and mainframe terminals
3	Up to 16 MHz	10Base-T Ethernet; 4Mbps Token Ring
4	Up to 20 MHz	16 Mbps Token Ring
5	Up to 100 MHz	100Base-TX
5e	Up to 1000 MHz	1000Base-T (Gigabit Ethernet)
6	Up to 1000 MHz	1000Base-T (Gigabit Ethernet)

- Categories 1 and 2 were used for telephony and early experiments in networking.

- Category 3 was used for telephony before being taken up for network use. Because it was in common (non-network) use, it was cheap and this contributed to its popularity. However, 10 Mbps is too slow by modern standards so, for new installations, Category 5 rapidly became the preferred standard.

- Category 5e is rapidly gaining in popularity, and given the cost of premises cabling, it may well be a preferred option for a new installation even if the initial network is intended only to run at 100 Mbps.

- Category 6 cable is faster than Cat 5e and supports Gigabit Ethernet more reliably. Its structure is fundamentally similar to the earlier specifications and it uses the same connectors.

- Category 7 – not yet released – will use a different connector and will not, therefore, be backward-compatible.

STP

Shielded Twisted Pair (STP) cables are essentially similar in their construction to their UTP counterparts. However, as an extra measure against electromagnetic interference, each of the twisted pairs has its own layer of insulation. This makes it slightly less flexible to use and it is somewhat more expensive than UTP. It is sometimes deployed where there is a risk of electromagnetic interference. However, the increased availability of fibre optic cables means that it is no longer as commonly used in these circumstances.

Fibre (e.g. single-mode and multi-mode)

Fibre optic (or optical fibre, or even 'fiber' (US usage)) refers to both the medium and, more generally, the technology used to transmit data as light pulses rather than electrical signals.

Because optical fibre technologies do not suffer from the kind if signal attenuation associated with copper wires, it can, depending on the type, carry data over much larger distances than copper cables. The nature of the signal – light – also means that it is not subject to ElectroMagnetic Interference (EMI). It is also more secure than copper cable because it is less easily tapped or scanned. The main disadvantages of optical fibre are the higher cost than copper media and greater difficulty in handling the components.

The two fibre optic cable types are multi-mode and single-mode (sometimes called mono-mode) fibre.

Multi-mode fibre is designed to carry multiple streams of light simultaneously, each at a slightly different reflection angle within the fibre optic cable core. This cable type is used for shorter transmission distances.

Single-mode fibre is used for longer distances.

The distances that can be achieved by the various cable types depend on the exact specification and detailed knowledge of this is beyond the terms of reference for A+. Multi-mode fibres generally support lengths in the range 550–2000 metres. Single mode fibre cables – depending on type – can cover distances of 10–40 kilometres.

Network connectors

Network (and other) cables are associated with different connector types and you should know them and be able to distinguish them by sight for exam purposes.

The BNC connector (Bayonet Neill-Concelman connector) – though there are several variations on the name – is used (in networking) in association with thinnet – RG58 cabling. Connection is through a T-connector – never direct to the NIC – and the last connector in the bus topology needs a terminator. This is rarely encountered, and is generally regarded as a legacy technology.

The RJ-11 (RJ = Registered Jack) is not a network connector but could be confused with an RJ-45 which is. The RJ-11 is a US phone connector with four wires and is sometimes found in the UK on some modem cables.

The RJ-45 connector is associated with twisted pair cable types. It has eight wires and is used on nearly all UTP cables, even though most of them only use four wires for signalling. (The connector that it fits into is, by the way, known as an 8P8C connector.)

The ST (Straight Tip) connector is a widely used fibre optic connector developed by AT&T. It uses a BNC-style bayonet connector that makes connection and diskonnection relatively easy.

The SC connector (Subscriber – or Square – connector) is a latched connector, that is, there is a latch mechanism which holds it in place. They will generally survive around 1000 connections / diskonnections. The SC connector is less popular than ST for LANs. They work with both single-mode and multi-mode optical fibre cables.

The LC connector – this is a small form-factor fibre optic connector from Lucent Technologies. It is similar in appearance to the SC connector.

Figure 13.4 shows the commonly used network connectors that are listed in the A+ exam specification. In addition to these, you should also be aware of the BT connector which is the standard phone plug in the UK. This is not part of the A+ specification and is mentioned here only because there is a possibility of confusing it with the RJ45.

USB, IEEE 1394 / FireWire

USB and IEEE 1394 / FireWire ports and cables are familiar from Chapters 1 and 5. They are, of course, both general purpose high-speed serial ports and may be used to connect network adapters to a PC. They are not, however, dedicated network ports or cables.

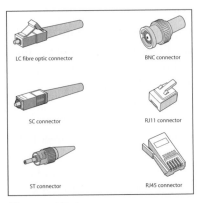

LC fibre optic connector

BNC connector

SC connector

RJ11 connector

ST connector

RJ45 connector

Figure 13.4

SUMMARY

This chapter has looked at the fundamental principles of networks. In terms of what you need to know for exam purposes, you should be familiar with protocols, and cabling and connectors in particular. You should know the characteristics of the cable types – transmission speeds, maximum segment lengths, etc. and which cable types are used with which connectors. You should also be able to distinguish the various connector types by sight.

QUESTIONS

1   You have been asked to connect a Microsoft Windows® XP PC to a Novell Netware® 4.x network. Which additional protocol would you need to install to achieve this?

   a) NWLink

   b) NetBEUI

   c) IPv6

   d) None of the above

2   Which of the following subnet masks indicates a Class B network?

   a) 255.255.255.0

   b) 255.255.0.0

   c) 255. 255.255.255

   d) 255.255.0.255

---

3   Which of the following connectors is used with coaxial cabling?

    a) RJ45

    b) RJ11

    c) BNC

    d) ST

4   A LAN that has no central server to control access to it by users is best described as

    a) A star network

    b) A peer-to-peer network

    c) A client / server network

    d) A bus network

5   The maximum data transmission speed of a Category 3 UTP cable is

    a) 100 Mbps

    b) 10 Mbps

    c) 1000 Mbps

    d) 24 Mbps

ANSWERS / EXPLANATIONS

1   You have been asked to connect a Microsoft Windows® XP PC to a Novell Netware® 4.x network. Which additional protocol would you need to install to achieve this?

    a) NWLink

2   Which of the following subnet masks indicates a Class B network?

    b) 255.255.0.0

3   Which of the following connectors is used with coaxial cabling?

    c) BNC

4   A LAN that has no central server to control access to it by users is best described as?

    b) A peer-to-peer network

5   The maximum data transmission speed of a Category 3 UTP cable is?

    b) 10 Mbps

CHAPTER 14
Network connectivity

Connectivity is essentially what networks are about. In this chapter we will look at the technologies that are used to connect to the Internet – the biggest Wide Area Network (WAN) of them all – and the technologies such as wireless, etc., which are used to connect PCs and other devices to a Local Area Network (LAN).

Exam objective 5.1 (part)
Identify names, purposes and characteristics (e.g. definition, speed and connections) of technologies for establishing connectivity, for example:

LAN / WAN
ISDN
Broadband (e.g. DSL, cable, satellite)
Dial-up
Wireless (all 802.11)
Infrared
Bluetooth
Cellular
VoIP

Network connectivity

LAN / WAN

Although the distinction between a Local Area Network (LAN) and a Wide Area Network (WAN) is a fundamental one, there is no simple clear-cut definition of either technology. Generally speaking a LAN is small – it may be confined to a single room (as in a small or home office) or it may occupy a whole building or even span several buildings. A large LAN may incorporate multiple servers, routers, etc. which are more often associated with WANs.

A WAN is the means by which LANs may be connected. It will probably use a protocol such as the Point-to-Point Protocol (PPP) and commonly uses leased telecommunication lines for the internetwork connections. The connection of networks to other networks – internetworking – is, arguably, the defining characteristic of a WAN.

Integrated Services Digital Network (ISDN)

This is a digital point-to-point network that normally operates at 128 Kbps (that is around twice the speed of a standard dial-up connection). ISDN uses the same copper wiring as a normal dial-up connection, but uses it to send digital signals through an ISDN terminal adapter. This is frequently, and inaccurately, referred to as a 'modem' – it is a digital device that neither MODulates nor DEModulates.

An ISDN Basic Rate Interface (BRI) connection has two 'Bearer' '(B)' channels capable of carrying 64 Kbps of data, which can be combined to a single 128 Kbps connection. There is also a 'Delta' '(D)' channel with 16 kbps used for call setup and link management – this is also known as the 'signalling channel'. The two 'B' channels give the user the choice of a data channel of 64 Kbps that can be used simultaneously with the other channel carrying voice signals, or a single 128 Kbps data connection.

The main advantages of ISDN are:

- Faster connection – i.e. time taken to establish the connection – than a dial-up

- Faster data transfers (around double that of a dial-up)

- No digital / analogue conversions, i.e. not a modem

Its main disadvantages are:

- More expensive

- Needs specialised equipment at both ends of the connection

- Not all equipment is compatible with other ISDN equipment

- It is still a type of dial-up – so a connection must be initiated (see the first 'advantage point' above)

Broadband (DSL, cable, satellite)

Digital Subscriber Line (DSL)

The Digital Subscriber Line (DSL) is a high-speed 'always on' Internet connection that uses the Public Switched Telephone Network to deliver connection speeds of 10, 20 or more times that of a normal dial-up connection. This technology has been widely adopted, and by the middle of 2005 there were more DSL than dial-up connections in the UK.

DSL is a broadband technology and is often referred to simply as 'broadband'. The most popular broadband type for domestic or small office use is the Asymmetric Digital Subscriber Line (ADSL). As the name implies, the width of the 'pipe' connecting to the Internet is not symmetric. Because most connections to the Internet require a lot of information to be downloaded, but relatively little to be uploaded (usually just the requests to initiate downloads) ADSL has a 'narrow pipe' on the upload side and a 'fat pipe' on the download side.

Typical connection speeds for an ADSL connection are 512 Kbps (often referred to as 10-speed) and 1Mbps (20-speed). Higher-speed connections – up to 8 Mbps are increasingly available in some areas.

In order to use the voice capacity of the line at the same time, connection is made through a splitter or filter that allows a separate voice channel on the same connection.

To connect the PC to the ADSL service requires a DSL 'modem'. This connects to the phone line at one end and the PC at the other, either through a USB port or an Ethernet (RJ-45) connector. This (see cable modems below) should normally be a straight-through LAN cable.

There are other DSL connection types, such as Symmetric DSL where greater upload capacity is needed, for example where you want to provide services, such as a website, to the Internet. Detailed knowledge of this is not necessary for A+ exams.

The distance limit between subscriber and exchange for ADSL service is 18,000 feet (5460 metres).This is a technical limit – part of the technology – and many ADSL providers place a lower limit on the distances for their service. This is because customers at the extreme range may experience significantly lower connection speeds than those who are close to the exchange and may regard the service as unacceptably slow.

Cable modem

A cable modem is a digital device and is not strictly speaking a modem. It is a means of connecting to cable television infrastructure for Internet access.

The specification for cable services was agreed between the major companies involved and is called Data Over Cable Service Interface Specification (DOCSIS) – most cable modems adhere to this standard.

As with an ADSL modem, connection between modem and PC may be through USB or Ethernet ports. The cable modem's RJ-45 port will be a Medium Dependent Interface-Crossover (MDI-X) – the same as the ports on a hub or switch so connection should be through a straight-through cable.

Connection speeds currently range between 128 Kbps and 10 Mbps and seem likely to increase further and connections, at any speed, are generally asymmetric, that is the download channel is greater than the upload channel.

Although they deliver broadly comparable high-speed always-on connections, there are some important differences between cable modems and ADSL. An ADSL connection, though distance dependent for speed, is nevertheless a point-to-point connection. A cable connection is not limited by distance, but each subscriber is part of a LAN. This means that connection speeds will degrade as more people log in and that the (shared) connection is potentially less secure than a PPP ADSL connection.

Satellite

Satellites placed in an orbit which makes them stationary with respect to the Earth's surface, geosynchronous orbits can be used to transmit and receive signals in various frequency bands.

Table 14.1

L-band	1.5 – 2.7 GHz
S-band	2.7 – 3.5 GHz
C-band	3.4 – 6.7 GHz
Ku-band	12 – 18 GHz
Ka-band	18 – 40 GHz

Satellite Internet access requires the user to have a satellite dish positioned to access the ISP's satellite. Services are either dial return or satellite return. Using dial return, the user sends data (typically requests for pages) through a dial-up connection with a downlink from the satellite of 400–500 Kbps – an asymmetric technology. Satellite return uses the satellite link in both directions and is symmetric at 400–500 Kbps. These are 'advertised' speeds and actual speeds may, in practice, reach 1 Mbps.

Connections between antenna and PC are through a PCI expansion card or a device attached to a USB or IEEE 1394 port.

Dial-up

The dial-up connection is still the most widely used of the Internet connection technologies worldwide. It uses the Public Switched Telephone Network (PSTN) – also known as the Plain Old Telephone Service (POTS) – to send and receive data.

The telephone network is 'public' in the sense that users pay a charge to access the system without owning any of the infrastructure. In the UK, this consists of line rental – the right to access the system – and call charges for actual use.

The system is 'switched' in as much as it relies on temporary connections between end points. Because not every subscriber will want to access the system at the same time, there are more 'phone numbers' – subscriber accounts – than there are available circuits.

Although the bulk of the modern telephone network is in fact digital, the connection between the end user and the exchange is still an analogue connection over copper wire. This means that we need to use a modem to modulate / demodulate the digital signals used by digital equipment.

A modem is a device that modulates the digital data in a PC into an analogue wave form, which can be sent over the telephone network. At the receiving end, another modem demodulates the analogue signal into a digital form suitable for the PC.

Although it is a slow connection method (56 Kbps in theory, less in practice) it has some advantages:

- It is cheap to set up. Most people – in developed countries at least – have access to an analogue telephone line and these are usually fairly reliable.

- There are no additional cabling costs – just a cable from modem to phone jack.

- Connections are available almost everywhere, for example a typical ADSL service (see above) is tied to a particular line – a dial-up can be connected wherever there is a working phone connection.

Wireless

There are three *wireless networking standards* defined by the Institute of Electrical and Electronic Engineers (IEEE) in common commercial and / or domestic use. These are:

- 802.11a

- 802.11b

- 802.11g

There is a fourth standard under development, 802.11n, which is not yet in widespread use.

These are all wireless Ethernet standards with strong similarities to the wired Ethernet standard 802.3. The similarities are necessary to make interconnection of wireless and wired systems because, although 'pure' wireless networks are feasible, they are much more commonly used to connect to a wired network backbone at some point (or points).

The 802.11b and 802.11g standards are the most frequently used standards at present. These operate on the same radio frequency (2.4 GHz) at speeds of 11 Mbps – the 'b' standard – and 56 Mbps – the 'g' standard.

802.11a (and the emerging 802.11n) use the 5 GHz frequency and are compatible with each other, though not with the 'b' and 'g' standards unless you use 'dual-band' equipment. Two of the major manufacturers supply equipment of this type: Linksys Wireless A+G and Netgear's Double range, which promises a maximum data transmission speed of 104 Mbps.

The wide adoption of the 2.4 GHz technologies means that there are already problems with congestion and interference between equipment, and the 5 GHz technologies and 'dual' technologies are expected (by Linksys and Netgear at least) to be the basis of the next generation of wireless networks for both business and domestic use. The chip manufacturer Atheros has invested heavily in this technology and 'supplies the silicon' for the Netgear dual-band range of products.

The original 802.11 specification (1997) used the 2.4–2.5 GHz band and is now regarded as a legacy technology.

Infrared

The specification for infrared devices is published by the Infrared Data Association (IrDA). Infrared is usually seen as a means of communicating wirelessly with infrared devices such as cameras and printers. Provided that infrared support is enabled through the CMOS set-up utility, then IrDA devices are much like wired devices in terms of installation, supplying drivers, etc. There is scope for attaching multiple computers to a hub or switch, but the fact that infrared only works on line-of-sight over short distances limits its usefulness for networking.

Bluetooth

Bluetooth is a wireless technology that supports up to eight simultaneous connections between Bluetooth-enabled devices that are within a range of 10 metres (32 feet) of each other. Unlike infrared, it does not require line-of-sight to work. The small-scale networks created by Bluetooth devices are sometimes known as Personal Area Networks (PANs) or piconets.

The original Bluetooth 1 specification (1998) allowed for a data transmission rate of 1 Mbps. This was increased to 3 Mbps with the release of Bluetooth 2. Version 2 devices are backward-compatible with version 1.

Bluetooth devices communicate in the frequency range 2.402 GHz 2.480 GHz – a range that is reserved for this type of device by international agreement.

Bluetooth requires little in the way of user intervention – devices 'discover' one another when they are in range. Rather than assigning a fixed channel between devices, Bluetooth uses spread-spectrum frequency hopping, changing frequency 1600 times per second. This minimises the effect of any interference on any given frequency. Bluetooth supports both half-duplex and full-duplex communications and is frequently used to connect a Personal Digital Assistant (PDA) with a PC, though it can, of course, be used for other communications such as between a headset and a Bluetooth-enabled mobile phone, or a keyboard and / or mouse and its PC.

Cellular

Cellular networks are by their nature asymmetric. A number of fixed transceivers are distributed across a geographic area and each transceiver communicates on a different frequency to that of its neighbours – this is the principle that governs non-satellite mobile phone networks.

Although it is possible to connect fixed-location devices to a cellular network, its real strength is the ability to connect mobile devices. Provided there is sufficient overlap between the cells served by the fixed transceivers, devices can always connect when they are in range. In order to avoid interference at the boundaries of the cells, neighbouring transceivers use different frequencies. To make best use of available frequencies, each one may be reused in non-neighbouring cells.

VoIP

The Voice over Internet Protocol (VoIP) is the means by which voice signals (i.e. telephony) can be routed over an IP network. In practice this is usually used for calls over the Internet, although it can also be used on an IP-based LAN.

A VoIP network can support three types of client:

- Traditional telephone

- IP telephone

- PC with additional software and hardware

Connecting a traditional phone to a VoIP network requires analogue to digital conversion and this can be achieved by connecting the phone to an RJ11 jack on an expansion card in a PC, connecting to a switch or router that accepts this kind of call (a digital Private Branch Exchange – PBX) or connection to an analogue PBX, which then connects to a voice–data gateway.

On new VoIP installations in particular, it is common to use IP phones that use only digital signals. Phones of this type each have their own IP address and plug straight into a standard Ethernet connection like any other network device. Because it has its own IP address, it is possible to plug the IP phone into any IP network and use it without further configuration.

A popular low-cost alternative is a softphone. This uses a standard PC that is equipped with a full-duplex sound card, speaker and microphone, and appropriate VoIP client software.

SUMMARY

There is a great deal more to know about network connection technologies than is required by the A+ specification. This chapter has examined the connection technologies required for the A+ exam and you should be aware of their characteristics – be able to recognise their various acronyms, transmission speeds and typical applications. In this area, however, there is considerable scope for additional private study, particularly if you intend to progress to further qualifications such as CompTIA Network+.

QUESTIONS

1 An ISDN connection requires the PC to connect through?

   a) A modem

   b) A terminal adapter

   c) A LAN port

   d) A cable modem

2 The maximum connection speed for a dial-up connection is?

   a) 46.9 Kbps

   b) 56 Kbps

   c) 128 Kbps

   d) 256 Kbps

3 Which of the following is NOT a wireless networking standard?

   a) 802.11

   b) 802.11b

   c) 802.3

   d) 802.11g

▶

4   The maximum range of a Bluetooth 2 piconet is?

   a) 5 metres

   b) 10 metres

   c) 15 metres

   d) 25 metres

5   A dedicated VoIP phone connects through?

   a) RJ11

   b) RJ45

   c) The sound card on the PC

   d) A PBX private exchange

ANSWERS / EXPLANATIONS

1   An ISDN connection requires the PC to connect through?
   b) A terminal adapter

2   The maximum connection speed for a dial-up connection is?
   b) 56 Kbps

3   Which of the following is NOT a wireless networking standard?
   c) 802.3

4   The maximum range of a Bluetooth 2 piconet is?
   b) 10 metres

5   A dedicated VoIP phone connects through?
   b) RJ45

CHAPTER 15
Installing, configuring and troubleshooting networks

As a working A+ technician, you will be required to install network adapter cards in PCs and to connect them to a network. You will also be expected to be able to diagnose and troubleshoot network connections. The A+ exam tests these skills under objectives 5.2 and 5.3.

Exam objectives 5.2 and 5.3
5.2 Install, configure, optimise and upgrade networks
Install and configure network cards (physical address).
Install, identify and obtain wired and wireless connection.

5.3 Identify tools, diagnostic procedures and troubleshooting techniques for networks
Explain status indicators, for example speed, connection and activity lights and wireless signal strength.

Install and configure a network adapter

Many modern PCs, especially laptop / notebook computers, have network connectivity built into the motherboard. This is almost invariably a port for an RJ45 connector, supporting 10/100 Mbps Ethernet connections, though 1000 Mbps (1 Gigabit) connections are increasingly common.

Where there is no on-board LAN connector, it is necessary to install a Network Interface Card (NIC). This will fit into one of the standard expansion slots, usually a Peripheral Component Interconnect (PCI) slot or Peripheral Component Interconnect Express (PCI-E) slot, although you may still occasionally encounter cards that fit into the obsolescent Industry Standard Architecture (ISA) slot. Most modern cards use the RJ45 connector, although thinnet (coaxial) may still be supported by some older cards. Figure 15.1 shows an ISA dual-use card, which supports both standards.

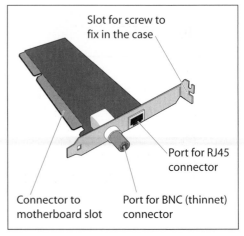

Figure 15.1

Fitting the card

In order to fit the card, power down the machine and (following the standard antistatic precautions):

1   Remove the case lid / side.

2   Locate an unused expansion slot and remove the cover plate.

3   Fit the new card in the free slot and secure the screw that holds it to the case. Replace the lid / side and start up the machine.

4   As the machine boots, you should see a message indicating that Microsoft Windows® has found new hardware. Microsoft Windows® XP is generally better than 2000 in this respect and modern cards (PCI) are more likely to plug and play than ISA cards. Depending on the operating system version and the card, it may just work 'out of the box'. If it does not, you will have to provide drivers from a manufacturer's disk or download them from the manufacturer's site. Wireless network cards in particular may require you to install software drivers before fitting the card in the motherboard slot – consult the manufacturer's documentation before you start.

Addressing

Modern Microsoft Windows® versions – particularly XP – are normally quite good at automatically configuring the necessary resources. You can examine these through the XP Device Manager.

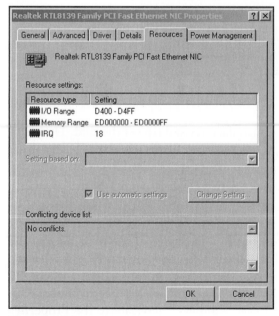

Figure 15.2

It is not necessary to change the system-determined settings unless Device Manager is reporting a conflict, or there are other operational problems with resources. If such adjustments are necessary, consult the manufacturer's documentation. It is very occasionally necessary to change physical jumpers on the card, although operating system software is usually sufficient to do the job.

A further addressing task may be necessary to bind the hardware (MAC) address of the card to a higher-level addressing scheme such as Internet Protocol (IP) addressing or an IPX address in Netware®. These topics are examined in Chapter 13.

Install, identify and obtain wired and wireless connection

With the network card physically installed, simply connecting to the existing LAN – whether wired or wireless – is usually automatic. By default, Microsoft Windows® allocates an IP address either through the Dynamic Host Configuration Protocol (DHCP) where there is a DHCP server on the network, or Automatic Private IP Addressing (APIPA) where there is not. The alternative to these addressing methods is to use Static IP addressing.

IP address assignments

To check the status of a network card, navigate through the Microsoft Windows® Control Panel and look at its properties, or use the command IPCONFIG /ALL from a system prompt. Figure 15.3 shows the output of this command on a PC running Microsoft Windows® XP and using static IP addressing.

```
Ethernet adapter Local Area Connection 1:

        Connection-specific DNS Suffix  . :
        Description . . . . . . . . . . . : Intel(R) PRO/100+ PCI Adapter
        Physical Address. . . . . . . . . : 00-A0-C9-E6-23-F9
        Dhcp Enabled. . . . . . . . . . . : No
        IP Address. . . . . . . . . . . . : 192.168.2.25
        Subnet Mask . . . . . . . . . . . : 255.255.255.0
        Default Gateway . . . . . . . . . : 192.168.2.1
        DNS Servers . . . . . . . . . . . : 192.168.2.1
```

Figure 15.3

The description field in the figure tells us the manufacturer and type of the card. The physical address is the burnt-on, hardware, or MAC address, and the next field – DHCP enabled: 'No' – tells us that the IP address has been allocated manually – a static IP address.

Static IP addressing

In a static IP addressing scheme, all that is necessary to obtain a connection is that the newly added PC is given a static IP address in the same range as the remainder of the network and that this address is unique. For a small network – say ten PCs in the same room – this can work quite well. However, once the network becomes larger, it becomes difficult to keep track of the IP addresses and to ensure that each of them is unique. In order to allocate a static IP address in Microsoft Windows®, navigate to the **Properties** sheet of the network adapter and change the default value from **Obtain an IP address automatically** to **Use the following IP address**, and allocate a static IP address in the correct range.

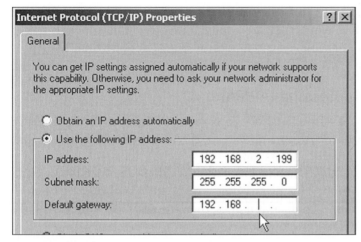

Figure 15.4

Figure 15.4 shows the process of allocating a static IP address to an adapter in Microsoft Windows® 2000 Professional. The process is all but identical in XP.

Dynamic Host Configuration Protocol (DHCP)

As noted earlier, the default setting for Microsoft Windows® systems is to obtain an IP address automatically and the most effective (and most commonly used) method is DHCP. Figure 15.5 shows the output of the IPCONFIG /ALL command for an Microsoft Windows® XP PC which is set up in this way.

```
Ethernet adapter Local Area Connection 1:

        Connection-specific DNS Suffix  . : elenmar
        Description . . . . . . . . . . . : Intel(R) PRO/100+ PCI Adapter
        Physical Address. . . . . . . . . : 00-A0-C9-E6-23-F9
        Dhcp Enabled. . . . . . . . . . . : Yes
        Autoconfiguration Enabled . . . . : Yes
        IP Address. . . . . . . . . . . . : 192.168.2.101
        Subnet Mask . . . . . . . . . . . : 255.255.255.0
        Default Gateway . . . . . . . . . : 192.168.2.1
        DHCP Server . . . . . . . . . . . : 192.168.2.1
        DNS Servers . . . . . . . . . . . : 192.168.2.1
        Lease Obtained. . . . . . . . . . : 09 October 2006 08:19:09
        Lease Expires . . . . . . . . . . : 16 October 2006 08:19:09
```

Figure 15.5

This setting causes Microsoft Windows® to look for a DHCP server on the network. If it finds a DHCP server, it requests an IP address from it. The DHCP server selects an unused IP address from its pool of addresses and offers it to the requesting node. If this is accepted, then the node becomes the 'bound client' of that server. The server will provide as a minimum:

- IP address

- Subnet mask

- Default gateway (address for connection to other network segments)

Other settings may be provided, but this will depend on the configuration of the DHCP server.

Where a node is set up to obtain an IP address automatically, it will look for a DHCP server and will use its services when they are available. However, if a DHCP server cannot be found (if it does not exist, or is temporarily out of action) then Microsoft Windows® will use Automatic Private IP Addressing (APIPA).

Automatic Private IP Addressing (APIPA)

The address range 169.254.0.0–169.254.255.255 is reserved (by IANA the Internet Assigned Numbers Authority) for Automatic Private IP Addressing. This means that there is no conflict with any other IP address range.

The subnet mask for the APIPA range is 255.255.0.0 so there are 65,534 available node addresses for self-allocation. This means that a node address chosen at random from this pool is unlikely to cause a conflict. If it does, then the node will simply try again until it can establish a unique IP address on the LAN.

Once the APIPA address has been established, then the node can communicate with other nodes on the same subnet – that is, with addresses in the APIPA-defined range – even if these addresses have in fact been allocated statically.

To tell if a node is using an APIPA address, run IPCONFIG /ALL. If DHCP Enabled is set to 'Yes' and the address starts 169.254, then the node is using APIPA. If the address starts 169.254, but DHCP Enabled is set to 'No', then the IP address has been allocated manually: a static IP address compatible with the APIPA range.

Note: APIPA is not available in either Microsoft Windows® 95 or NT 4.

Obtaining a connection

Once the NIC has been physically installed and the PC powered up again, you should be able to connect to an existing network simply by attaching the appropriate cable type to the port on the PC and plugging it into the network. In the case of a wireless network, providing that the PC is within range of a base station / wireless access point, connection should be more or less automatic (more on wireless connections later).

If you do not obtain a connection after rebooting the PC, you will need to check a few basic items:

1   Check physical connections – that the NIC is properly seated and that the cable is of the correct type. Use a 'known good' cable from another PC if necessary. Check that the NIC is listed in Microsoft Windows® Device Manager.

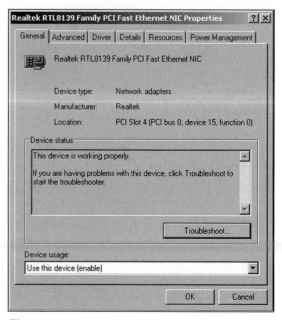

Figure 15.6

2   Figure 15.6 shows a functioning network card as it appears in the General tab of Device Manager. Other information and settings can be viewed or modified through the other tabs.

3   Check that you are using the appropriate addressing scheme for the network to which you are connecting. Use the IPCONFIG command to determine whether you are using dynamic or static addressing and make any necessary changes.

4   On a TCP / IP network, use the command PING 127.0.0.1 to verify that you have a working TCP / IP installation. Note that this does not test the NIC as such, merely that the PING command can elicit a response from the reserved loopback IP address, which is a diagnostic tool available on all TCP / IP networks.

```
C:\>PING 127.0.0.1

Pinging 127.0.0.1 with 32 bytes of data:

Reply from 127.0.0.1: bytes=32 time<1ms TTL=128
Reply from 127.0.0.1: bytes=32 time<1ms TTL=128
Reply from 127.0.0.1: bytes=32 time<1ms TTL=128
Reply from 127.0.0.1: bytes=32 time<1ms TTL=128

Ping statistics for 127.0.0.1:
    Packets: Sent = 4, Received = 4, Lost = 0 (0% loss),
Approximate round trip times in milli-seconds:
    Minimum = 0ms, Maximum = 0ms, Average = 0ms
```

Figure 15.7

Figure 15.7 shows a successful PING of the loopback address on a Microsoft Windows® XP PC.

Obtaining a wireless connection

The checks in Device Manager and the use of the PING command are both useful if you are having difficulty in obtaining a wireless connection. Generally, however, Microsoft

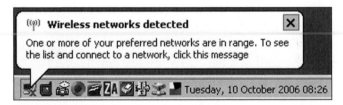

Figure 15.8

Windows® will find an available wireless network and alert you to this. Figure 15.8 shows such an alert in the notification area / system tray of a Microsoft Windows® XP system.

As an alternative, in XP navigate to the **Control Panel** and select the applet for **Network Connections**. Right-click on the icon for the connection and select the **View available wireless networks** option from the context menu. This will present you with a list of available wireless networks. Select your preferred network from the list and click on the **Connect** button.

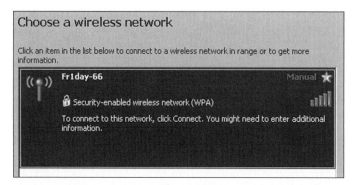

Figure 15.9

Microsoft Windows® 2000 does not provide this interface as part of Microsoft Windows®, but you can obtain the same functionality through the wireless NIC manufacturer's software utilities.

If you are unable to connect to the listed network, then you probably have a problem with security settings. Security – including wireless network security – is the subject of Chapter 16.

If no wireless networks are listed and you have checked Device Manager, the addressing scheme and used the PING command on the loopback address successfully, then you have the wireless equivalent of a cabling problem. Check the antennae at either end of the connection and try relocating the PC. When working in the field, it is also worth checking for possible outside factors such as cordless phones, mobiles, microwaves, etc. that may be in the next office or even the next building!

Status indicators

Network cards have LEDs that indicate the status of various variables. These will vary from card to card and it may be necessary to consult the manufacturer's documentation for details. However, as a minimum you should expect a *link indicator* and an *activity indicator*. The link indicator will show a steady light to indicate that the NIC is connected to a valid network connection and the activity indicator flashes as network data is sent or received. Because many NICs are dual speed, 10/100 Mbps or 100/1000 Mbps, there may be an indicator to show the operation speed of the card in a particular installation. There may be other indicators to show, for example, collision detection and whether the card is working in full- or half-duplex mode. In full-duplex mode, a card can send and receive data simultaneously; in half-duplex, it can either transmit or receive, but not both simultaneously. There may also be status indicators on the switch or hub used to connect the PCs.

Wireless signal strength

Wireless signal strength is typically reported through software – either Microsoft Windows® or management software from the card's manufacturer. The strength of the signal is a measure of how fast data can be transferred and obviously the stronger / faster the connection the better. In practice, quite small changes in the position of the equipment or orientation of the antennae can make significant differences to reported signal strengths. Figure 15.10 shows a less than perfect connection speed as reported by Microsoft Windows® XP and Figure 15.11 shows the full strength signal after a reorientation of the antenna on the wireless NIC in the PC.

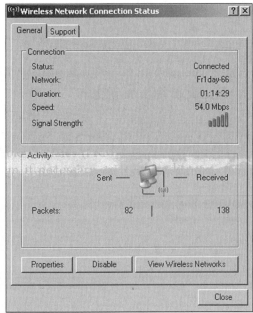

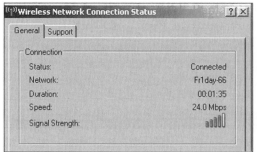

Figure 15.10   Figure 15.11

Troubleshooting guidelines

The key to any form of troubleshooting is to adopt a systematic approach. Chapter 7 looks at troubleshooting PC hardware and Chapter 10 deals with fault diagnosis in operating systems. You may find it useful to refer to these chapters.

Start with the obvious

Many faults with PCs – networked or otherwise – arise from really simple things: loose connectors, lack of power, incorrect passwords, so the first step in troubleshooting is to check the obvious. Does the faulty device – PC, printer, router, etc. – have power and a connection to the network?

- Check for mains power.
- Reseat any cables that may be loose.
- Reboot.
- Check status indicators, LEDs, etc.

All devices on your network have volatile RAM memory and this can become fragmented, corrupted or misallocated in the course of day-to-day operations. The cure for this is simply to reboot the device. This will restore the contents of RAM and can fix many problems. If it does not fix the problem, you will have eliminated one of the possibilities, and that is the key to successful fault diagnosis – patient systematic investigation of the possibilities and eliminating the possibilities one by one until a solution is found.

Once you have checked for physical connections and rebooted the PC, the next step is to reproduce the problem. Where the problem has been reported by a user, enlisting their cooperation is one of the 'soft skills' that is sometimes underestimated in the troubleshooting process.

Reproduce the problem

The most important question that you ask the user is Can you show me? If you haven't already done so, reboot the machine and ask the user to demonstrate the problem. Check that they are logging in to the system with a correct user name and password and note any error message that may be displayed at the point of failure.

Isolate the problem

The most commonly reported problem from users is the inability to log in to the network. A useful method to determine whether this is a node problem, a network problem, or a user account problem is:

1   Log in to the network using your own credentials. If you can log in, but the user can not, then the hardware is functioning properly.

2   Ask the user to log in from another node on the network. If he or she can log in from a different point on the network, then the problem is with the PC. If not, then it is probably a password problem. As an A+ working tech you probably will not have sufficient network rights to reset the user's password so at this point you would probably refer the problem to the network administrator.

Some more troubleshooting tools

One of the most common network problems that you will encounter is simple lack of connectivity arising from either a failed NIC or a defective cable, so a 'known good' spare of each of these can be useful tools in the working technician's kit.

Spare network card

If there are no lights on the existing card, power down and replace with a new one. Power up, configure as necessary for your network, and then try again. If this works, fine. If not, you may well have a cable problem.

Spare cable

The patch cables that attach the workstation PCs to the wall jacks are a common point of failure. Replacing a suspect patch cable with a known good replacement is the work of a few seconds. Another useful tool is a spare crossover cable. Detach the workstation from the network and connect to a spare PC or a laptop with a crossover cable. If, with a new NIC and a known good patch cable, you cannot connect to the network, but you can connect over a crossover cable, then you are probably looking at a problem with the main premises' cabling.

Beyond essentials

There are two useful system-level commands that we have already mentioned in passing that you will find useful when troubleshooting network problems. These are PING and IPCONFIG. Although you are not required to know them for the Essentials exam, they are too useful to ignore.

PING

The software tool PING is available on all operating systems – including Microsoft Windows® – for diagnosing TCP / IP networks. You can ping a remote system by name or by IP address. If you cannot ping a device on your network, then you have a basic connectivity problem – check cable, card and configuration, in that order.

If you successfully ping by name, the command will show the numeric IP address of the remote machine. If you ping across the Internet, and you find that you can ping a site by its IP address but not its name, then you probably have an incorrect setting for the Domain Name Service (DNS) so check your settings against those given to you by your network administrator.

IPCONFIG

The IPCONFIG command can be used at a system prompt to show the current configuration of the system. Every node on your network needs to be on the same network – that is have an IP address and settings that are compatible with everything else. Suppose, for example, that you have checked cable and card and established that you have connectivity at the hardware level, a possible cause may be wrong settings. Use IPCONFIG to check them. On a network that uses DHCP to allocate IP addresses, you can use this command to obtain a new IP address like this:

1 IPCONFIG /RELEASE – clears the current settings

2 IPCONFIG /RENEW – obtains new settings from the DHCP server

3 IPCONFIG – to view the new settings

Knowledge of the PING and IPCONFIG commands – along with some others – is required for both the Field Service Technician (220-602) exam and the Remote Support Technician (220-603) exam, so by getting to grips with them now you are not wasting your time.

SUMMARY

In this chapter we have looked at the basics of installing, configuring and troubleshooting networks. The A+ certified technician is not required to know any advanced network material – there are other qualifications such as Network+ or Server+ which cover this. For both the exams and the practicalities of the workplace, you should concentrate your efforts on knowing how to connect a node to an existing network. You should be able to fit a network card and configure it according to values (such as the IP addressing scheme) provided by your network administrator. You also need to be able to diagnose problems with connectivity – physical or logical – using the tools and techniques outlined in this chapter. The key to troubleshooting anything is a patient logical approach: start with the obvious, ask questions, and isolate symptoms until you converge on a solution. Typically, exam questions test these skills by giving you a scenario, perhaps outlining some of the steps already taken, and asking 'what do you do next?' or 'what is the most likely cause?'

QUESTIONS

1   You have been asked to connect a PC to a small workplace LAN, but there is no LAN port visible on the back of the machine. You install a new LAN card of the correct type and reboot the PC. It Plugs & Plays the new hardware. You attach the PC to the wall jack, but are unable to connect to the network. Status lights on the card show signs of activity. What do you check next?

a) The patch cable

b) The seating of the card on the motherboard

c) The IP addressing scheme for the network

d) The availability of the DHCP server

2   A PC has been returned from the base workshop after repairs. You attach it to the LAN, but it cannot see other nodes on the network. You test the physical connections and they are OK. What is the most likely cause of the failure?

a) Static IP address in the wrong range

b) Wrong subnet mask

d) DHCP server has failed

d) Wrong type of network card

▶

3 A user reports that they cannot connect to the network. You visit them at their desk and, after introducing yourself and asking the nature of the problem, what do you do next?

a) Check the activity lights on the network card

b) Attempt to log in to the network yourself

c) Ask the user to show you the problem

d) Replace the patch cable

ANSWERS / EXPLANATION

1 You have been asked to connect a PC to a small workplace LAN, but there is no LAN port visible on the back of the machine. You install a new LAN card of the correct type and reboot the PC. It Plugs & Plays the new hardware. You attach the PC to the wall jack, but are unable to connect to the network. Status lights on the card show signs of activity. What do you check next?

a) The patch cable

This is the next logical step. b is unlikely because you have working activity lights. c and d are possible, but less fundamental than a. Therefore A is the best answer

2 A PC has been returned from the base workshop after repairs. You attach it to the LAN, but it cannot see other nodes on the network. You test the physical connections and they are OK. What is the most likely cause of the failure?

a) Static IP address in the wrong range.

3 A user reports that they cannot connect to the network. You visit them at their desk and, after introducing yourself and asking the nature of the problem, what do you do next?

c) Ask the user to show you the problem

Always ask the customer to reproduce the problem first.

CHAPTER 16
Principles of security

Security is a major concern for all PC users, particularly in industry and commerce. There is a Security+ exam that tests knowledge of security in depth, but the A+ technician needs to be familiar with the fundamentals. The A+ Essentials exam gives security an 11 per cent weighting. All of the Elective exams have a Security domain, so whatever combination of exams you choose as your route to A+ certification, learning the material presented in this chapter will be well worth the effort.

Exam objective 6.1
6.1 Identify the fundamental principles of security

Identify names, purposes and characteristics of hardware and software security, for example:

> Hardware deconstruction / recycling
> Smart cards / biometrics (e.g. key fobs, cards, chips and scans)
> Authentication technologies (e.g. user name, password, biometrics, smart cards)
> Malicious software protection (e.g. viruses, Trojans, worms, spam, spyware, adware, greyware)
> Software firewalls
> File system security (e.g. FAT32 and NTFS)

Identify names, purposes and characteristics of wireless security, for example:

> Wireless encryption (e.g. WEP.x and WPA.x) and client configuration
> Access points (e.g. disable DHCP / use static IP, change SSID from default, disable SSID broadcast, MAC filtering, change default username and password, update firmware, firewall)

Identify names, purposes and characteristics of data and physical security:

> Data access (basic local security policy)
> Encryption technologies
> Back-ups
> Data migration

▶

Data / remnant removal
Password management
Locking workstation (e.g. hardware, operating system)
Describe importance and process of incidence reporting.
Recognise and respond appropriately to social engineering situations.

Security

Security in its various forms is an area of increasing interest and concern throughout the computer industry, which is why CompTIA have added a Security domain to the new 2006 exam specification. As mentioned above, the subject accounts for 11 per cent of the marks for the Essentials exam and is featured in all the other A+ exams as well. This is an important area of knowledge in the workplace too.

Hardware and software security

One of the purposes of security measures is to prevent access to information by unauthorised persons while making data easily available to legitimate users. In order to achieve this, we have to pay attention to both the physical media (hardware) on which the information is stored as well as the various technologies – hardware and software – that are used to regulate access.

Hardware deconstruction / recycling

All of the information on a computer system is encoded as zeroes and ones on hardware storage media. This includes removable media such as back-up tapes, DVDs, CDs and even floppy disks, as well as internal and external storage media such as hard disk drives.

Removable media should be stored securely when in use and destroyed when no longer required. Reusable media such as back-up tapes or hard drives can be recycled provided sufficient precautions are taken. Hard disks for example, even if they have been reformatted using normal operating system tools, may still contain data which is recoverable with the appropriate specialist tools. If it is policy in your workplace to recycle old storage media, particularly if they are to be reused outside the organisation by selling them or donating them to third parties, they will require special treatment. Proprietary software tools are available for disk erasure and there are standards set by various organisations, such as the United States National Computer Security Centre and European government agencies, to ensure proper levels of security in erasure procedures. Failure to erase data effectively can compromise data security for your whole organisation.

Smart cards / biometrics

At its simplest, a smart card is an electronic key which unlocks an electronic lock to give the holder access to various resources from buildings, or parts of buildings, or computer systems. The card contains information about the holder's identity, access privileges and so on, which can be checked by a card-reading device attached to the protected area or system. The main disadvantage to this is that if the card is stolen, the thief has access to the resources that are supposed to be protected.

A more sophisticated approach is to add details of the card that are known only to the authorised holder, such as a password or PIN, which act as a check that the person using the card is the legitimate owner. An everyday example of this approach is the chip and PIN credit cards that have been widely adopted in recent years.

The principle of authenticating the user as the legitimate owner of the card can be extended further by encoding biometric data such as fingerprints or the retinal patterns of the owner's eyes on the smart card.

Key fobs are small hardware devices that incorporate rapidly changing codes and can be used along with a PIN (or other code) known only to the card holder. The fundamental principle of all of these approaches is that they combine the possession of an object (card, fob, etc.) with information known only to the legitimate user or based on their personal characteristics.

Authentication technologies

Authentication is the process of checking that the user is, in fact, the person that they claim to be. The most familiar example of this is the requirement that each user of a system has a user name and password, and the detail of how this is implemented has implications for security. If you allow 'easy' passwords, then the whole system is compromised. It only requires one person to think that they are the first person to think that DROWSSAP (password backwards) is difficult to guess and you have a huge hole in your security. On the other hand, if you have a policy (which can be implemented through the Microsoft Windows® operating system) that forces users to use complex passwords and to change them from time to time, there will be an increase in users asking for forgotten passwords to be reset or – worse – an outbreak of sticky labels on the sides of monitors proclaiming the password to the world. As we will see later in the chapter, it is important for users to understand the nature of security and the part that 'social engineering' can play in a security attack.

Malicious software protection: viruses, Trojans, etc.

Malicious software – often known by the collective name of *malware* – has been an increasing nuisance over recent years. Protection against the various viruses, Trojans, worms etc., is a necessary part of security whether at the level of an individual system or an entire network. Viruses – malicious programs that replicate themselves and damage systems – have been with us for years and more sophisticated approaches such as spyware and root kits can conceal themselves on systems for the purposes of identity theft.

The most basic form of protection against malware is to maintain up-to-date scanner software and to use it. Users should also be made aware of the dangers of downloading, installing (or attempting to install) unauthorised software or even visiting certain 'dodgy' sites at all.

Malicious software and the measures that you can take to counter it are discussed more fully in Chapter 17.

Software firewalls

A firewall – hardware or software based – is the first line of defence for a network when it connects to another network such as the Internet. Its role is roughly that of a door-keeper – to allow in only that which has been requested and to reject (or simply drop) unsolicited material from external sources. A firewall may be implemented as a dedicated stand-alone device or as a piece of software running on a gateway or router, or simply as an application on a PC.

Packet filtering

TCP / IP networks route data in packets. Each packet contains both data and addressing information such as the IP address of the sender, the protocol used to send the packet, the port number, and so on. Filtering based on this information is known (unsurprisingly) as *packet filtering*. It is frequently implemented on the router that controls access to external networks such as the Internet. For example, port 23 is used by the Telnet proto-col for communications between systems. This is an insecure transfer method, so you may want to block it. To do this, the filter is set up either to reject packets on port 23 or simply to drop them without a response. Most packet filtering systems can be set to allow or deny traffic on particular ports or from particular IP addresses.

A *proxy firewall* is an intermediary that stands between your network and the outside world. It intercepts all communications and makes rule-based decisions about which packets should be forwarded and which should be rejected or dropped. It also performs Network Address Translation (NAT) between the systems so that the internal addresses of your network nodes are never seen by the other end of the network connection – these are translated to and from a 'public' IP address on the Internet side of the firewall.

Stateful packet filtering adds a further layer to the process of packet filtering. Whereas packet filtering processes each packet then forgets about it, a stateful system keeps a state table of all transactions between the systems.

File system security

The default, and preferred, file system for Microsoft Windows® 2000 and XP operating systems is the NT file system (NTFS), which was developed by Microsoft for their NT family of operating systems. From the outset, it was intended to provide the sort of secu-rity features required in business. Earlier 'home user' Microsoft Windows® versions – 98 and Millennium, for example – used a File Allocation Table system (FAT) for organising files on hard disks. The 32-bit version of this was known as FAT 32 and this is still avail-able as an option when installing modern Microsoft Windows® versions (2000 and XP) and when formatting disks for use on those systems.

FAT systems are inherently insecure, particularly in network terms. The only types of protection available are at share level or user level on a drive or directory (folder) on the target system. Under these arrangements, anyone who has (say) read / write access to a particular directory has that level of access to all of its contents – subdirectories, files, etc.

NTFS implements its security through Access Control Lists (ACLs) and can apply these at the level of volumes, directories or even individual files. It can also specify the type of access at each of these levels: Read Only, Change, or Full Control.

NTFS security can be applied to both local volumes and disks as well as on network shares. It also supports file encryption.

In addition to the improved security that NTFS offers in terms of security, it is also more efficient in handling large disks and offers greater stability than the older FAT-based systems.

Practical exercise with file systems

This is a long exercise and could well be done in conjunction with the operating system material presented in Chapters 8 and 9.

1 Install either Microsoft Windows® 2000 or XP on a FAT32 partition.
2 Create user accounts on the system.
3 Create shares, change user permissions, etc.
4 Test shares and access rights locally and, if possible, on your network.
5 Run the drive conversion utility to (non-destructively) convert the volume to NTFS.
6 Repeat the tests at 2, 3 and 4 above and note the results.

Wireless security

All of the security considerations that apply to wired networks – physical security, password policies, protection from malware, etc. – apply in equal measure to wireless networks. In addition, though, the process of sending data across wireless links is more susceptible to interception than similar transmissions over wired or fibre-optic media. In order to close the security gap between wired and wireless networks, two encryption standards have been devised by the industry. These are Wired Equivalent Privacy (WEP) and Wi-Fi Protected Access (WPA).

Wired Equivalent Privacy (WEP)

Wireless networking standards are specified in the Institute of Electrical and Electronics Engineers (IEEE) standard IEEE 802.11. Part of the specification is the security measures known as Wired Equivalent Privacy (WEP). As the name suggests, this was intended to give a degree of security to wireless networks similar to that provided by wired networks.

One of the weaknesses of the 802.11 standard is that it does not require any form of security by default. A wireless access point broadcasts its Service Set Identifier (SSID) and any client within range can connect to it at the click of a mouse. The WEP standard imposes a requirement to provide a network key both to authenticate the user (like a password) and to encrypt the data as it passes over the network.

WEP originally used a 64-bit key, though this was later upgraded to 128-bit, and some systems support a 256-bit key. An encryption key is set up by the network administrator and users who wish to access the network need to provide it in order to connect to the network. This is reasonable security if all you need to do is to prevent casual unauthorised access, but even where long encryption keys are used, it has been demonstrated that it can be cracked in a matter of hours (sometimes less) using easily available software tools on a standard PC or laptop.

As a stop-gap measure, WEP2 was introduced and this made 128-bit encryption mandatory. However, it doesn't run on all hardware and can still be cracked by using the appropriate tools. WEP+ is a proprietary standard enhancement of WEP, but is of limited use because it has to be used on both ends of the connection.

Wi-Fi Protected Access (WPA)

WPA was created by the Wi-Fi Alliance – the trade association that owns the Wi-Fi trade mark – in order to close the gaps that had been discovered in the WEP standard. WPA was introduced in advance of the final version of the IEEE 802.11i standard and implements most of the requirements of that standard. It is designed for use with an authentication server, which provides a different key for each user. There is also a less secure mode of operation which uses a Pre-shared Key (PSK), which is given to all users of the system. The PSK mode is also known as 'personal mode' and can be used by households or small businesses who are unwilling (or unable) to deploy an authentication server. In this mode, the PSK is held on the Wireless Access Point and must be entered by the user in order to access the network. It is generally possible to store the PSK on the user's workstation to avoid the need for re-entry at each connection.

WPA2 is a further development of the standard (published in June 2004) that uses the Advanced Encryption Standard (AES) to deliver a greater level of security. There may be compatibility problems with WPA / WPA2 with older Wireless Access Points and network cards. They may need new drivers, a firmware upgrade, or even to be replaced altogether. Microsoft Windows® XP operating system support for WPA2 was officially announced in May 2005 and, after March 2006, WPA2 certification will be required for new devices that wish to be sold as Wi-Fi Certified.

Wireless Access Points

Although it is possible to network a handful of PCs using Wi-Fi without a Wireless Access Point (ad hoc networking) most wireless networks are organised through a Wireless Access Point (WAP), which is – roughly speaking – the equivalent of a workgroup hub or switch. In order to make set-up and connectivity as easy as possible, most WAPs have default settings that are insecure. There is usually a default IP address for the WAP and a default SSID, which it broadcasts. There may also be default (or even blank) passwords and user names that make access to the WAP's settings easy. Because these defaults are stated in the manufacturer's documentation and are widely available on the Internet, it is strongly recommended that you change them. It is also good practice to update firmware for these devices on installation or as required.

Once you have set non-default user names and passwords and carried out any firmware update that may be needed, there are a number of steps that you can take to improve basic security.

- **Disable DHCP / use static IP**. By default, Microsoft Windows® clients are set to obtain an IP address automatically. If the WAP is running a DHCP server (many do, by default), then any wireless-enabled PC / laptop that comes into range will obtain an IP address from it. If you turn off DHCP services on the access point, each node trying to join the network will have to be configured with a static IP address in the appropriate range. This imposes an administrative overhead – someone has to manage the static IPs – but it makes casual (even accidental) access to the network less likely.

- **Change SSID and disable SSID broadcast**. As we have noted earlier in the chapter, a wireless access point broadcasts its Service Set Identifier (SSID) and any client within range can connect to it at the click of a mouse. The SSID has a default value – often based on the manufacturer's name – which will be widely known, and this is broadcast for the benefit of any node in range. Changing the SSID to something difficult to guess and disabling broadcasting of the SSID effectively makes the hidden SSID into a password, that is the user needs to know the SSID in order to connect and, because it is held on the WAP, it can be changed from time to time.

- **MAC address filtering**. Each network adapter has a unique Media Access Control (MAC) address that is burned on to the hardware when it is manufactured. You can specify which MAC addresses will be given access to the network by filtering on the WAP so that only listed devices can have access. This means that, even with otherwise similar hardware and operating system configurations, a node that is not on the list of permitted MAC addresses will not be given access to the network.

- **Firewall**. Many WAPs – especially combination devices acting as routers or Internet gateways – have a built-in firewall. Enabling this can improve security by providing a first line of defence between your LAN and other networks such as the Internet. A hardware firewall of this type is sometimes used in addition to a software firewall that may be running elsewhere on the system.

Data and physical security

Unless you have basic physical security in place, your data is at risk of theft. Software tools are freely available that make it possible to crack the administrator password on any NT-based system in under five minutes. This means that an intruder can have access to all your data either on site or simply be stealing the equipment and cracking it at leisure later. Even where the motive is not data theft as such, if your hardware is stolen, dismantled and sold at a fraction of its worth, you will still be facing a severe test of your back-up strategy (see page 276 for more on back-ups).

A great deal of physical security needs to be implemented at the level of premises management and the A+ technician should (like all staff) be aware of the measures that are in place. For the most part, these are quite obvious measures such as restricting access to critical areas, locks, security patrols, cameras and other forms of electronic surveillance. Details will vary from installation to installation, depending on the perceived needs of the organisation and the importance or sensitivity of the data.

Detection of a security breach is also important. In the event of a breach, you need to know what was accessed and how so that you can plug the gap in security and minimise the consequences of the event. Security cameras that capture to tape can be useful in this respect.

A third component of physical security is planning a recovery strategy in the event of a loss. You should know how long it will take to replace stolen or vandalised equipment and how long it will take to reconfigure it and replace data from back-up.

With physical security in place, logical security of the data is achieved through password policies and the file system security described earlier. A further level of data security can be achieved by using encryption technologies.

Encryption technologies

Both Microsoft Windows® 2000 and XP support encryption of files and folders and encryption can be implemented with a couple of mouse clicks. Where a folder is encrypted, any file created in or moved to it will be encrypted as a matter of course. By default, Microsoft Windows® will identify encrypted files by showing their names in a different colour.

Other encryption technologies you may encounter are based on various hashing algorithms. The principle underlying these is simple, even though the mathematics may be difficult: a clear text message is encoded using a key that can be used to decrypt and reconstruct the original message by the recipient. The encryption methods that you encounter most often are Secure Hash Algorithm (SHA) and variations on the Message Digest Algorithm (MDA) such as MD5, MD4 and MD2.

Back-ups

A back-up is a copy of information which is independent of its source. It could consist of paper-based records as well as electronic files, though in computer terms we are usually interested in electronic copies of electronic data. These should normally be stored away from the computer system, in another room, in a fireproof safe, or on different premises altogether. The last option – storage on different premises – may include backing up over a network to a secure storage facility, which may even be owned by a third party.

Disaster recovery strategies depend heavily on the existence of back-up copies of data that can be restored in the event of catastrophic equipment failures, fire, theft or damage by malware or other attacks.

Various media may be used for the storage of back-up information, from burning to CD / DVD in a small office, to tape drives on servers or even redundant copies of entire servers. The backed-up data may be stored on site, or off site, or some combination of the two. What is important for back-ups is to have a thought-out system that is properly implemented.

Working / shadow copies

These are usually held on site and are performed frequently. They allow for the replacement of files that are corrupted, lost or accidentally deleted. These shadow copies are operationally useful, but are not adequate to protect all data from all potential disasters. In order to protect all data – and that will include metadata such as user account details and configuration settings – you need an organised system that covers all of the data, all of the time. This is normally achieved by a combination of three types of back-up:

- Full back-up
- Incremental back-up
- Differential back-up

Full back-up

As the name suggests, this consists of backing up all data files to removable media suitable for off-site storage. If you are using an automated overnight back-up system, you can simply do a full back-up overnight, every night. This means that in the event of data loss you can restore all data (up to the previous night's back-up) from a single tape or other storage medium. If you are also operating shadow copies, you may be able to recover data almost to the time of the loss.

Incremental back-up

This backs up only those files that have been modified since the last back-up of any kind. For example, if you did a full back-up on Monday, followed by incremental back-ups on Tuesday and Wednesday, the Wednesday back-up would not include files modified on Tuesday. In the event of a failure, you would need to restore from three tapes. First, you would restore from the full back-up that you made on Monday, then from the Tuesday tape to recover files backed up on Tuesday, then from the Wednesday tape, and so on until you have restored from the entire series from the last full back-up to the last incremental back-up.

Differential back-up

This backs up all files that have been changed since the last full back-up. In the event of data loss, you can restore all data by restoring the last full back-up, followed by restoring the last differential back-up – that is, you need to restore from two tapes (or other storage media) to recover all of your backed-up data.

Media rotation

It is advisable to have more than one back-up of your data because, if one set of back-up media is lost or destroyed, then restoring from an earlier version is considerably better than nothing.

The most common rotation system is generally known as *grandfather, father, son*. As the name suggests, there are three back-ups – or if you are using a mixture of full and differential / incremental back-ups – three back-up sets.

For the sake of simplicity, we will assume that you are using a tape drive to back up all your data every day – that is, a full back-up, possibly as an automated overnight job.

1　On day 1, make a full back-up to tape 1 (grandfather). Label it and store it somewhere safe where it will not be subjected to extremes of temperature, or strong magnetic fields.

2　On day 2, make a further back-up to tape 2 (father). Label it and store it.

3　On day 3, make a further back-up to tape 3 (son). Label it and store it.

4　On day 4, overwrite the data of the grandfather tape, tape 1. You have now established a rotating three-tape set: grandfather, father and son.

Using this system, you will always have a back-up that is no more than 24 hours old and two further back-ups that are 24 and 48 hours old respectively. In the event of the last tape being lost, destroyed or corrupted, you can still recover the bulk of your data from one of the earlier tapes. It is good practice to keep at least one generation of the tapes – usually the 'father' tape in secure off-site storage, if only by taking it home. This means that even if your premises are burgled, bombed or struck by lightning, the bulk of your data will survive.

Network back-up

As a supplement to back-up systems that use various removable media, some people set up a system that copies files from the central file store to another machine on the network. This can be a useful supplement to backing up to removable storage, but it is not a satisfactory substitute for it unless you are able to back up to remote storage. If you really need it, there are companies that will rent you remote storage in secure off-site data centres.

Data migration

It is necessary to migrate data between systems from time to time. The process involves backing up data to removable media and reinstating it on the target system. From a security point of view, you need to be sure that the two systems make this possible, particularly that the access controls on the new system give the same levels of data access to the correct groups of users. Obviously, it is good practice to migrate the data and test that the migration has been successful – probably on a test system first – before considering what to do with old or intermediate media.

Data / remnant removal

Once data has been successfully migrated, old storage media from the old system and any intermediate storage used in the process – disks etc. – need to be cleaned up so that data cannot be recovered from them. Earlier in the chapter (see page 257) we looked at hardware deconstruction and recycling. The techniques outlined there are fundamental to the proper completion of a data migration exercise.

Password management

The management of passwords is achieved through the operating system. By default Microsoft Windows® 2003 servers will require a password to have both length and complexity requirements. It must not be based on the user's account name and must contain at least six characters. It must contain a mixture of upper- and lower-case letters, at least one numeral and one non-alphanumeric character. These requirements may be strengthened or weakened by the network administrator, who needs to find a balance between ease of access (easy passwords that suit users) and complexity which, if it is overdone, will result in people writing down passwords on or near their workstations. Other adjustments are also possible, for example forcing users to change passwords every few weeks, not allowing password changes too frequently, and so on. As an A+ technician, you are unlikely to be involved in setting password policies, but you should be aware of what they are in order to support users who may experience difficulty with them.

Locking workstations

At its simplest, this is just a setting in Microsoft Windows® that requires a password to be re-entered if the workstation has not been used for some predetermined length of time. On more sensitive systems, this approach may be complemented by the technologies such as smart cards, biometrics, etc. that we looked at earlier in the chapter.

Incident reporting

Large organisations frequently have detailed policies on incident reporting, including some definition of what constitutes a reportable incident. Smaller organisations may have less detailed policies and the way in which policies are framed and implemented may vary between different legislations. As a working technician, you need to know the incident reporting policies for your organisation and be able to implement them.

For our present purposes, we may regard an incident as being any attempt – successful or otherwise – to access a system for anything but legitimate use. This includes unauthorised access to data, introducing malicious code or attacks (such as Denial of Service attacks) intended to disrupt the normal functioning of the system. In some organisations, it may even include some types of equipment failure that expose weaknesses in the disaster recovery procedures of the organisation.

Regardless of how an 'incident' is defined in a particular organisation, a working A+ technician needs to know and be able to implement the relevant policy. In particular, you need to know:

- Resources used to deal with an incident
- Procedures to collect and secure evidence
- Which outside agencies should be contacted (and in what circumstances)

As a working technician, you are unlikely to have much (or any) input into the formulation of the policies. Your role is to know them and to implement them.

Social engineering

Social engineering is the term used to describe attempts to obtain information by non-technical means. Typically, the attacker will attempt to obtain information such as a password by social means – a form of confidence trick. This could take the form of a call to a help desk claiming to be a member of staff who has forgotten a password, or someone from a maintenance company who needs remote access to carry out urgent work. The rule here is simple: do not go along with it. No matter what the purported situation, no matter how urgent it is claimed to be, your company will have procedures for the issuing of passwords and credentials and these must be adhered to. The best response is to refer the enquirer to the relevant person in the company – network manager or system administrator, for example – and to log the call as an incident under your company's incident reporting procedures.

SUMMARY

This chapter has introduced the fundamentals of security principles and practices as required by the CompTIA A+ Essentials exam specification. In the workplace, the A+ certified technician will probably have little input into determining security policies, but will be required to know them and implement them for their own organisation. In terms of exam questions, you need to know the general principles for systems, not organisation-specific policies.

QUESTIONS

1   Your organisation has decided to decommission some systems and intends to donate the equipment to a local school. In order to protect the data that was on the system you need to?

   a) Reformat the hard disks

   b) Use specialist disk-cleaning software

   c) Remove the network adapter

   d) All of the above

2   You have been asked to implement a firewall on a Microsoft Windows® 2000 PC that connects directly to the Internet through a modem. Which of the following statements are true?

   a) The Microsoft Windows® built-in firewall is adequate for the job

   b) You need a third-party firewall package

   c) You need a separate hardware firewall device

   d) You need to connect through a router

3   You fit a recycled hard disk as secondary storage in a Microsoft Windows® XP PC. It has been formatted with the FAT 32 file system. In order to improve the security of the system, which of the following measures are appropriate?

    a) Convert the file system to NTFS

    b) Reformat the disk using NTFS

    c) Leave it as FAT 32

    d) Reformat the disk using HPFS

4   You have set up a small wireless network using a wireless access point. Now that you have a working network, what additional steps can you take to increase your security?

    a) Nothing. Default security settings are adequate

    b) Disable SSID broadcasting on the WAP

    c) Implement MAC address filtering for all users

    d) Disable DHCP

5   You receive an out-of-hours emergency call from the Managing Director of your company requesting her password which she has forgotten. You recognise her voice and she gives you personal details which confirm her identity. Do you?

    a) Give her the password

    b) Reset her password and give her access to the system

    c) Offer to obtain the information and call back

    d) Refuse and log the call as an attempted security breach

ANSWERS / EXPLANATIONS

1 Your organisation has decided to decommission some systems and intends to donate the equipment to a local school. In order to protect the data that was on the system you need to?

b) Use specialist disk-cleaning software

2 You have been asked to implement a firewall on a Microsoft Windows® 2000 PC that connects directly to the Internet through a modem. Which of the following statements are true?

b) You need a third-party firewall package

Microsoft Windows® 2000 doesn't have a built-in firewall. Neither a hardware firewall nor a router are necessary in this scenario.

3 You fit a recycled hard disk as secondary storage in a Microsoft Windows® XP PC. It has been formatted with the FAT 32 file system. In order to improve the security of the system, which of the following measures are appropriate?

a) Convert the file system to NTFS

OR

b) Reformat the disk using NTFS

4 You have set up a small wireless network using a wireless access point. Now that you have a working network, what additional steps can you take to increase your security?

b) Disable SSID broadcasting on the WAP

c) Implement MAC address filtering for all users

d) Disable DHCP

5 You receive an out-of-hours emergency call from the Managing Director of your company requesting her password which she has forgotten. You recognise her voice and she gives you personal details which confirm her identity. Do you?

d) Refuse and log the call as an attempted security breach.

Even if the call is genuine, any response but d would be a breach of security.

CHAPTER 17
Install and optimise security

The previous chapter looked at the principles of security This chapter looks at much of the same material from a slightly more practical point of view, though there is a fair amount of crossover between them. There is also a lot of overlap between the exam objectives in this chapter.

Exam objectives 6.2, 6.3 and 6.4
6.2 Install, configure, upgrade and optimise security
Install, configure, upgrade and optimise hardware, software and data security, for example:

BIOS
Smart cards
Authentication technologies
Malicious software protection
Data access (basic local security policy)
Back-up procedures and access to back-ups
Data migration
Data / remnant removal

6.3 Identify tool, diagnostic procedures and troubleshooting techniques for security
Diagnose and troubleshoot hardware, software and data security issues, for example:

BIOS
Smart cards, biometrics
Authentication technologies
Malicious software
File system (e.g. FAT 32, NTFS)
Data access (e.g. basic local security policy)
Back-up
Data migration

▶

6.4 Perform preventative maintenance for computer security

Implement software security preventative maintenance techniques such as installing service packs and patches and training users about malicious software prevention technologies.

Security

BIOS

BIOS – the Basic Input Output System – is the set of microcode programs stored on the BIOS chip that run at boot time. The information used by the BIOS programs, such as the order in which the system looks for boot devices, is stored in a table in CMOS (Complementary Metal Oxide Semiconductor) memory and this can be password protected against unauthorised changes by adding a password – a supervisor password. It is also possible to add a user password, which requires a password to be used in order for the boot sequence to proceed. Because these passwords, and other settings, are held in CMOS – a form of volatile memory – they can be blanked simply by removing the CMOS battery. Some motherboards have a jumper that can be used to reset the BIOS to default values, there are software utilities widely available to blank passwords and some BIOS manufacturers even ship their product with known default master passwords. BIOS security will delay a determined attempt to bypass it for a few minutes if the intruder has unsupervised physical access to the PC. Like many security features, BIOS security can only work properly where there is adequate physical security.

Smart cards, biometrics

Smart cards and biometrics have been described in Chapter 16. A straightforward swipe-card with no personal information is relatively easy to replicate and can be used by anyone if stolen. Chip and PIN – or cards containing biometric data – are considerably more secure, but still need to be managed. The general principle of security is this: make a better lock and someone, somewhere will make a key for it. Support staff – indeed all staff – need to be security conscious and to report anything suspicious.

Authentication technologies

As noted in Chapter 16, the most common form of authentication is the requirement to have a user name and password to access the system. There are, however, some security protocols used in the log on process that you need to be aware of.

Password Authentication Protocol (PAP)

Under the PAP system, a user name and password are sent across the network to the logon server as plain text and if they match, the user is given access. Obviously, plain text messages are susceptible to interception, so PAP is considered to be unacceptably insecure for secure networks.

Challenge Handshake Authentication Protocol (CHAP)

Under this system, the workstation sends a log on request to the server which responds with a challenge. The challenge is encrypted at the workstation end of the dialogue and sent back to the server. The encrypted values are compared and, if there is a match, then the log on can proceed. Because the authentication process uses encrypted values, it is obviously more secure than PAP.

Kerberos

The Kerberos protocol was originally developed at the Massachusetts Institute of Technology (MIT) and has been widely adopted for network security. It uses a security server – known as a Key Distribution Centre – to issue tickets. Under this system, a principal – which may be a user, a program or even a system – is authenticated and issued with a ticket. This ticket is then valid on all parts of the network. The main drawback of this system is that it requires the Key Distribution Centre to be continuously available – if the Kerberos server fails then no one has access to the network.

Certificates

Digital certificates may be physical devices or electronic certificates. Their key characteristic is that they are issued by a trusted third party known as a Certificate Authority (CA). Large institutions and government departments may have their own CA – there are also commercial CAs such as Verisign or Thawte, which are widely used on the Internet.

Security tokens

These are similar in operation to certificates. After a successful log on, the operating system issues a token that defines the user's access rights on the network. At the end of the session, the token is destroyed and a new one must be generated at the next log on.

Multi-factor authentication

This is a variation on 'belt and braces'. It is common to use more than one authentication method – for example, you may require users to have a smart card to access the workstation and then use Kerberos (or CHAP) to authenticate against the network server.

Malicious software

Malicious software – malware – is at best a nuisance, and at its worst may be a serious threat to the stability and security of your system. The first line of defence against these threats is appropriate up-to-date scanner software. A virus or adware scanner that has a definition file that is a week out of date is a security hole that must be plugged. A scanner that is a month out of date is worse than useless – it offers no protection from new threats and encourages a false sense of security.

Viruses, Trojans and worms

These are all terms for malicious code which, if run, may damage the infected system. Until they are run they are, of course, harmless.

Computer viruses are never naturally occurring; they are always man-made. Once created and released, however, their spread is not directly under human control.

Viruses, Trojans and worms are all written with malicious intent and it is illegal to distribute them. Their key characteristics are replication and some sort of payload. Unless the program replicated itself by some means, it would not be a problem and if it did not do something, we would not even know it was there. The replication aspect of a virus is also a major clue in its detection – the fact that a problem appears to be spreading across a group of PCs indicates a virus rather than (say) a hardware fault.

Virus types

Viruses are commonly classified according to their type and their means of distribution.

- **Boot sector viruses** infect or substitute their own code for either the DOS boot sector or the Master Boot Record (MBR) of a PC. The MBR is a small program that runs every time the computer starts up. It controls the boot sequence and determines which partition the computer boots from. The MBR generally resides on the first sector of the hard disk. Because the MBR executes every time a computer is started, a boot sector virus is extremely infectious. Once the boot code on the drive is infected, the virus will be loaded into memory on every start-up. From memory, the boot virus can spread to every writeable disk that the system reads.

- **File / Executable Viruses** are pieces of code that hide themselves in infected executable files: EXE, COM, OVL extensions are common targets. When an infected program is run, the virus loads into memory and infects other files of a similar type. Like a biological virus, which can only live inside a host cell, file viruses can only exist within host executable files.

- **Macro viruses** consist of code that can be embedded in a data file. Some word processors (e.g. Microsoft Word®) and spreadsheet programs (e.g. Microsoft Excel®) allow you to attach macros to the documents they create. This may be something quite simple and harmless such as a document template that automatically inserts the current date when it is opened. However, it is equally possible to embed malicious code in a document – the Melissa macro virus was an example of this.

- **Email viruses** are not really a separate type. They are usually malicious scripts embedded in attached documents and are properly regarded as macro viruses.

Trojan horses

Trojans were named after the Trojan horse that the Greeks used to enter Troy by deception. Although there are differing definitions of a Trojan, a widely accepted one is that of: 'a program that does something undocumented, which the programmer intended, but that the user would not approve of if he or she knew about it'. An example of this sort of program would be a program that appeared to be a game but which in fact carried a destructive payload. Trojans are not usually self- replicating and some people would not regard them as 'true' viruses.

Worms

Unlike viruses, worms exist as separate entities; they do not attach themselves to other files or programs. However, because of their similarity to viruses, worms are often also referred to as viruses.

Worms are similar to viruses in that they are programs that replicate functional copies of themselves (usually to other computer systems via network connections) and often, but not always, contain some functionality that will interfere with the normal use of a computer or a program.

Root kits

The key characteristic of a root kit is its ability to hide itself. The root kit takes over part of the operating system so that when you check what processes are running (using Task Manager in Microsoft Windows® or the ps command in Unix® or Linux), it is not visible. Apart from the concealment, the root kit may create back doors that allow exploitation of the system: data and identity theft. Because of the root kit's ability to conceal itself, it can be difficult to remove even after it has been detected by software tools available for the purpose. Many techs prefer to cut their losses by reinstalling the operating system after an infection has been discovered.

Spyware / adware / grayware

These are related pieces of software that are usually installed on a system by social engineering methods. The user downloads something – a utility say – and it is covertly bundled with code that sends information back to the originator, listing sites visited, log giving key strokes, etc. They are frequently used to send targeted advertising, pop-ups and other annoyances. In some respects these types of malware are more of a threat than viruses because they are developed by professional coders for commercial gain. There are a number of detection and removal programs available and, like virus scanners, these should be kept up to date and used as a matter of routine.

Spam

This is the popular name for unsolicited commercial email – frequently offering drugs, get-rich-quick schemes or free access to pornography. Apart from the time and bandwidth eaten up by spam, it is often associated with sites which are a source of viruses and other malware. Many ISPs have spam filtering as part of their email services and larger organisations running their own mail servers implement screening procedures. There is also scope for training users and discouraging them from opening emails that may contain malware attachments that will compromise the system. Some client programs can be set up to detect potentially harmful attachments such as documents with embedded macros, and issue a warning to the user or even to prevent download altogether.

Malware – prevention and cure

Prevention

Prevention is not 100 per cent possible unless you are prepared to lock the computer away and never connect to any other system or disk drive. In reality, the probability of infection is reduced by adopting some common-sense procedures, such as employing a stand-alone 'sheepdip' machine to scan all incoming media with an up-to-date virus scanner and virus scanning on network servers. Individual machines need also to be equipped with an up–to-date scanner, preferably one that can be updated over the network by the network administrator. It is also important to train users in the basics of malware detection and to encourage early reporting of virus-like symptoms.

Cure

The cure for any form of malware, once detected, is its removal from the system, followed by the systematic checking of all media that may have been the source of the infection. Having cleaned up the system, it is especially important to scan all back-up media before restoring files from them as it is possible that a virus / Trojan / worm may have inadvertently been backed up along with the legitimate data.

File system (e.g. FAT 32, NTFS)

File system security has been discussed in Chapter 16. From the point of view of optimising security, it is important to bear in mind that FAT 32 is an insecure legacy file system and that NTFS is the native (and strongly preferred) file system for all modern Microsoft Windows® versions.

Data access (e.g. basic local security policy)

Most security work is the domain of system administrators, though the A+ technician needs to be aware of the basics of how local security policies are implemented. The key operating system utility in Microsoft Windows® XP and 2000 for implementing security policies is the Group Policy Editor. In order to use this utility, you will need administrator rights. The Group Policy Editor is not a feature in Microsoft Windows® XP Home edition.

To start the Group Policy Editor, type GPEDIT.MSC at a prompt or in a 'Run' box; note, you will need to type in the .MSC extension as well as the file name.

Figure 17.1 shows the Group Policy Editor in Microsoft Windows® XP; it is all but identical to its Microsoft Windows® 2000 counterpart.

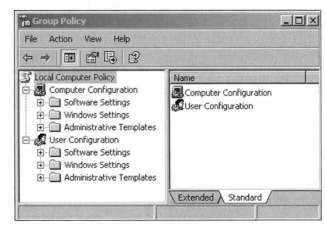

Figure 17.1

The Group Policy Editor uses the familiar Explorer-style interface: clicking on an item with a + sign will open up available sub-options.

The two main headings in the Explorer-style interface are Computer Configuration and User Configuration. Settings that are made under the Computer Configuration apply to all users of that particular PC; User Configuration settings apply to a particular user when he or she logs on to the system.

Computer configuration policies include the facility to run scripts at start-up and shut-down and the ability to set password policies. Figure 17.2 shows the default password policies on a newly installed version of Microsoft Windows® XP Professional.

Policy △	Security Setting
Enforce password history	0 passwords remem...
Maximum password age	42 days
Minimum password age	0 days
Minimum password length	0 characters
Password must meet complexity re...	Disabled
Store password using reversible e...	Disabled

Figure 17.2

Depending on the security requirements of your workplace, you may need to reset values such as maximum password age or complexity requirements to enforce 'strong' passwords.

The Local Policies section is located at:

Computer configuration | Microsoft Windows® settings | Security settings | Local policies and contains three sub-sections: **Audit policy, User rights assignment** and **Security options** as shown in Figure 17.3.

Most of these settings have default values that are set when the operating system is installed and are probably best left alone unless you are specifically instructed to change them in line with the policies of the organisation where you work.

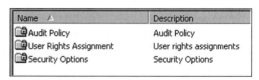

Name △	Description
Audit Policy	Audit Policy
User Rights Assignment	User rights assignments
Security Options	Security Options

Figure 17.3

In most workplaces, security polices are implemented at the network level on the server, so there are only a few security policies which are of interest to the technician working on the local machine.

Back-ups and back-up procedures

Back-ups and back-up procedures have been discussed in Chapter 16. Optimal security requires that back-ups – particularly back-up media and intermediate copies – are properly managed and accounted for. Both on-site and off-site storage of disks, tapes, etc. should be secure – stored in a fireproof safe, for example – and only accessed by authorised personnel. Where there is a back-up to any form of online or network back-up storage, this should be password protected and access limited to authorised personnel. Both Microsoft Windows® 2000 and XP have a predefined user group called Back-up Operators, who have sufficient rights to back up and restore local data regardless of the file permissions on the data being backed up or restored.

Data migration

Data migration – also discussed in Chapter 16 – produces intermediate data sets. Once a migration has been completed and tested and you are 100 per cent sure that the new data set is complete, uncorrupted and has been backed up on the new system, then the media used for the migration can be cleaned up, recycled or destroyed. Until this is done, the intermediate data / storage media should be treated with the same regard for security as back-up media.

Data / remnant removal

Old storage media – whether intermediate data from a migration, or back-up tapes, or hard disks that have been removed from a system – will contain copies of at least some of the data held on the system. In Chapter 16, we looked at the processes of hardware deconstruction and these are fundamental to the effective removal of all data from the media. Unless you can be completely sure that all data has been removed permanently and irrecoverably, it is better to destroy the media concerned than to compromise security by reusing it.

Preventive maintenance for security

Preventive maintenance is part of the duties of any working technician. Chapter 7 looks at this in terms of hardware maintenance and Chapter 10 considers it in the context of operating systems. From a security point of view, you need to consider:

- Patches
- Service packs
- Malware detection programs
- User awareness

Patches

Modern operating systems are complex and constantly evolving. New security vulnerabilities are discovered from time to time and patches are released in order to fix them. In the case of Microsoft Windows® systems, these are available for free download from the Microsoft site and should be applied as soon as they are available. The update process can be automated for individual machines or you can download the patches and either burn them to CD or make them available from a network share for other PCs on your network.

Another important, and often overlooked, source of vulnerabilities is applications software. Mail clients, word-processor packages, etc. all need to be updated for security vulnerabilities from time to time. Where automatic notifications are available, use them. Otherwise, visit manufacturers' and vendors' sites.

Service packs

Service packs are collections of updates – patches – which are bundled into a single update package. They are available for free download and if you have more than a couple of PCs in need of the latest service pack, it can save time and bandwidth to download a stand-alone executable file version which can be burned to disk or deployed from a network share.

Malware detection programs

An important part of malware detection programs are 'definition files', which are used to detect known virus and malware types. It is important to keep these up to date and most programs have an automatic update facility.

There is an important difference between antivirus programs and other malware detection programs. Once you have decided which antivirus package to use, then you need to stick with it or change it altogether. If you add a second antivirus program, the two packages may conflict – possibly each will 'detect' the other as a virus. Adware scanners, on the other hand, complement one another and it is generally possible to run them side by side for additional protection.

User awareness

Security is everyone's concern – or at least it should be. Technical support staff are primarily responsible of course, but users should be encouraged to report any concerns that they have. In order to do this, they need to know at least the basics of how your malware protection policies and technologies are implemented and why. Even where you have a policy such as 'no games' or 'no private software', it should be made clear to all staff that reports of virus-like activity, for example, will be treated in confidence and without penalty. An unreported malware attack can only be made worse by delays in reporting and implementing a clean-up.

SUMMARY

This chapter has looked at security issues from the point of view of how to apply the principles outlined in Chapter 16. In preparing for the exam, you should thoroughly review the contents of both chapters – don't forget that more than one mark in ten of the Essentials exam is for knowing the contents of these two chapters.

QUESTIONS

1 You need to change the boot order on a PC in order to install an operating system from CD, but the setup utility is password protected. The person who set the password has left the company. Which of the following are possible solutions to your problem?

  a) Remove the CMOS battery

  b) Search the Internet for a utility to remove the password

  c) Find the password-clearing jumper on the motherboard

  d) Any of the above

2 A user reports that he is unable to access the network from his workstation. You attempt to log on and this fails also. You move to a different workstation where you can log on but the user is still locked out. Which is the most likely combination of factors to explain this?

  a) Kerberos server has failed

  b) Faulty network card on the first workstation

  c) Bad user name / password combination for the user

  d) The network is using CHAP rather than Kerberos

3 A user reports a number of disk errors on a PC. You replace the machine with a swap-out from your base workshop, but within hours other users are reporting similar problems. You run a virus check and find that there is a virus infection. You clean up the affected PCs. When you have done this, which of the following should you also do?

  a) Scan all removable media

  b) Scan all back-up media

  c) Alert all staff to the problem and ask for increased vigilance

  d) Inform the technical support services at any other centres with whom you share data

4 Question 3 omits an important action that you should take. What is it?

▶

5   You type GPEDIT.MSC at a command prompt on a Microsoft Windows® XP machine but when you do so you see an error message stating that the command is not found. What it is the most probable cause for this?

a) This program does not work from a command prompt – only from a 'Run' box

b) The GPEDIT utility requires that you have administrator privileges and you don't

c) This is a Microsoft Windows® XP Home system, which doesn't have GPEDIT available

d) The GPEDIT utility can only be accessed through the GUI

ANSWERS / EXPLANATIONS

1   You need to change the boot order on a PC in order to install an operating system from CD, but the setup utility is password protected. The person who set the password has left the company. Which of the following are possible solutions to your problem?

d) Any of the above

In practice answer a is probably the easiest.

2   A user reports that he is unable to access the network from his workstation. You attempt to log on and this fails also. You move to a different workstation where you can log on but the user is still locked out. Which is the most likely combination of factor to explain this?

b) Faulty network card on the first workstation

AND

c) Bad user name / password combination for the user

Answer a would affect all users and all workstations. Answer d is irrelevant.

▶

3 A user reports a number of disk errors on a PC. You replace the machine with a swap out from you base workshop, but within hours other users are reporting similar problems. You run a virus check and find that there is a virus infection. You clean up the affected PCs. When you have done this, which of the following should you also do?

a) Scan all removable media

b) Scan all back-up media

c) Alert all staff to the problem and ask for increased vigilance

d) Inform the technical support services at any other centres with whom you share data

You should do all of these.

4 Question 3 omits an important action that you should take. What is it?

You should also scan and clean up the machine that you swapped out. It has a virus and will be a source of reinfection if it is not cleaned up.

5 You type GPEDIT.MSC at a command prompt on a Microsoft Windows® XP machine but when you do so you see an error message stating that the command is not found. What it is the most probable cause for this?

c) This is a Microsoft Windows® XP Home machine, which doesn't have GPEDIT available

CHAPTER 18
Safety and environmental issues

Safety and the environment are areas that concern us all. In order to be an effective working PC technician, you need to be able to work on a PC without harming yourself or others. You also need to know the procedures to identify and deal with some of the potentially harmful products used in the manufacture of PCs. With 10 per cent of the marks for the Essentials exam available for this knowledge, it is also well worth studying this subject as part of your exam preparation.

Exam objectives 7.1, 7.2 and 7.3
7.1 Describe the aspects and importance of safety and environmental issues

Identify potential safety hazards and take preventative action:

> Use Material Safety Data Sheets (MSDS) or equivalent documentation and appropriate equipment documentation
> Use appropriate repair tools

Describe methods to handle environmental and human (e.g. electrical, chemical, physical) accidents including incident reporting.

7.2 Identify potential hazards and implement proper safety procedures including ESD precautions and procedures, safe work environment and equipment handling

7.3 Identify proper disposal procedures for batteries, display devices and chemical solvents and cans

Working safely

Wherever you live and work as a PC technician, you will be subject to various laws and regulations concerning how you go about the job, your consideration for others – co-workers and customers – and how you handle and dispose of potentially harmful products. These conditions will be different in different localities and workplaces and may also change over time. You need, therefore, to be aware of what applies to you in your workplace as well as local laws and regulations. However, although details may vary from place to place and time to time, there are some fundamentals that you need to know, and which are examined by the Essentials exam.

Potential hazards

Mains electricity

PCs use mains electricity so an obvious safety precaution is to disconnect from the mains supply before removing any covers or working on the inside of the case. CRT monitors and Power Supply Units (PSUs) have internal capacitors that store electricity even when they are turned off. They are also capable of generating considerable heat in operation; sufficient to cause burns if they are not handled with care. Both CRT monitors and power supplies are regarded as Field Replaceable Modules (FRMs) and the rule is simple: never open them in the field. Replace them if necessary and either dispose of the unwanted unit or send it to a base workshop for specialist work.

The case and internal components

PC cases are not always as well finished as they might be and may have sharp edges. While you are unlikely to cause yourself life-threatening harm, you may well cut yourself if you do not work with care. Internal components have solder points (aka 'the knobbly bits') and these can cause abrasions if handled incorrectly. If you look at the underside of a motherboard, for example, you will see thousands of solder points, which have the potential to cause abrasions. Some components, such as heat sinks and disk drives, run hot, so a PC that has been in recent use is also a potential source of burns. CD and DVD drives use laser light in operation and need to be serviced with care. They can be removed and replaced easily enough, but if you want to strip one down in order to clean it, make sure that it is disconnected, and do not peer into the lens.

External components

Most external components are attached by cables of some sort and these can be tripped over. When you disconnect anything from a PC, store it somewhere safe – preferably in an antistatic bag – where it cannot be a hazard to you or anyone else.

Printers

Laser printers in particular use high voltages and have many hot-running components. The toner that they use is also a toxic compound that should be handled carefully and, if necessary, disposed of according to the legal requirements of the place where you work. Never wear a wrist strap when working on a laser printer: static is not much of a problem (unless you are doing a RAM upgrade) and a wrist strap is more likely to conduct power to you than away when you are working on high-voltage equipment like a laser printer or a CRT monitor.

Fire safety

PCs are not particularly prone to bursting into flames but a shorted-out wire can be the cause of a minor fire. Using the wrong type of fire extinguisher can cause far more problems than the original short; a water-based extinguisher will almost certainly make a bad situation worse. Class C fire extinguishers are the only type designed for use with electrical fires, though there are also general purpose ABC extinguishers that can be used safely. When you are working in the field, it is sensible to find (or ask for) the location of the nearest fire extinguisher of the correct type.

The work environment

Obviously, if you are in a workshop or depot that is used exclusively for PC repair, it should be set up so that it is a safe and healthy environment. PCs require much the same levels of humidity and temperature ranges as humans so as a general rule of thumb, if you are happy, the PC will be OK. Work surfaces should be well lit, uncluttered and at a comfortable working height; tools need to be stored neatly and properly when not in use; and where cables have to run across walkways, they need to be covered with a floor cable guard.

When you are working in someone else's space – doing a field repair in someone's office for example – you have less direct control over your environment. In these circumstances, it is important to adopt safe working practices to suit your situation. For example, if you are working on a PC and you are called away, do not leave an unprotected open case; the very minimum that you should do is to place the lid loosely over the machine and, if possible, ask someone to keep an eye on it while you are away. If you are called upon to install a PC or other equipment, you should ensure that it will not cause a safety hazard by its positioning or the positioning of the cables that are used to connect it.

Preventive action

Part of your job is to foresee and avoid potential health, safety or environmental concerns: ask where the nearest fire extinguisher is, check for cracked insulation on cables, look out for trip hazards, etc. It is also bad practice to eat, drink or smoke in the vicinity of a PC. Above all, always try to exercise some imagination and common sense and, if there is any doubt, seek the guidance of your immediate supervisor.

Material Safety Data Sheets and product documentation

Material Safety Data Sheets (MSDSs) are required by United States law where the material concerned is considered to be hazardous and where employees may be exposed under normal conditions or in an emergency. MSDSs are widely available on the Internet and include information about the characteristics – melting point, toxicity etc. – for hazardous substances. These sheets are available to anyone and some companies make them available for any of their products, usually through their websites. However, there is no legal obligation to provide this information to the end user; MSDSs are intended for emergency services personnel or workers who come into contact with the hazardous substances in the course of their work. Where someone's job may bring them into contact with a hazardous substance, they have a right to access to the relevant MSDS.

As a working technician, it is part of your job to be aware of MSDSs as well as product manuals that contain this type of information. The equivalent safety legislation in the United Kingdom is the Control Of Substances Hazardous to Health (COSHH) regulations. You need to be aware of, keep up to date with and, where necessary, make available to others, all relevant safety information.

Use appropriate repair tools

The main tool for working on a PC is a Phillips #2 screwdriver because it fits the most common screw type that you will encounter in your everyday work. You will also need to supplement this with other tools such as: flat-bladed screwdrivers, Torx drivers, hex drivers, smaller Phillips drivers, pliers, wire cutters, a mirror and a flashlight for looking in inaccessible places, canned air, an antistatic vacuum cleaner and a multimeter. Some screwdrivers have a mildly magnetic tip to make it easy to pick up dropped screws, although it is generally preferable to use a non-magnetic screwdriver and carry a simple retrieval tool as part of your toolkit. One or more antistatic wrist straps should also be part of your toolkit; just remember not to use it if you are working on high-voltage equipment.

Dealing with accidents

No matter how careful and conscientious you and your colleagues are, accidents will happen from time to time. These may be environmental – a power surge, an electrical storm or a flood – or they may be human, such as a chemical spill. The first rule, of course, is do not panic. In the event of electrical or water problems, turn off all affected equipment and deal with the cause. This may be as simple as waiting for a storm to subside (and checking the status of any power conditioning equipment such as Uninterruptible Power Supplies (UPSs)) or calling an emergency repair service to deal with a leak. Only when the accident has been dealt with should you turn your attention to the affected PCs.

Where an accident involves a hazardous substance, shut down all equipment, cordon off the area and check the MSDS. Inform your supervisors, building security and possibly the local authority. The exact clean-up procedures will depend on the nature of the substance and in all but the most trivial of cases should be left to the emergency services or other qualified professionals.

After an accident – or even a near miss – you should use your company's reporting procedures to record it and, if there is any doubt at all, take qualified medical advice.

Other accidents, someone tripping over a cable for example, should also be recorded so that preventative measures can be put in place to prevent further instances; failure to do this could later be construed as negligence on your part.

Identify potential hazards

Hazards to you, your colleagues and customers are best avoided through the exercise of common sense and observing the work practices outlined earlier in the chapter. Other hazards to components in particular require their own approach.

Electrostatic discharge (ESD)

The main cause of damage to components is static electricity and the worst culprit (unless you are careful) is you. We all have static electricity on our bodies and if this runs to earth (ground) through a component, the result is damage. If you are lucky, the component will be a write-off, and the sole expense will be the time and cost of a replacement. More insidious is the component that appears to work but is in fact damaged. A damaged stick of RAM may, for example, work for most of the time but fail occasionally; often such failures will generate error messages that suggest something else such as a disk error. Intermittent faults of this type can take a long time to track down even if, when identified as in the RAM example, they are easy enough to fix.

WRIST STRAPS

The first line of defence for the working technician is to wear an antistatic wrist strap. This may be connected to earth (ground) or attached to a bare metal part of the PC case. Either way, its purpose is to drain away any static charge so that it cannot discharge itself through a component that it will damage in the process.

ANTISTATIC MATS

This is the equivalent to a wrist strap for the components. A component is placed on a grounded mat which drains away static. Most mats are intended for use on a workbench, but there are also floor mats for the technician to stand on. Mats may be used in conjunction with a wrist strap and may be connected to provide a static-free working area.

ANTI-STATIC BAGS

Nearly all new components are packed in antistatic bags in order to protect them in transit and in storage. Always leave components in their antistatic bags until you are ready to use them and save the bags so that they can be reused. If necessary, additional bags can be bought.

OTHER MEASURES

Your working environment can contribute to the possibility of ESD, particularly if the level of humidity is too high or too low. The ideal is around 50 per cent, so adjusting the air conditioning can be a useful thing to do. You can prevent the build up of static on carpets and other fabrics by using an antistatic spray, which you can either buy or make with water and fabric conditioner in a 50 / 50 mix; be careful though only to use a light mist when applying it.

A safe working environment

You can ensure a safe working environment by adopting the measures outlined earlier in the chapter: disconnecting the mains electricity supply before working on the inside of a machine, handling components which may have sharp edges with care, ensuring that you have the appropriate type of fire extinguisher available. Cleanliness and tidiness in any work environment – whether workshop or in the field – can make a significant contribution to workplace safety. Preventive measures are, of course, essential: if a power cable crosses a floor, either re-route it or protect it with a cable guard before any problems arise. Similarly, you should always be on the look out for everyday problems such as cracked insulation, trip hazards, or even wrongly rated fuses in mains plugs. In addition you should be aware of laws and regulations which apply where you are working and be aware of your rights and responsibilities as an employee. Your company should have a safety plan or a safety policy and you should be aware of its provisions.

Equipment handling

When handling equipment, there are two considerations: safety of the equipment and safety of the person handling it. We have considered the main threat to equipment – electrostatic discharge (ESD) – at some length earlier in the chapter. However, in addition to the safety of the equipment, we need to consider the safety of the technicians carrying out the work. Obviously, you should observe all of the antistatic precautions when handling components, but you should also be careful when lifting heavy objects: that is lift with a straight back or ask for help if a task is beyond your physical capacity. You should also bear in mind that some equipment, such as CRT monitors or Power Supply Units (PSUs) can contain hazardous levels of electricity even when they have been turned off for hours (or even days) and should be handled with appropriate care. Similarly, laser printers are high-voltage equipment and often have hot-running components when in use: they need to be treated with care. If you are in doubt about the proper handling procedures for a particular piece of equipment, consult the manufacturer's documentation or manuals or simply ask what the procedures are in the organisation where you are working.

Disposal procedures

Nearly all computer components contain potentially hazardous substances: various plastics and metals, lead and mercury in batteries. These are not 'dangerous' in the same way as we would describe nuclear waste as dangerous, but they need to be disposed of with care where they cannot be recycled. Like most of the material presented in this chapter, disposal procedures are subject to legal requirements, which vary between regions and which are subject to periodic revision.

Batteries

Batteries, especially the batteries from portable systems, contain significant quantities of lead, cadmium, lithium, mercury and manganese. Rather than dumping them in a landfill site, they should be taken to an appropriate centre for recycling where possible and special disposal where not.

Printer cartridges

Toner cartridges from laser printers can be refilled and reused. Even where you don't want to use a recycled product yourself, they are probably saleable to a company specialising in this sort of material. Inkjet cartridges can also be refilled: you can buy kits to do this yourself, though it can be a fairly messy procedure.

CRT monitors

Cathode Ray Tube (CRT) monitors contain toxic materials and high voltages. They are therefore potentially dangerous to handle. Breaking the tube of a CRT monitor results in an implosion which will shower the area with shards of razor-sharp glass. Regulations for disposal of CRT monitors have recently been updated in the UK under European law.

This means that there are fewer landfill sites able to accept monitors and it is illegal to dispose of a CRT monitor through anything but a Licensed Waste Carrier approved by the Environment Agency. (This does not currently apply to private individuals.)

Solvents and cans

Various chemical solvents and cans – even depleted compressed-air cans – need to be disposed of safely. In the UK, the handling, disposal and labelling of potentially harmful materials is regulated by the Control Of Substances Hazardous to Health (COSHH) regulations. The International / US equivalent requires there to be a Material Safety Data Sheet (MSDS) for all potentially hazardous materials. Suppliers are required to provide this documentation whenever they supply materials or products of a potentially hazardous nature. MSDSs must inform workers and management about hazards associated with the product, how to handle it safely and procedures in the event of an accident. Use this information to determine the appropriate disposal procedure for each product.

SUMMARY

In this chapter, we have considered the hazards that PCs can present to both individuals and to the environment as a whole. We have looked at the practical means of dealing with these in terms of work practices, documentation and incident reporting. We have considered disposal procedures for batteries and other potential pollutants and noted that legislation and practices vary from time to time and place to place. With a growing awareness of environmental and safety issues in society as a whole, you need to be aware of current environmental and safety requirements for your workplace and location in order to do the job of a PC technician. There are also marks to be had (10 per cent of the examination) for knowing the material covered in this chapter.

QUESTIONS

1 You have been asked to diagnose problems with a PC and, in the course of your diagnostic work, you find that the PSU cooling fan isn't working. Do you?

  a) Replace the PSU

  b) Remove the PSU, strip it down and fix the fan

  c) Fit an additional case fan to compensate for the broken one

  d) Swap out the defective PC and send it to a base depot to be fixed

2 You arrive at an office in order to fix a defective PC. The room where you are working has a fire extinguisher on the wall and it is labelled as being type ABC. Is this suitable for emergency use in the event of an electrical short in the PC starting a fire?

  a) Yes

  b) No. Only a type C extinguisher should be used on an electrical fire

  c) No. Only a type A extinguisher should be used on an electrical fire

  d) No. The best way to deal with this type of fire is to let it burn itself out

3 There is a spillage of a compound in an area where you work and you believe that it may be toxic. What do you do first?

  a) Close off the area to the best of your ability

  b) Report the incident to building security

  c) Start to clean up

  d) Look up the MSDS for the compound in order to assess the level of hazard

4 You should wear a wrist strap when?

  a) Doing a RAM upgrade

  b) Replacing a hard disk drive

  c) Cleaning a CRT monitor

  d) Replacing a graphics adapter card

5 An empty toner cartridge from a laser printer should be?

  a) Thrown in the bin

  b) Refilled

  c) Sold

  d) Burned

ANSWERS / EXPLANATIONS

1   You have been asked to diagnose problems with a PC and, in the course of your diagnostic work, you find that the PSU cooling fan isn't working. Do you?

a) Replace the PSU

A PSU is a Field Replaceable Module and the standard procedure is to replace it in the field.

2   You arrive at an office in order to fix a defective PC. The room where you are working has a fire extinguisher on the wall and it is labelled as being type ABC. Is this suitable for emergency use in the event of an electrical short in the PC starting a fire?

a) Yes.

A type C extinguisher should be used for a PC fire, but a type ABC can also be used.

3   There is a spillage of a compound in an area where you work and you believe that it may be toxic. What do you do first?

a) Close off the area to the best of your ability

Answer b will probably be your second step, but only after you have secured the area to the best of your ability.

4   You should wear a wrist strap when?

a) Doing a RAM upgrade

b) Replacing a hard disk drive

d) Replacing a graphics adapter card

Answer c is wrong because a CRT monitor contains high voltages even when disconnected and the wrist strap could conduct a lethal voltage to you.

5   An empty toner cartridge from a laser printer should be?

b) Refilled

c) Sold

Answers a and d are both inadvisable and are probably illegal.

CHAPTER 19
Communication and professionalism

Customer care is an important aspect of every business, and effective communication and professional attitudes and practices are as important for the PC technician as any other professional. The Communication and Professionalism domain of the Essentials exam accounts for 5 per cent of the marks for the exam as a whole. The material in this chapter deserves attention not just for the exam marks but also because the skills it examines are necessary for a successful career as a support technician.

Exam objectives 8.1 and 8.2
8.1 Use good communication skills including listening and tact / discretion, when communicating with customers and colleagues

Use clear, concise and direct statements.
Allow the customer to complete statements – avoid interrupting.
Clarify customer statements – ask pertinent questions.
Avoid using jargon, abbreviations and acronyms.
Listen to customers.

8.2 Use job-related professional behaviour including notation of privacy, confidentiality and respect for the customer and customers' property
Behaviour:

Maintain a positive attitude and tone of voice
Avoid arguing with customers and / or becoming defensive
Do not minimise customers' problems
Avoid being judgemental and / or insulting or calling the customer names
Avoid distractions and / or interruptions when talking with customers

Property:

Telephone, laptop, desktop computer, printer, monitor, etc.

Customer satisfaction

If you are a freelance technician, you will be aware of the need for customer satisfaction; satisfied customers are what keep you in business. If you work for someone else, even a huge corporation where you are part of an in-house support team, the people who use your services are still your 'customers' even if they don't directly pay the bills. Fixing the PC problem is a major goal – that is what you are paid for – but the overarching aim must be a satisfied customer; someone who can say that you achieved the required technical outcome and that you did so efficiently and professionally.

Communicating with customers and colleagues

Communication is at the heart of just about everything we do in business, and much of what we do in life. Many of the problems that we experience in work (or life) are the result of misunderstandings: 'I thought you meant....' is an indication – often too late – of a failure of communication. Given the amount of technical terms (jargon) that we use every day – almost without thinking – when working in PC technical support, it is necessary to be aware of the difficulties and misunderstandings that may arise. The specialist terms that you may use are, to most customers, 'technobabble'. Tell a customer that the cache size on their SATA drive is the cause of excessive latency in operation and they will probably be confused. They may also feel embarrassed at their 'ignorance' and resentful of you for making then feel that way. That is not how you wish to be perceived by your customers.

A further practical reason for developing communication skills is that the customer is one of the best sources of information about the problem that you are trying to fix; alienate them and you are (at best) creating extra work for yourself.

Clear, concise and direct statements

Whether you are communicating face to face, over the phone, or by email, the purpose of what you say or write is to communicate information to the customer and (often) to elicit a useful reply from them. You need to engage their interest and cooperation, not to impress them with your knowledge and expertise. Consequently, you need to translate your technical terms to something less specialised without talking down to the customer. The best way to do this is to use clear, concise and direct statements, ideally making one point at a time and confirming that it has been understood, possibly by asking supplementary questions and listening to the answers.

If you tell the customer, 'The 12-volt DC output on your PSU is delivering sub-optimal power levels', you will probably be met with a look of incomprehension and confirm the customer's worst fears that technical support people speak entirely in jargon and quite possibly come from another planet. Tell them, 'There's a problem with the power supply' (and point to it if you are there in person), then add 'I can fit a new one in about ten minutes', and you are on your way to having a satisfied customer, not just a working PC.

Allow the customer to complete statements

This is just basic courtesy. No one likes to be interrupted or have their sentences completed for them. If the question that you have asked is pertinent, direct and relevant to the problem you are investigating (and if it is not, then why did you ask it?) then the answer is worthy of your attention, just as the customer is worthy of your attention and respect. When you are troubleshooting a PC, a customer who is 'on side' can be a useful source of information. If you can ask questions, listen and be appreciative of their help, you will be able to fix the problem more quickly and you will end up with a working PC and a satisfied customer.

Clarify customer statements

In the early stages of troubleshooting a PC, you are trying to narrow down the range of possibilities until you arrive at a result. A typical dialogue may be along the lines of the following:

Tech: I hear you are having problems printing.

Customer: Yes. And I need this document by lunch time today.

Tech: Well that gives us an hour. And if we can't find a fix by then, we'll send it to a different printer. When did the problem start?

Customer: Not sure exactly, but it was working okay yesterday. I printed several things yesterday afternoon.

Tech: Can you show me the problem?

Customer: Okay.

Note that the technician has addressed the customer's problem – the need for a document by lunch time – not the technical problem with that particular printer. The language is inclusive – we can do this or that – win the customer's confidence and get them involved. The supplementary question elicits some additional information about the technical problem and leads naturally toward the most useful troubleshooting question of them all: 'Can you show me?'

Avoid using jargon

This can be difficult. Technical terms are a useful shorthand for talking and thinking about problems and it is all too easy to slip into using jargon, abbreviations and acronyms without realising it. Sensitivity to the customer is the best line of defence against this. Be aware, as you speak, of the effect that you are having and watch for signs of boredom, irritation, or incomprehension from the customer. Above all, do not be afraid to apologise and explain properly. The customer has probably made the same mistake in terms of using the technical terms of their profession inappropriately at some time. An accountant, say, who occasionally slips into accountant-speak and confuses their customers, will probably recognise your slip as a human quality that you share. If you make the mistake of slipping into jargon: recognise it, apologise, explain and use it, if you can, to get the customer on side.

Listen to customers

Communication is a two-way process; talking and listening are the two sides of any dialogue. When you are investigating a problem with a PC, the customer knows more about the problem than you do. Your job is to turn their knowledge of the problem – such as 'it won't print' – into technical terms that suggest a workable solution. The key to this is listening, interpreting the replies, framing supplementary questions and listening again. It has been said that you are born with two ears and one mouth and you should use them in roughly that proportion; that may not be the whole truth about anything, but it is worth bearing in mind.

Job-related professional behaviour

The customer pays your wages – directly or indirectly – and the customer has the right to expect you to behave professionally at all times and in all circumstances. Whether you are a PC technician, a dentist or a taxi driver, the customer, who pays, is entitled to expect civility, tact, discretion, punctuality and respect for them and for their property. As a technician, you will have access to data and possibly passwords, user account information, etc. and you may be required to back it up or restore it; this may well involve reading it if only to check the success of a back-up or restore operation. This does not, however, give you any rights to use, discuss or disclose any of the information. Respect for confidentiality is an absolute requirement of the technician's role.

Maintain a positive attitude

Your job is to solve problems, not to create more of them. Whether you are taking a phone call or visiting the customer in person, they expect – and have the right to expect – a competent professional who will listen and respond in a positive way. The customer has a problem; that's why they called. The problem is a technical one from your point of view, but an operational one from theirs. A printing problem, for example, may well be a problem with the printer, but to the customer the problem is not being able to print a document that they need for a meeting or a report. They may well be distressed by this or even angry over the failure. Without making a punch-bag of yourself, part of the technician's job is to listen, to accept that the customer may have negative feelings and allow them to express them. In the course of your initial contact, you need to be able to reassure the customer that the problem can and will be solved. On the telephone, especially, your tone of voice can be vital. The customer cannot see your body language or react favourably to your bright, confident smile; they can only judge by your voice. When taking a support call, you should answer promptly, give your name and ask something like 'how can I help'. In some organisations, there is a formal script for answering calls and this, too, can be a trap. If you have uttered the same standard phrases every day for weeks, it is all too easy to go through the motions, to say the words, but still appear to be bored or insincere. Maintaining a positive attitude and making sure that it shows in your tone of voice and choice of words is not always easy, but it is always part of the job.

Avoid arguing with customers

Customers can be argumentative and downright hostile at times; just bear in mind that they are under pressure to get their job done. A technology failure at a vital point in the working day can feel like a disaster and the frustration can easily spill over into blaming not just the technology but also the team who support it. If you are contacted by a customer who is agitated, your first task is to calm them down, to listen (again) and not to be drawn into mutual recrimination. Arguing with the customer can only make things worse and will do nothing to fix the problem. If the customer is accusatory – 'If the support operations were properly organised....' – your best bet is to sidestep: – 'There may be something in what you say....' – then get back to the problem in hand. The minute that you become defensive, you have been drawn into an argument. That will not fix the problem; all you will end up with is a dissatisfied customer, an unresolved problem and, quite possibly, a complaint about your lack of professionalism.

Do not minimise customers' problems

Whatever the problem is, the chances are that you have seen it before; just remember that the customer probably has not. Your customer is trying to do something and they are being prevented from doing so by an equipment failure, and from their point of view, there is no such thing as a trivial problem. How you deal with this is largely a matter of presentation. The fact that the problem is familiar and relatively easy to fix doesn't make it trivial for the customer. First of all, put yourself in the customer's place: how would you feel if your car simply stopped working for no apparent reason just when you needed it most? Frustrated and annoyed, probably. Now imagine how you would want to be treated by the vehicle technician. You would probably want someone who could answer your questions, assure you that it could be fixed and, if it is a big job, arrange for a courtesy car until yours is fixed. The familiarity of the problem is your key to showing the customer that you know and that you care. In practice, customers need reassurance that someone is taking their problem seriously and is capable of dealing with it, and that begins with listening and is achieved by maintaining a positive attitude, not arguing and not minimising the impact of the problem on the customer.

Avoid being judgemental

Your private judgement may be that the customer is partly or even wholly responsible for their problems and at a later date you may be able to suggest improved staff training to someone in your organisation. However, at the time of the call, your main concern is to diagnose and fix the problem that has been reported and to leave a customer who is satisfied and productive as a result. Blaming the customer, disparaging them, insulting them or calling them names won't fix the problem; it will simply make the situation worse.

Avoid distractions and / or interruptions

This is not always easy. You probably have a cell phone or a pager and you are generally required to respond to work-related messages promptly. If you take a call, you should apologise to the customer but explain that it is necessary, then take the call and explain that you are with a customer, that you will return the call as soon as you are free and could all future calls be held until then. This course of action keeps you in touch with your office and demonstrates to the customer that you can prioritise your work and that they have top priority. Any other call or demand on your time that is not work related should simply be ignored; you are at work and personal matters should be dealt with in your leisure time. The customer pays for, and deserves, your undivided attention.

Property

Respect for the customer includes respect for their property. On a typical desktop, support call, the customer will have an array of equipment: a telephone, a laptop or a desktop PC, a printer, a monitor, etc. None of this equipment belongs to you! You may need to make a phone call: use your own phone or, if this is not possible, ask the customer's permission to make a call on their phone and explain that it is not just a work-related matter but a matter that is related to their problem and your attempts to fix it. Similarly, you may have to 'take their computer to pieces' to track a hardware fault. It is good practice to explain what you are doing and why; to reassure them that your actions are necessary and are part of the search for the answer to their problem. Always ask if the computer is covered by a warranty before piling in and possibly voiding it. If necessary, check the warranty status with the vendor.

Customer respect

Customer care is an important aspect of all business and is one that needs to be taken seriously at all levels of your organisation. The Customer Respect Group is a US-based consultancy firm that measures the performance of websites in terms of how the online customer is treated. It calculates a Customer Respect Index for each company, based on these criteria: Privacy, Responsiveness, Attitude, Simplicity, Transparency and Business Principles. These principles apply in equal measure to how you conduct yourself as a working technician. A visit to www.customerrespect.com will give you an insight into the principles of customer care whether online, over the phone or in person.

SUMMARY

In this chapter we have looked at the need for a technician to use appropriate communication skills and professional behaviour when dealing with customers. The principles that have been outlined are a requirement of the PC technician's role and you need to understand them and be able to apply them both for the Essentials exam and in your working life. If we step back from the details for a moment, there is one straightforward guiding principle: treat other people as you would like to be treated yourself in similar circumstances. Bear that in mind and you won't go far wrong.

QUESTIONS

1 You are taking a phone call from a customer and they ask for your name. Do you?

a) Give your name and continue with the call

b) Ask why they want to know

c) Refuse to tell them

d) Drop the phone

2 You have been called in to investigate a network problem and need to logon with the user's name and password. Do you?

a) Ask the user for the password

b) Ask the user to logon using the password

c) Logon using your own credentials

d) Any of the above

3 A customer on a desktop support call-out is trying to impress you with their knowledge and using a lot of jargon. It is plain that they don't really know what they are talking about. Do you?

a) Ignore they

b) Respond with even more jargon

c) Ask them to explain a little more slowly

d) Ask them to show you the problem

4 You have finished a repair job and the customer has tested your work and is satisfied. You are about to leave when you are asked 'While you are here can you look at....' Do you?

a) Call your base and tell them that you are running late, then do the extra work

b) Tell the customer to log a fresh support call

c) Take a quick look, then suggest a fresh support call

d) Any of the above – it depends on the circumstances

5 You complete a support call only to find that the customer has gone home and there is no one to test and sign off your work. Do you?

a) Leave a note for the customer

b) Inform the customer's supervisor or manager

c) Inform your supervisor or manager

d) Go home

ANSWERS / EXPLANATIONS

1   You are taking a phone call from a customer and they ask for your name. Do you?

a) Give your name and continue with the call

In many organisations, you would be expected to give your name at the beginning of the call. Even where you are not, using names can be a useful way of creating rapport with the customer.

2   You have been called in to investigate a network problem and need to logon with the user's name and password. Do you?

b) Ask the user to log on using the password

Option a would be breach of privacy and probably a breach of the law. Option c is not appropriate because the problem outlined in the question requires that you log on with the user's credentials.

3   A customer on a desktop support call out is trying to impress you with their knowledge and using a lot of jargon. It is plain that they don't really know what they are talking about. Do you?

d) Ask them to show you the problem

'Can you show me?' is the best troubleshooting question of them all.

4   You have finished a repair job and the customer has tested your work and is satisfied. You are about to leave when you are asked 'while you are here can you look at...' Do you?

c) Take a quick look, then suggest a fresh support call

This balances the need to show concern with the customer's problem with the need to attend your next call to fix their problem.

5   You complete a support call, only to find that the customer has gone home and there is no one to test and sign off your work. Do you?

a) Leave a note for the customer

b) Inform the customer's supervisor or manager

c) Inform your supervisor or manager

d) Go home

Yes, all of them. In that order.

APPENDIX 1
Additional practical exercises

(This appendix can also be downloaded in PDF format from www.aplusforstudents.co.uk)

The best way of learning anything is probably by doing it, so although you will need to learn and memorise a lot of information for exam purposes, doing some practical exercises will help to reinforce your knowledge. You will find suggestions for practicals in the body of the book, which you may like to try or to adapt to your own circumstances. This appendix contains some additional ideas.

Before you start

There is nothing particularly hazardous about practical work with PCs but before you start any further practicals you should review the notes on practical exercises, working safely, setting up a lab and tools in the introduction to the book. You may also like to review other parts of the text as needed.

Domain 1 – Personal computer components

21 per cent of marks

With 21 per cent of the marks available, this is a major component of the exams. This weighting also reflects the importance of these topics in the life of a working technician. Probably the best way of learning the components is to handle them and this can be done by removing and changing various components on a practice machine. Ideally, this should be an old PC, where it does not really matter if it is broken; not so much because you are likely to damage it (though accidents happen) but because using old kit for this type of exercise puts you under less pressure.

A radical rebuild

This is something that you may have to do in the course of your work at some point. It is also a useful and informative exercise. At its simplest, all you do is reduce a PC to its component parts, then reassemble and test it. If you are working in a group or instructor-led class, you can add a dimension by swapping parts with other students as you rebuild. In order to do a rebuild, you will need the basic tools of the trade – screwdrivers, etc. – and either notebook and pen or a camera to record the position and orientation of cables and components.

1   Using appropriate antistatic precautions and work practices, strip a PC down to its constituent parts.

2   If you are working in a group, place all the parts in a single place; all the graphics cards together, all the RAM sticks together, and so on.

3   Rebuild the PC from the parts using the notes / photos that you made to ensure proper location / orientation of components.

4   Test everything.

With the exercise complete, consider how you would replace or upgrade various components. Check for availability and price of components on the Internet. For example, check the existing graphics card. What is its type? Is that type currently available? How much does it cost? Similarly with the hard disk: what type is it? If it is an old slow EIDE disk type, would the motherboard support an upgrade to something faster? What are the implications for BIOS compatibility, etc?

If you are not feeling sufficiently confident to undertake a radical rebuild at first, experiment with simply swapping components. However you approach these exercises, you will learn and practise antistatic handling techniques, the characteristics of the components that you are using and the upgrade options open to you. Variations on the radical rebuild exercise can be the basis for several practical lab sessions; what you make of them will depend to some extent on what equipment you have available and the time that you want to spend on it.

Domain 2 – Laptop and portable devices

11 per cent of marks
The difficulty here is equipment. Laptops have changed significantly over the years and really old 'chuck-out' kit is not particularly representative of modern systems. If you do have old laptop systems, by all means have a go; you may be able to access system RAM and there are, of course, the whole range of PCMCIA card accessories to consider.

In the course of your work as a technician, you may well be asked to assess laptop machines and comment on their future upgradeability. Try researching – probably on the Internet – to find which of the currently available systems use ZIF socket for their CPUs, what RAM type they use, and its availability and price. You may even like to do a comparative evaluation of two or three different systems as if you were preparing a report for a customer, taking into account acquisition costs and upgrade paths. There are no definite right or wrong answers in an exercise like this, so if you are working in a group, there is ample scope for discussion.

Domain 3 – Operating systems

21 per cent of marks
This is the other 'big' domain in terms of marks and the scope for practical exercises is more or less unlimited.

Basic installation

1   Partition a hard disk on a working PC so that you have two partitions.

2   Format the first partition with the FAT 32 file system.

3   Install Microsoft Windows® 2000.

4   Set up user accounts and look at the security settings for files and folders.

5   Use the Microsoft Windows® file system conversion utility to convert the FAT 32 partition to NTFS and examine how security is implemented. If you are working in a group, this can be the basis for a discussion.(Note: steps 2–5 are considered more fully under the File System Security heading in Chapter 16.)

6   Install Microsoft Windows® XP on the second partition. How many ways are there of doing this?(Hint: there are at least two.)

If you carry out this practical over one or more sessions, it raises questions about file system types, minimum hardware requirements, upgrade paths, etc.

Other installation methods

How many installation methods are there for Microsoft Windows® 2000 and XP? Review the material in Chapter 9 and try one or more of the other installation methods. In particular, have a go at one of the unattended installation methods and consider the security issues that it raises. Which installation methods are suitable for which scenarios? Do the practicals and discuss your results.

Configuration

Set up user accounts on a Microsoft Windows® 2000 or XP system. Give some users full privileges (i.e. Administrator rights) and others restricted rights. Experiment in order to find out who can do what.

Security

1   Create a password-protected user account called (say) 'Fred' on two Microsoft Windows XP or 2000 PCs that are using the security features of the NTFS file system.

2   Remove the hard disk from the second PC and put it in the first PC as a second hard disk.

3   Once it has been physically fitted, you will be able to see the new disk. However, even though both disks belong to the user 'Fred', you will not be able to access the contents.

4   What does this tell you about the relationship between user names and Security IDs (SIDs)?

5   How do you make the files available? Hint – you need to be an Administrator to do this and the key phrase is 'take ownership'.

Domain 4 – Printers and scanners

9 per cent of marks

Printers and scanners are other items of equipment that may be more difficult to obtain for practice sessions so you will have to work with whatever is available. Depending on what you have available, you could download manuals and drivers from the Internet and install the printer and update its drivers. If you have a network, you can attach to it, set up a share and do some test prints. Most of this material is outlined in Chapter 12.

If you have a 'true' network printer available (that is one that needs its own IP address) you could try setting it up. The exact details will vary according to the make and model of the printer. The example that follows is based on a Hewlett-Packard Laser Jet printer. Treat it as an outline that may need to be adapted for your particular circumstances.

1   Disconnect the printer from the network and reboot it.

2   Use the menu button to display – or print out – the current IP settings. You can probably find out how to do this by experimentation or you could, of course, read the manual!

3   Now that you know the printer's default IP address, connect a PC (or your laptop) to it with a crossover cable.

4   Assign a static IP address to the PC so that it has an IP address that is compatible with that of the printer.

5   Type the IP address of the printer into the address bar of your browser to access the printer's set-up page.

6   Assign a static IP address and any other configuration details to your printer, making sure that these are compatible with your network. Save these settings.

7   Disconnect your temporary connection and reconnect your printer to your network.

8   Use the PING command with your new printer's IP address as its argument, to test that it is visible on your network.

The next step will be to install the new printer on your PC clients on the network. Hint: although this is a network printer, you will need to select the 'local printer' option as you step through the Printer Wizard on the client PC – Microsoft Windows® XP's online documentation is pretty good on this.

Domain 5 – Networks

12 per cent of marks

How you approach practical work with networks will depend to some extent on what you have available. The good news is that, even if you have access to a large profession-ally managed network, it is probably not the best place to carry out practical exercises; for sound operational and security reasons, you will not have sufficient rights to do any-thing interesting! What you can do, though, is to set up a small LAN of your own. This can be anything from two PCs linked on a crossover cable to a small LAN connected through a workgroup hub or switch. Within this framework, you can:

▢ Add / remove / configure a network adapter; both PCI internal adapters and / or USB adapters.

▢ Assign static or dynamic IP addressing schemes.

▢ Use the diagnostic commands such as PING, IPCONFIG and NET VIEW to check your work.

▢ Install and share a printer or a scanner on the network.

Experiment with user rights on shared resources. How does the security of your small peer-to-peer network compare to a professionally managed client / server network?
If you have Internet access from your LAN, you can consider and experiment with Internet access sharing in Microsoft Windows® and use the diagnostic commands such as PING and TRACERT to see how your connection works.

Domain 6 – Security

11 per cent of marks
One of the problems that you may experience in approaching security is that if you 'test' the security of your workplace or college network you could be breaking the law. In most countries, it is illegal even to attempt to access a network in breach of security procedures and no one will thank you for triggering a hacker alert. What you can usefully consider, though, is the security status of your own practice LAN and the PCs attached to it.

▢ Have up-to-date service packs been applied?

▢ What is the status of malware protection software?

▢ What is the status of the firewall on your Internet gateway box?

You may also find it useful to experiment with user accounts and permissions.

Domain 7 – Safety and environmental issues

10 per cent of marks
In terms of safety, you could carry out a safety review or audit of your own workplace.

▢ If you are working in a classroom or lab, do you have the tools and facilities to work safely?

▢ How good are your antistatic measures?

▢ Is there a fire extinguisher of the correct type?

This could be the starting point for preparing a written report with sub-headings cross-referenced to the exam objectives.

In terms of environmental considerations, you need to bear in mind that the CompTIA exams reflect US law at the time that the specification was drawn up. It can be useful to review US practice and compare it with the law as it applies now where you live and work. For example, in the US there are more stringent requirements for network cables that are run though ventilation ducts (a common practice, particularly in older buildings) than in the UK. What other regional variations can you find?

All potentially hazardous substances are the subject of Material Safety Data Sheets and these are available on the Internet. These reflect US law and practices; what are the regional variations? How, for example, do they relate to the Control Of Substances Hazardous to Health (COSHH) regulations in the UK?

Legislation and practice are all subject to change, especially where hazards arising from PC use and disposal are concerned. Check on the disposal facilities available in your area. What are the legal requirements? Are there any proposed changes in law or practice in the pipeline?

The object of these exercises is to create an awareness of the continuing safety and environmental debate and to establish best practice in your place of work. However, you are preparing for an exam, so do not neglect the details required by the exam specification.

Domain 8 – Communication and professionalism

5 per cent of marks

It can be quite difficult to devise a practical exercise that does not involve making a nuisance of yourself! Calling help desks with fictitious 'problems' is at best antisocial. However, the exam is not concerned exclusively with computer-related topics. A worthwhile exercise can be to pick a topic of which you have little or no knowledge and to research it as if you were going to produce a 'beginner's guide' or a one-page fact sheet. Choose your topic – it can be anything from how to bake a cake to how to draw a pencil sketch – and research it. This may involve visiting web sites, libraries or book shops in search of information.

- How clear was the website?

- How helpful were the library / bookshop staff?

- When your research is complete, consider how you will write up the results.

- Do you explain the real basics; how to sharpen a pencil before you start?

- How much knowledge do you assume; where do you draw the line between explaining the basics and patronising the reader with things they already know?

The object of this exercise is not to find definite answers but to consider the processes of communication and how they can be improved. Ultimately, it's not about right and wrong answers for a particular topic but in realising the simple truth that if you treat others as you would wish to be treated yourself, you will be well on your way to mastering the basics of customer care. Once you have cultivated the customer- focused mindset, ticking the right boxes to pass the exam should be relatively straightforward.

Exam technique

No matter how much you know in terms of facts and figures or however much practical experience you have, your A+ certification requires you to pass exams. It can be useful, then, to try thinking like a question setter. An A+ exam question consists of a scenario and four possible answers and you are required to choose the correct answer or to 'choose all that apply'. The questions often include what CompTIA call a 'distracter'; that is, a superficially plausible wrong answer. Bearing in mind that the question, the set of possible answers and all the navigation controls for the test all have to fit on a monitor, questions cannot be more that a few sentences in length at most and, given the time span of the test, they need to be answered at the rate of almost one per minute. Bearing these constraints in mind, it can be a useful exercise to make up your own test questions; this can be a particularly useful group exercise for a class and can lead to some interesting and informative discussions. Obviously, you can do this by making up test questions as a pen-and-paper exercise; and there is a lot to be said for the pen-and-paper approach even in the digital age. There are also test- and quiz-setting software applications available for download, so that you can implement your tests on a PC if you want to. Some of these programs are available as trial versions or as shareware or with a limited free use licence. Providing that you check (and comply with) the licensing conditions for the product that you choose, you can produce some useful mock tests. What matters here is not simulating the real CompTIA test – you are unlikely to be able to do that – but stepping through the process of devising test questions and answers and reviewing your own 'knowledge base' of A+ facts and information. You can also test the validity of your questions and answers by trying them out in practice. Devise a question, say, about the syntax of the PING command, then see how it works on your own LAN, then repeat the exercise over your Internet connection. This is a straightforward-enough approach, but it combines theory, practice and exam technique in a way that you may find useful.

Objective	Topic	Chapter	Pages
3.1	Names and locations of operating system files	8	123–124
3.1	Creating, viewing and managing disks, directories and files	8	125–127
3.1	Working with files	8	127–128
3.2	Hardware compatibility and requirements for Windows 2000 and XP	9	134–135
3.2	Installation methods	9	135–138
3.2	Drive imaging: creating and deploying	9	138–141
3.2	Installation options/unattended installation	9	141–144
3.2	Upgrading operating systems	9	144–145
3.2	Installing devices and drivers	9	145–147
3.2	Optimising the operating system	9	147–149
3.3	Boot sequences and methods	10	154–160
3.3	Diagnostic procedures and troubleshooting	10	160–166
3.3	Operating system utilities	10	167–169
3.3	System management tools	10	169–174
3.4	Preventive maintenance on operating systems	10	174–176
2.1	Laptop specifics/form factors/RAM	11	181–183
2.1	Laptop hard drives	11	183
2.1	Form factors for other components	11	184
2.1	Docking stations and port replicators	11	184
2.1	Expansion slots and ports	11	185–186
2.1	Communication connections	11	186–188
2.1	Power and electrical input devices	11	188–189
2.1	Laptop displays	11	189–191
2.1	Input devices	11	191–192
2.1	Motherboards/processors/throttling	11	192–194
2.2	Power management	11	194–197
2.2	Safely removing hardware	11	198–199
2.3	Diagnosing and troubleshooting laptops	11	199–201
2.4	Preventive maintenance on laptops	11	201–202
4.1	Printer and scanner technologies	12	208–210

INDEX

wired networks, installing, 246–248
Wired Equivalent Privacy. *See* WEP
wireless
  connections for printers and scanners, 216
  installing wired and wireless network connections, 246–248
  network connectivity, 240
  obtaining a connection, 249–251
  security, 260–262

Wireless Access Points, 261–262
working copies, 263–264
worms, 273, 274
WPA (Wi-Fi Protected Access), 261
wrist straps 286
WUPDMGR, 174

XGA standard, 56

yearly preventive maintenance, 105